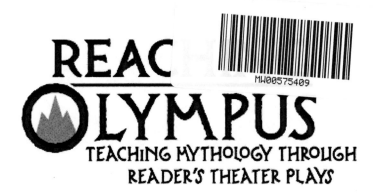

REACH OLYMPUS

TEACHING MYTHOLOGY THROUGH
READER'S THEATER PLAYS

REACHING OLYMPUS

THE GREEK MYTHS VOL. II
THE SAGA OF THE TROJAN WAR

WRITTEN AND ILLUSTRATED BY ZACHARY HAMBY

For Baby Jane

ISBN-10   0982704917
ISBN-13   978-0-9827049-1-2
LCCN   2012901373

Reaching Olympus: Teaching Mythology Through Reader's Theater Plays, The Greek Myths Volume II

Written and Illustrated by Zachary Hamby

Edited by Rachel Hamby

Published by Hamby Publishing in the United States of America

TABLE OF CONTENTS

INTRODUCTORY MATERIALS

READER'S THEATER PLAYS

SUPPLEMENTAL MATERIALS

APPENDICES

REACHING OLYMPUS

The faces of the souls of the Underworld could not have been more death-like. It was five years ago, but I remember it well. In a matter of weeks, I had gone from inexperienced student to full-time teacher. Smack dab in the midst of my student teaching experience, my cooperating teacher gave me some startling news. Because of a worsening medical condition, she would be leaving soon—then it would be *all me*. Even more startling: four long years of college had not prepared me for the subject matter I would be required to teach—a class called World Short Stories and (gulp) Mythology. I remembered a few short stories from my survey literature courses, but with mythology, I was drawing a blank. In my cobwebbed memory there stood a woman with snake-hair and a psychedelic image of a wingéd horse—but that was it. Not to worry though. I had *two whole weeks* to prepare. After that I needed to fill a whole semester with mythological learning.

As any competent educator would, I turned to my textbook for aid. At first things looked promising. The book had a classy cover—black with the aforementioned wingéd horse on it. Bold gold letters tastefully titled it *Mythology. Edith Hamilton*—in the same lettering—was apparently the author. Yes, my judgment of the cover was encouraging, but what I found inside was anything but.

When I opened the text to read, I quickly realized I was doomed. Edith Hamilton had written her book in code. It was the same indecipherable language used by those who write literary criticism or owner manuals for electronic devices. Every sentence was a labyrinth, curving back in on itself, confusing the reader with many a subordinate clause and cutting him off completely from context with an outdated aphorism. If she wasn't randomly quoting Milton or Shakespeare, she was spending a paragraph differentiating between the poetic styles of Pindar and Ovid. It was as if Edith Hamilton was annoyed at having been born in the twentieth century and was using her writing style as some kind of literary time travel. Originally published in 1942, *Mythology* reflects the writing style of the day—a style that has grown increasingly more difficult for modern readers to comprehend. I knew if *I* could barely understand Hamilton's language, my students were going to be even more lost than I was.

Designed for average learners, Mythology was a junior-senior elective—the kind of class that was supposed to be entertaining and somewhat interesting. With Edith Hamilton tied around my neck, I was going down—and going down fast. It was at this point that the stupidly optimistic part of my brain cut in. "Maybe it won't be so bad," it said. "Don't underestimate your students." My ambitions renewed thanks to this still, small voice, and I laid Edith to the side, somehow sure that everything would turn out all right in the end. This was still more proof that I knew nothing about mythology.

Before I continue to tell how my tragic flaw of youthful optimism led to my ultimate downfall, I should take a minute to say a kind word about Edith Hamilton. In a time when interest in the classical writings of Greece and Rome was waning, Edith Hamilton revitalized this interest by writing several works that attempted to capture the creativity and majesty of Greco-Roman civilization. Hamilton's *Mythology* was one of the first books to take a comprehensive look at the Greco-Roman myths. The popularity of mythology today owes a great deal of debt to this book and its author. Fifty years after its publication, it is still the most commonly used mythology textbook in high school classrooms. Ironically, *Mythology* is no longer on an average high-schooler's reading level. As I mentioned earlier, Hamilton's writing style, with its ponderous vocabulary and sphinx-worthy inscrutability, further alienates any but the most intrepid of readers.

My first semester of teaching Mythology was a disaster. If I hadn't been so idealistic and gung-ho, I probably would have given up. Instead the new teacher within me stood up and said, "No! I'm going to do this, and we're going to make it fun! After all, Mythology is filled with all kinds of teenage interests: family murder, bestiality, incest, etc. It'll be just like watching *MTV* for them."

Utilizing every creative project idea under the sun, I threw myself into making the class work. We drew pictures, we read aloud, we watched related videos, wrote alternate endings to the stories—yet every time I kept coming up against the same brick wall: the text. It did not matter how enjoyable the activities were. Whenever we turned to the actual stories and cracked open that dreaded book, the life was sucked out of my students, and I was staring at their Underworld faces once again.

My last resort was boiling the stories down to outlines and writing these out on the whiteboard. Even *that* was better than actually reading them. At least the students would get the basic facts of the story. One student, possibly sensing I was seconds away from the breaking point, made the comment, "I didn't know this class would be a bunch of notes. I thought it would be fun."

Then I gave up.

When I look back on that semester, I realize that I failed a whole batch of students. They came and went thinking that studying mythology was a brainless exercise in rote memorization. Perhaps the failure of that first experience would not have been so stark if a success hadn't come along the next year.

The second time through the class, I was determined to *not* repeat the mistakes of the past. There must be some way of avoiding the text—somehow relating the stories without actually reading them. But then I thought, "Isn't this supposed to be an English class? If we don't actually read, can it be called *English*? What has this outdated text driven me to?"

When *I* looked into the stories, I could see excellent tales trapped behind stuffy prose. How could I get the students to see what I saw? How could I set those good stories free?

On a whim I decided to try my hand at rewriting one of the myths. I had dabbled in creative writing in college, so surely I could spin one of these tales better than Edith Hamilton had. The idea of dividing the story into parts struck me as a good one. Maybe that would foster more student involvement. A few hours later, I had created my first Reader's Theater script. (At the time I had no idea that there was an actual term for this type of thing or that there was sound educational research behind reading aloud.) Part of me was excited. The other part was skeptical. "These kids are high-schoolers," I said to myself. "They'll never go for this." I looked at some of the elements I had included in my script: overly-dramatic dialogue, sound effects, cheesy jokes. What was I thinking? Since I had already spent the time and energy, I decided to give it a shot.

There are those grand moments in education when something clicks, and those moments are the reason that teachers teach. My script clicked. It clicked quite well, in fact. The students *loved* reading aloud. They were thrilled beyond belief to not be reading silently or taking notes or even watching a video. They performed better than I ever dreamed possible. They did funny voices. They laughed at the cheesy jokes. They inhabited the characters. They even did the sound effects.

As I looked around the room, I noticed something that was a rarity: My students were having fun. Not only that, but they were getting all the information that Edith Hamilton could have offered them. When the script was done, I encountered a barrage of questions: "Why did Zeus act like that to Hera? What is an *heir*? Why did Aphrodite choose to marry Hephaestus? Did the Greeks have *any* respect for marriage?" Did my ears deceive me? Intelligent questions—questions about character motivation, vocabulary, and even historical context? I couldn't believe it.

I was also struck by another startling fact: They were asking about these characters as if they were real people. The students were able to treat the characters as real people because real people had inhabited their roles. Zeus was not some dusty god from 3,000 years ago. He was Joe in the second row doing a funny voice. Something had come from the abstract world of mythology and become real. And as for the quiz scores, my students might not remember the difference between Perseus and Theseus, but they definitely remembered the difference between Josh and Eric, the two students who played those roles. On top of all this, the class had changed from a group of isolated learners to a team that experiences, laughs, and learns together.

After the success of that first script, I realized I had created some kind of teaching drug. It was an incredible teaching experience, one that I wanted to recreate over and over again. I wouldn't and *couldn't* go back to the old world of bland reading. So I didn't.

The great moments of Greek mythology flew from my keyboard, and I created play after play. Despite my overweening enthusiasm, I knew that too much of a good thing could definitely be bad, so I chose stories that would spread out the read-aloud experience. We would still use Edith Hamilton in moderation. After all, a few vegetables make you enjoy the sweet stuff all the more.

Over the course of that semester, I discovered a new enthusiasm in the students *and* myself. They enjoyed learning, and I enjoyed teaching. I had students arguing over who would read which parts—an unbelievable sight for juniors and seniors. Laughter was a constant in the classroom. As the Greeks would say, it was a golden age of learning.

Now I have the chance to share this technique with other teachers. With these plays, I hope my experiences will be recreated in other classrooms. Mythology should not be an old dead thing of the past, but a living, breathing, *exciting* experience.

USING READER'S THEATER IN THE CLASSROOM

Reader's Theater is a highly motivational strategy that blends oral reading, literature, and drama. Unlike traditional theater, Reader's Theater does not require costumes, make-up, props, stage sets, or memorization. Only a script is needed. As students read the script aloud, they interpret the emotions, beliefs, attitudes, and motives of the characters. A narrator conveys the story's setting and action and provides the commentary necessary for the transitions between scenes.

While this strategy has been enormously successful with lower grade-levels, it may not seem like a good fit for secondary students. This could not be further from the truth. Students of any age enjoy and appreciate the chance to *experience* a story rather than having it read to them. For years now Reader's Theater has been the tool that I use to teach mythology to high-schoolers. I wouldn't have it any other way. Below are the answers to some of the most frequently asked questions concerning Reader's Theater in the classroom.

How do you stage these stories in the classroom? Hand out photocopies of the particular script for that day. (Note: It is perfectly legal for you to photocopy pages from this book. That is what it was designed for!) Certain copies of the plays should be highlighted for particular characters, so that whichever students you pick to read parts will have their lines readily available. (This is not necessary, but it does make things run more smoothly.) Some teachers who use Reader's Theater require their students to stand when reading their lines or even incorporate physical acting. As for the sound effects in the plays (*fanfare*), noisemakers can be distributed to the students and used when prompted. Otherwise, students can make the noises with their own voices.

How do you structure a class around Reader's Theater? How much do you use the plays? As with anything, too much of a good thing can be bad. In my own classroom I do employ the plays frequently—in some units we read a play every day of the week—but I do supplement with other notes, texts, activities, and self-created worksheets. Some of these activities are included in the back of the book. For other examples of these activities, check out my website located at www.mythologyteacher.com.

How do you assess Reader's Theater? A quick reading quiz after the completion of a script is an easy way to assess comprehension. In my own classroom I ask five questions that hit the high-points of the story. I never make the questions overly specific (for example, asking a student to remember a character's name like Agamemnon or Polydectes). Each play in this book comes with five recall questions for this purpose.

Another form of assessment is by trying to foster as much discussion as possible. How well students discuss will tell you how well they have comprehended the story. The discussion questions included in this book have seen success in my own classroom.

I hope you find this book to be a great resource. It was designed with the intent of helping a much wider audience experience the timeless tales of world mythology in a new manner. On the next page I have listed some further notes concerning the Reader's Theater plays. Thanks for purchasing the book. Please feel free to contact me if you have any questions.

Sincerely,

Zachary Hamby
mr.mythology@gmail.com

FURTHER NOTES

INTENDED AUDIENCE: 6th-12th grade

LENGTH: Plays range between 25-45 minutes in length

PROCESS

- Every student will need a copy of the script.
- Reading parts may be highlighted for greater reading ease.
- As the teacher, you are the casting director. Assign the parts as you deem best.
- Give your largest parts to your strongest readers but still try to draw out the reluctant participant.
- As the teacher, you should take the part of the narrator. Actively participating only makes it more fun for you and the students.
- Cut loose and have fun. Reader's Theater allows students to see their teacher in a whole new light.

POSSIBLE MODIFICATIONS

- Costumes, props, and even sets can be added to any script to make it more engaging.
- Requiring the students to stand while reading their parts creates a stronger dynamic between speaking roles.
- Encouraging students to write their own Reader's Theater plays gets them thinking about the elements of storytelling and the use of dialogue.
- Assigning one student to be responsible for all the sound effects in a play can involve someone who is not a strong reader in the performance. Including certain tools that actually make the indicated sound effects (noise-makers, coconuts, etc.) is another excellent way to add interest.

THE TROJAN WAR: AN INTRODUCTION

"Let me die…in some great clash of arms that
even men to come will hear of
down the years!"

—Prince Hector, the *Iliad*—

When the Trojan prince Hector utters these lines, he seems to be predicting the future: Poets have been singing of Troy and its great "clash of arms" for over 3,000 years. Even the poet Homer, who wrote the *Iliad* probably around 850 B.C., considered the war to be ancient history since the events that inspired the Trojan War most likely occurred around 1,250 B.C. Now, a couple thousand years later, the story and its characters still have the power to captivate. We are just as entranced as the ancient Greeks were by the powerful Achilles, preening Paris, noble Hector, the wily trickster Odysseus, and Helen, the woman whose beauty launched a thousand ships.

According to the many legends concerning it, Troy was a city-state on the western tip of Asia (modern-day Turkey). The horse-lords of Troy (or Ilium as it also called) were known for their great wealth in gold. As the story goes, Paris, prince of Troy, "kidnaps" the Greek princess Helen while he visits her husband, Menelaus, in Greece. Menelaus and his powerful brother Agamemnon recruit the other Greek kings to cross the sea and retrieve his beautiful wife. Launching a thousand ships, the Greeks sail to Troy with revenge as their goal. What they think will be a quick skirmish turns into a ten-year war.

While there were many poems written about ancient Troy, the Greeks' favorite version was Homer's *Iliad* (a title meaning "a poem about Ilium"). The *Iliad* with its passionate speeches, glorious victories, and violent deaths made the Greeks idolize the heroes of the Trojan War. If a Greek orator wished to prove a point, he would quote Achilles, Hector, or even Zeus himself from the pages of the *Iliad*. Homer's poetry was revered as the pinnacle of art and was used in the education of every Greek child. For this reason, the *Iliad* is often called the "Bible of the Greeks."

In spite of its excellent storytelling qualities, the *Iliad* tells only a fraction of the ten-year war, beginning nine years into the conflict and focusing on a brief, but eventful, period of time. The poem ends with the death of the Trojan prince Hector and leaves the war still unresolved. For ancient readers this was no problem: Everyone knew the rest of the story by heart. But for modern readers, the rest of the war must be fleshed out by consulting other sources and lesser storytellers.

The saga of the Trojan War is the most famous legend to come from Greek mythology (and according to many, the best). The war and its aftermath form a sprawling, beautifully complicated tale. It's no wonder that Homer chose to tell only a part of it.

Follow-up legends to the Trojan War tell how many of the victorious Greek veterans do not make it back home without a few adventures. Odysseus, the most notorious of the delayed homecomers, wanders for ten years before reaching Greece. His travels are recounted in Homer's second epic poem, the *Odyssey*. While this poem was also a favorite of the ancient Greeks, it never achieved the same central status as the war-oriented *Iliad*.

In these plays I have tried to harmonize the various versions and sources for the legends to form a cohesive whole. Different writers often have contradictory conceptions of the same characters and events. What I have tried to do is resolve them to one another, smooth the lines between, or at the very least, explain why characters change drastically from one portion of the story to another.

My ultimate goal has been to stay as faithful to the source material as possible while still making the legend accessible and coherent to a middle-school and high-school audience. I have rarely censored the gory details. After all, this *is* a tale about war—with all its brutal force—and it should not lose its impact. Inevitably, this has become my own personal version of an ancient story. For the full-flavor of the originals, seek them out. Homer will never disappoint you. There's a reason he's been on the bestseller list for 3,000 years.

Since the saga of the Trojan War encompasses an enormous cast of characters, a reference sheet "Who's Who in the Trojan War" has been included in the supplemental materials of this book. Making this sheet available to your students or giving the information as notes before they read may aid in comprehension. Below is also a list of books, which I recommend to teachers and students who wish to increase their background knowledge of the *Iliad* and *Odyssey*.

RECOMMENDED READING

- Homer. The *Iliad*. Trans. Robert Fagles. New York: Penguin Books, 1990.
- Homer. The *Odyssey*. Trans. Robert Fagles. New York: Penguin Books, 1996.
- Huler, Scott. *No Man's Lands: One Man's Odyssey through The Odyssey*. New York: Random House, 2008.
- Seyffert, Oskar. *Dictionary of Classical Mythology, Religion, Literature & Art*. London: MacMillan & Company, 1891.
- Strauss, Barry. *The Trojan War: A New History*. New York: Simon & Schuster, 2006.

THE JUDGMENT OF PARIS
TEACHER GUIDE

BACKGROUND

Cause and effect are important when it comes to wars, and the cause of the Trojan War is a not a typical one. No other war can claim to have been started in the name of love. Many historians who believe in a historical Trojan War that occurred in the Bronze Age have scoffed at the Paris-Helen love affair as a fanciful addition. Yet it seems fitting that a legendary war should be started by a legendary love affair.

Helen, the face who launched a thousand ships, is one of mythology's most intriguing and elusive characters. She poses the reader with many questions: Why does she leave her husband and daughter behind in Greece? Why does she not give herself up even after the death of Paris? Why does she go back to her husband after the war is over? The stories offer us no answers. We are left to determine her psychology for ourselves.

For all of those who did not think that love (or even lust) provided a good enough reason for the Trojan War, another myth was invented. "The Judgment of Paris" explains that a beauty contest between three powerful goddesses was the actual reason behind the war. Many experts think that this story was written long *after* Homer wrote about the Trojan War in the *Iliad*. Why? Homer makes no mention of this episode in his epic poem. He only states that Paris had previously offended Hera and Athena.

Regardless of the *true* cause, the effect was ten years of bloodshed that claimed many Greek and Trojan lives. It is doubtful that any conflict—real or imagined—will ever achieve the same legendary status as the Trojan War.

SUMMARY

Even on Olympus, a wedding is a great occasion, and all the gods and goddesses are gathered to celebrate the marriage of Thetis the sea nymph to Peleus, a mortal man. A prophecy has said that the son of Thetis will be greater than his father, and for this reason, the gods decide to marry her off to a mortal man, rather than risk one mightier than the gods being born into existence. (Achilles, the son of Thetis and Peleus, does go on to be greater than his father, as he becomes the greatest warrior Greece has ever seen.)

The wedding celebration is marred though when Eris, the goddess of Discord, plays a trick by leaving an apple that reads "For the fairest" among the wedding presents. Three goddesses—Hera, Athena, and Aphrodite—spy the apple and begin to argue over who its true owner should be. They go to Zeus to solve their problem, but he abstains from judgment. Instead he tells them to ask Paris, a young Trojan prince who lives as a shepherd, to judge between them. Paris has lived his whole life ignorant of the fact that he is the son of Priam, the king of Troy. A prophecy that Paris would destroy Troy caused his father to banish him.

The goddesses appear to Paris, who agrees to judge between them. Instead of competing fairly, each of the goddesses offers Paris a bribe. Hera offers him the chance to be the ruler of Europe and Asia, Athena offers him the chance to be the greatest warrior known to man, and Aphrodite offers him the hand of the most beautiful woman in the world. Paris, being a lover and not a fighter, chooses Aphrodite. The other two goddesses vow revenge while Aphrodite spirits Paris away to view his newly-won prize. What Paris does not know—and Aphrodite temporarily forgets—is that the most beautiful woman in the world is Helen of

Sparta, a woman already married to Menelaus, the king of Sparta.

Aphrodite magically transports Paris to Helen's palace in Greece, where he beholds her as she sleeps. The goddess promises to arrange a reunion between the Trojan prince and his father, which will restore Paris to princehood. She also will see to it that Paris is sent to Sparta for a diplomatic mission. Then he will be able to seduce Helen and return to Troy with her.

Meanwhile, the infuriated Hera and Athena vow to stir up a war. They will make sure that the kings of Greece journey to Troy to retrieve the stolen wife of Menelaus—no matter what the cost.

ESSENTIAL QUESTIONS

- How important is physical beauty?
- What are the consequences of love?
- How are wars started?

ANTICIPATORY QUESTIONS

- Who was Helen of Troy?
- What was the Trojan War?
- Which Greek goddess do you think would be the most beautiful?
- What would happen if the gods got into an argument or a fight?
- What is an "Achilles Heel"?

CONNECTIONS

Helen of Troy (**TV miniseries, 2003**) This miniseries re-tells the entire saga of the Trojan War—including the Judgment of Paris, a portion often overlooked by other film versions. **Warning:** Many scenes are not appropriate for middle-school and high-school audiences.

Doctor Faustus Christopher Marlowe's 1604 play features a famous speech addressed to Helen of Troy. It begins "Was this the face that launch'd a thousand ships/ and burnt the topless towers of Ilium?" Read the full speech in Act V, Scene I of the play.

TEACHABLE TERMS

- **Cause and Effect** What negative effects will Paris' choice among the goddesses cause for others? Who will be most affected by the affair of Paris and Helen?
- **Characterization** How does the author characterize each of the goddesses differently? What are their individual characteristics? How do these characters play off one another?
- **Foreshadowing** On pg. 4 Thetis the sea nymph dips her son, Achilles, into the River Styx to make him invulnerable, yet she forgets to dip his heel. What does this foreshadow for Achilles?
- **Humor** What does humor add to this myth? What parts are the most humorous? How would the story be different if told seriously?

RECALL QUESTIONS

1. What message is engraved upon the golden apple?
2. Whom do the bickering goddesses *first* ask to judge between them?
3. Why is Paris living as a shepherd instead of a prince?
4. Which goddess does Paris choose as the fairest?
5. How will his choice start a war?

THE JUDGMENT OF PARIS

CAST

ERIS	*Goddess of Discord*
PARIS	*Exiled Prince of Troy*
APHRODITE	*Goddess of Love*
HERA	*Queen of the Gods*
ATHENA	*Goddess of Wisdom*
ZEUS	*Ruler of the Gods*
HERMES	*Messenger God*

NARRATOR: On the great mountain of Olympus, nothing was a more exciting event than a wedding, and this day a great crowd of immortals had gathered for the union between Thetis, a sea nymph, and Peleus, a mortal king. Thetis was a beautiful creature and had caught the eye of many a god, but a terrible prophecy haunted the one whom she married: The son of Thetis was destined to be greater than his father. As much as they admired Thetis, none of the gods would risk having a son born more powerful than he. So it had been decided that Thetis should be married off to a mortal and be done with it.

ZEUS: Greetings, guests! Welcome all gods, goddesses, nymphs, satyrs, centaurs, *et cetera!* We are gathered here today to witness a grand ceremony. The son of Thetis and Peleus will be legendary. I have foreseen it. So, let us drink to the happy couple! *(cheers from the crowd)*

NARRATOR: While this was a happy occasion, not everyone in attendance was pleased to be there. Eris the goddess of discord, who had been left off the guest list, was up to no good. She loved nothing more than to cause trouble—which is exactly why she had not been invited in the first place.

ERIS: Fools! Celebrating the marriage of a vain nymph and a mortal weakling! I'll ruin their little festival! Let's see them sort this one out.

NARRATOR: As the guests laughed and feasted, Eris pulled forth from her pocket a golden apple. Engraved upon it were the words:

ERIS: For the fairest. *(laughs)* This should get them going.

NARRATOR: Careful not to draw attention to herself, she placed the apple among the gifts for the newly-wedded couple. Just as Eris had planned, it did not take long for the golden apple to catch the eye of the Olympian goddesses. Aphrodite was the first to notice it there.

APHRODITE: *(cooing)* What a marvelous apple! And look, it's engraved: *(reading)* To the Fairest. Hmmm. There must be some mistake. This is among the gifts for Thetis, but someone has obviously placed this gift here for me.

ATHENA: And how can you be so sure?

NARRATOR: Athena, the goddess of battle and wisdom, had noticed Aphrodite fondling the golden apple.

APHRODITE: *(snidely)* Well, Athena. We can safely say it's not here for *you.*

ATHENA: *(growling)* And why wouldn't it be?

APHRODITE: *(giggling)* Don't you know? Beauty is not commonly associated with manliness.

ATHENA: I ought to box your ears!

NARRATOR: Hera the queen of the gods, who had been listening to the goddesses argue with cat-like interest, stepped forward.

HERA: Ladies, ladies. Calm yourself. I have a simple solution to this problem: I am the Queen of Heaven, so, therefore, the apple would naturally be for me.

APHRODITE: Oh, please! You look twice my age! The apple is obviously mine.

HERA: You insolent wench! Unhand that apple!

ATHENA: Yes, you're tarnishing it. Plus, there's no telling where you've been!

HERA: She's been off wooing other people's husbands, no doubt!

APHRODITE: Ha! The fact that you despise me for my own advantages with men should be proof enough that I am the fairest. Do not blame me, Hera, because your husband finds you undesirable. And, Athena, what man would find you attractive? Unless he loved women with shoulders twice as wide as his!

ATHENA: Why you—!

HERA: Tramp!

APHRODITE: Cow!

ATHENA: Tart!

(sounds of female squabbling)

NARRATOR: Now, since this was going to be no easy discussion and the guests started to feel a bit awkward, the wedding disbanded. The wedded couple left, their day ruined. Eris laughed to herself. Her plan had worked perfectly.

Time to the gods is but the blink of an eye, and as the goddesses argued, much time passed. Thetis and Peleus conceived a son. He truly was to be greater than his father—the greatest warrior Greece had ever seen. To insure his safety, Thetis took him, as a boy, into the dark Underworld to where the Styx twists like a dark snake.

There, holding him by the heel, she dipped him into the waters. This river had magical powers. It would bestow upon the boy invulnerability. No sword or spear would ever pierce his blessed skin. But foolish Thetis forgot to dip the heel by which she held him, and through this, her son, Achilles was doomed.

Back on Olympus, the argument of the

golden apple was still raging, but Zeus had exhausted his patience.

ZEUS: *(angrily)* Ladies! This bickering must stop! The apple belongs to no one! My head will split open if you do not stop this arguing!

ATHENA: Oh, Father, I have been insulted, and you're whining about a headache! What is a headache compared to my pride?

ZEUS: Silence! I would not take my headaches so lightly if I were you. It was from one of them that you were born.

HERA: Yes, and it was a foul day when she was born, too.

ZEUS: And you! Hera, my wife, the "queen" of Olympus! There's nothing royal or stately about your actions here!

HERA: Well, you, Zeus, are the *king* of Olympus, and yet you lack the gumption to do something about these two foul shrews who challenge me!

ZEUS: *(growling)* Do not make me angry! You *shall* regret it.

APHRODITE: Put her in her place, brother! She's been asking for it for a long time now!

ZEUS: And Aphrodite, my sister—goddess of "love"—this argument does not flatter you. Where is the love in your actions?

APHRODITE: *(huffily)* This argument may not concern love, but it *is* a question of beauty—and beauty trumps love any day!

ZEUS: *(yelling)* I have had enough! This fighting must cease!

HERA: Then, husband, you must choose between us. You must decide who is the fairest: the wife, the sister, or the daughter?

ATHENA: I agree.

APHRODITE: You *are* a good judge of beauty, brother.

HERA: *(hatefully)* A little too good at times…

ZEUS: I will do no such thing. How could I choose between you? You have said it. You are my wife, my sister, and my daughter. Such a choice would anger two and please only one. I could not win delivering such a verdict.

ATHENA: Then find us a judge or we shall come to blows, and our conflict will shake the very foundations of the earth.

ZEUS: *(sigh)* I will do what you ask.

HERA: Good! Now be off! Shoo!

ZEUS: Hmph. Women.

NARRATOR: Zeus looked down upon the earth. Where would he find a suitable judge? This contest must be fair. Three of the mightiest goddesses were involved. Only the most able connoisseur of beauty would appease them.

There was a kingdom that was dear to Zeus' heart—the great kingdom of Troy. Wise king Priam lived there, and he had amassed great wealth through wise ruling, but he was old, and his heart no longer pulsed with life as young ones did. He was no judge for this contest.

Priam had fifty strapping sons. Foremost of all was the great Hector. But to Zeus he seemed too serious—and married.

ZEUS: *(dry chuckle)* What do married men know of beauty? *(pause)* Wait a minute. Here we are.

NARRATOR: Zeus' eye peered into the Trojan countryside. One son of Priam lived apart—a youth named Paris. As a baby, his queenly mother had dreamed that he would bring about the destruction of Troy. Since Priam was a good man, he did not have the heart to put the child to death, so he sent him into exile instead.

There Paris had been raised by a kindly shepherd and now lived as a shepherd himself—ignorant of his true heritage. He was a romantic boy, one who was not very good at sheep-watching. He spent most of his time picking at his lyre and composing love songs for the girls and nymphs who lived nearby.

ZEUS: He will be my judge. *(clearing his throat)* Ladies!

HERA: Have you found us a judge, husband?

ZEUS: I have chosen Paris of Troy.

ATHENA: Does he know his women?

ZEUS: Does he? He is quite a Casanova. In the Trojan countryside he has romanced many beautiful women!

HERA: *(grumbling)* A man after your own heart.

APHRODITE: Let us go to him at once!

ZEUS: I will have Hermes guide you to him. Hermes!

NARRATOR: There was a zipping sound in the air, and the god Hermes appeared in their midst, floating inches above the ground. Tiny wings fluttered upon his cap and sandals.

HERMES: You rang?

ZEUS: Hermes, these goddesses have been having a disagreement—

HERMES: A disagreement? That's an understatement. Sounds like the catfight of the century! *(cat hissing sound)*

ZEUS: *(irritated)* Hermes…

HERMES: Don't tell me. Since I'm the cleverest, you want me to sort this all out, right? Well, I can tell you right now, I'm not stupid enough to get in the middle of this argument!

ZEUS: Listen! I want you to guide them to Troy—to the exiled prince Paris. He will resolve their conflict.

HERMES: Oh. Perfect plan, pops! He can judge between them, and then they can rip *his* lips off.

ZEUS: I guess you could say that.

HERMES: Ahem. Ladies, if you would be so kind as to collect your fuming selves, we will be departing shortly.

ZEUS: Goddesses of Olympus, take care. I love this land of Troy. Do nothing to harm it! Do not poison it with your jealousy.

NARRATOR: Hermes and the three goddesses disappeared in a cloud of smoke.

In the Trojan countryside the shepherd Paris sat on a rock, humming softly to his sheep. There was a loud clap of thunder. (clap of thunder) Four immortals stood before him.

PARIS: (startled) Ah!

NARRATOR: Terror-stricken, Paris fell to his face.

ATHENA: Mortal boy, do not fear. We are goddesses from Olympus, come with a task for your noble mind.

PARIS: I will do whatever you wish!

HERA: We have been having a bit of a disagreement, young Trojan. We wish you to settle it.

PARIS: But what do I know?

APHRODITE: (playfully) Beauty, silly.

ATHENA: Judge between us. We will each present ourselves in our best light, and you, Paris, will decide once and for all who is the fairest.

PARIS: I will try.

NARRATOR: Paris was frightened but sat himself back on the rock and waited for his next order.

HERMES: Mind if I sit in on this? I love a good pageant. C'mon, ladies! Strut your stuff!

HERA: I am Queen of Heaven. I shall go first.

NARRATOR: There was a flash, and Hera reappeared—furs dripping from her naked shoulders.

HERMES: Wow. She's half-attractive when she's not snarling.

NARRATOR: Her skin was milky white and her eyes piercing. She was stunning. She drew forward to Paris and leaned in. She smelled of fine wine.

HERA: (quietly) Young mortal, choose me in this contest, and I will make it worth your while. I will make you a lord of Europe and Asia—give you power beyond your wildest dreams. Do you want to be a shepherd your entire life? I know power, and I know how to get it. Choose me if you are wise.

APHRODITE: What are you saying up there?

ATHENA: You have had enough time!

HERA: I am finished.

NARRATOR: She backed away from Paris— her eyes never leaving his.

ATHENA: Now, it is my turn.

NARRATOR: There was a fluttering sound in the air. Athena appeared, as she never had before. Her helmet was gone. Her hair was piled into great amber mounds on top of her head. A shining robe clothed her lithe body. Her virgin beauty shone forth. Paris was speechless. She, too, advanced toward him and leaned in. She smelled of a grassy meadow—fresh and breathtaking.

ATHENA: Trojan youth, choose me in this contest. I will make you a mighty warrior! With me by your side, you will sail across the sea and conquer the armies of Greece. I am the goddess of war. It is in my power. Glory comes to Paris, the victorious warrior.

HERA: What lies are you telling the boy?

APHRODITE: Your time is up! It is my turn now.

ATHENA: I am finished.

NARRATOR: She retreated, her lips parted in a celestial smile.

HERMES: She's a bit beefy, but I don't know about you—I like a woman who can hold her own at arm-wrestling!

NARRATOR: The fragrance of nectar drew Paris' gaze. Aphrodite was advancing.

HERMES: *(whistles)*

NARRATOR: Flowers were dancing through her hair. She wore a gossamer gown that shifted and flowed as if it were weightless. Her face was the most glorious thing Paris had ever seen. Truly, she was the goddess of love. She leaned in, her cherry lips whispering in his ear.

APHRODITE: Don't be tricked by the others. They are dried up and foolish. I can see what you truly want. What else would any young, handsome boy such as yourself want? Love. It's what I do. Gorgeous Paris, if you chose me, I shall give you the hand of the most beautiful woman in the world. I swear it by the River Styx.

NARRATOR: Paris' heart stopped. His desire did not rest with glory or power—but with love. Aphrodite sensed this, and she smiled smartly as she backed away.

ATHENA: I hope you did not promise something that you cannot deliver.

APHRODITE: On the contrary.

NARRATOR: Excited—forgetting that he was in the presence of immortality—Paris jumped up.

PARIS: I have made my decision!

HERA: Remember, boy, we are powerful. To offend us would have great consequences.

NARRATOR: But it did not matter to the young Trojan. He had found the desire of his heart.

PARIS: I choose Aphrodite, goddess of love.

HERMES: Uh-oh. Watch out.

ATHENA: *(angry)* Fool! I knew you were worthless! I will remember this when you call upon my name! May Troy fall!

NARRATOR: With that, Athena disappeared in a huff.

HERA: I curse your marriage, Trojan whelp. Whatever future you have, I will do all in my power to make it a sad one.

NARRATOR: Hera, too, was gone in the blink of an eye. Only Aphrodite was left, holding the golden apple—a smile of triumph on her face.

HERMES: Well, Aphrodite, you have done it again—laid on the old charm. Made me wish *I* was the one judging this contest for a second there.

APHRODITE: Buzz off, Hermes!

HERMES: Ahem. All right. I'll leave you two kids here alone to work out the details of your little deal.

NARRATOR: With a flutter Hermes vanished.

APHRODITE: You have made a wise choice, Paris of Troy, and I will show you your reward. Prepare yourself. I will return momentarily to take you to your prize.

PARIS: Thank you! Thank you!

NARRATOR: As swiftly as she could, Aphrodite flew back to Mt. Olympus to announce her victory to Zeus. But he had already heard.

ZEUS: Aphrodite, I hear from my infuriated wife and daughter that you have won the competition.

APHRODITE: *(beaming)* I have!

ZEUS: Hopefully, you did not promise the boy something out of your means.

APHRODITE: No, no. It was a stroke of brilliance really. What else would a romantic young man want? The most beautiful woman in the world, of course!

ZEUS: *(pausing)* Oh, foolish Aphrodite. Tell me you did not.

APHRODITE: *(confused)* Why? What harm is there in that?

ZEUS: Do you know who this girl is?

APHRODITE: Not offhand…

ZEUS: She is my daughter, Helen—Helen of Sparta.

APHRODITE: So?

ZEUS: *(annoyed)* Aphrodite, she is already married!

APHRODITE: I don't see the big problem with this. Affairs happen all the time. *You* should know that. Don't be so uptight.

ZEUS: Her husband is the king of Sparta. He does not take sharing his wife lightly.

APHRODITE: *(flippantly)* The affairs of mortals do not trouble me. What do I care? I must keep my promise.

ZEUS: I will not let you keep this promise. It will start a war.

APHRODITE: *(confused)* But I have to. I have sworn by the River Styx…

ZEUS: Fool! *(sigh)* Go! Carry out your brainless errand. I fear I have doomed this boy and his kingdom with this burden.

APHRODITE: *(sing-song)*   Remember, brother, love conquers all!

ZEUS: No, it doesn't.

NARRATOR: Aphrodite reappeared in the Trojan countryside. Paris jumped up from the perch where he had been anxiously waiting.

PARIS: I thought maybe you weren't coming back.

APHRODITE: Don't be silly. Now, come to me. Hold on.

NARRATOR: A great cloud started to envelope the world around them, the sun was blotted out, and Paris got the sensation he was flying.

APHRODITE: Have you ever heard of Helen of Sparta? She's Zeus' daughter. *(whispering)* He visited her mother in the shape of a swan.

PARIS: If she is half as beautiful as you, I shall be pleased.

NARRATOR: The world materialized about them. They were in the foyer of a great hall. A humongous feast was going on through the half-opened doors.

APHRODITE: She is upstairs—asleep. Her husband, Menelaus—

PARIS: She's married?

APHRODITE: Don't worry. She's terribly unhappy. As I was saying, her husband, Menelaus, is an ugly, hulking man—very undesirable. As handsome as you are, you will have no trouble wooing her!

PARIS: But I'm a nobody!

APHRODITE: Oh yeah. Well, you're actually a prince. Didn't you know that?

PARIS: *(shocked)* A prince? My whole life I've been a shepherd!

APHRODITE: Don't be ridiculous! Shepherds are all sun-blasted prunes—never good-looking like you! Here's my plan: I will reunite you with your father, King Priam. Then once you're re-established as a prince, I'll put it into his head to send you here—to Sparta—so that you and Helen can meet and fall madly in love! *(pause)* Yes, yes. It will be perfect!

PARIS: Please let me see her!

APHRODITE: She is just upstairs.

NARRATOR: Paris' pounding heart overcame his fear of the strange palace, and he bolted up the stairs to Helen's room.

He found the beautiful girl asleep on her bed—golden hair, ruby lips. She was everything promised. Paris was overcome with passion. He leaned over and whispered into her ear.

PARIS: Helen, awake. Your love is here.

APHRODITE: Oh, not yet, loverboy. She can't hear you. You will have to come back to woo her in person.

PARIS: Please, goddess, soon! The sight of this woman is maddening.

APHRODITE: Oh please, Paris. As if her looks are anything compared to mine.

PARIS: You must take me back to Troy at once, and I will regain my title. Then I will cross the sea and claim this beautiful creature. I will steal her from her husband. I'll even kill him if I have to. I must have her! I must!

APHRODITE: *(sigh)* How romantic! All right. When you awake, you will be back in Troy. Head toward the city. There is a great festival going on. Enter the contests there, and while you compete, I will make sure you are recognized by your royal father.

NARRATOR: Paris was still staring at the sleeping princess.

PARIS: *(dreamily)* Will she truly love me, goddess?

APHRODITE: Your love will burn like a thousand suns—only hotter.

PARIS: I can barely tear my eyes away from her face.

APHRODITE: Well, hurry up. I have an apple to polish.

NARRATOR: Once again a fine mist began to shroud the prince.

APHRODITE: Remember my instructions.

PARIS: Remember your promise.

APHRODITE: *(grandly)* I will, young fair one!

NARRATOR: Paris was borne away to his home country.

On high Olympus the gods watched all this with dissatisfaction. Soon Aphrodite appeared there, displaying her golden apple with a coy grin.

ATHENA: There is the brainless hussy now! Aphrodite, do you have any idea what you have started?

APHRODITE: You mean Paris and Helen? Of course. I have started the greatest romance in all of history.

ATHENA: Their love will start a war!

APHRODITE: Oh. It will blow over. These mortal wars always do.

ATHENA: If Menelaus brings his Spartans after Helen, King Priam will have no choice but to protect Paris.

APHRODITE: *I* can protect Paris.

ATHENA: *(laughing)* Ha! I would like to see that!

HERA: You and your stupid stunt have angered me against these Trojans. I will send all of Greece after your two lovers!

ATHENA: As will I. It is not right what you have done!

APHRODITE: You two don't frighten me. Paris is brave and beautiful. He will fight for Helen.

HERA: He will die for her, and I will laugh when the crows pick his bones.

APHRODITE: Is that a fact? Well, I'll have you know that the God of War just so happens to be *my* lover.

ATHENA: One of many! But no matter how many gods you end up seducing to your cause, you *will* be outmatched. All of Olympus will soon be in an uproar.

HERA: Looks like, whelp, you have bitten off more than you can chew this time!

APHRODITE: We'll just see about that.

HERA: *(playfully)* What do you think, Athena? Will the mighty Aphrodite be remembered as the fairest of them all or the destroyer of many?

ATHENA: They will soon call her the goddess of death, I say.

HERA: Let the battle begin then. I am ready.

NARRATOR: As the other two goddess departed, Aphrodite looked down to the apple that still glistened in her hand. She slid her delicate finger across the sheen of its surface and smiled.

A chain of events had been set into motion. The greatest war of man was about to begin. The face that would launch a thousand ships would soon be taken. The fairest city ever built would soon be under attack. Thousands would die.

APHRODITE: *(musing)* And to think, it all began with a simple apple.

DISCUSSION QUESTIONS

- Should Zeus have ended the argument between the goddesses before it escalated? Explain.
- Is this contest between the goddesses a *fair* contest? Explain.
- Is it foolish to try to avoid a prophecy—as Paris' parents did? Explain.
- Is Paris selfish? Explain.
- Who do you think will suffer the most for Paris and Helen's affair? Explain.

THE TIDES OF WAR
TEACHER GUIDE

BACKGROUND

Not every Greek warrior was thrilled with the idea of fighting a war over the fate of a single woman, and, as this myth tells us, some tried to avoid the war in ingenious ways. This pre-war episode explains the treaty that binds the kings of Greece into fighting for Helen. It also sets up two important characters: Odysseus and Achilles.

Odysseus, a young intelligent king, emerges as one of the war's chief players. Initially reluctant to go to war, he becomes the man to finally bring Troy to its knees. To some Odysseus is a hero; to others he is a dishonorable, heartless villain. In spite of his tactics, Odysseus' motives are always pure: He misses his home—his wife and son he left behind.

Achilles is the supreme warrior of Greek mythology, so in this episode it is ironic to see him going into hiding dressed as a girl. For much of the span of the Trojan War, Achilles is at the mercy of his immortal mother, Thetis the sea-nymph, who is constantly trying to assure his survival. A prophecy has previously told her that her son will not return from Troy, but this does not stop her from trying every trick at her disposal to save his life. Achilles, even with all his brute strength, often becomes little more than a "mama's boy."

SUMMARY

Odysseus and his good friend Mentor enter the bustling city of Sparta. Nearly every king in Greece has come to see King Tyndareus choose a husband for his legendarily beautiful daughter, Helen.

As Odysseus passes by the palace, he spies a beautiful girl walking along the ramparts. Infatuated by her beauty, he decides to sneak inside the palace to speak with her. He meets with the girl and learns she is Penelope, the niece of King Tyndareus.

Odysseus then makes his way to the chamber of the king, who is in the midst of a dilemma. Every king of Greece has come to his doorstep—all contending for the hand of his daughter—but he doesn't know how to choose between them without starting a war. Odysseus interrupts his deliberation and proposes a cunning compromise: Having each of the kings swear to fight for the honor of the man Tyndareus chooses. That way if anyone tries to harm the winner, all the other kings will be obligated to retaliate. Tyndareus is delighted by this intelligent suggestion and agrees to give Odysseus his heart's desire—the hand of the beautiful Penelope.

Several years into their marriage, Odysseus and Penelope learn of Helen's abduction. This means all the former suitors of Helen will have to go to Troy to retrieve her. (Odysseus had also sworn to fight for Helen's cause.) Odysseus decides that he will devise a clever trick to avoid the war.

When Odysseus does not report to the port of Aulis as King Agamemnon has commanded, the king dispatches a crafty young man named Palamedes to Ithaca, Odysseus' island kingdom. When Palamedes arrives there, he is greeted by a strange sight: Odysseus has yoked an ox and a donkey to his plow and is driving the team haphazardly through the field, slinging salt from a pouch at his side. Penelope and the servants tell Palamedes that Odysseus has gone mad.

Doubting Odysseus' madness, Palamedes grabs Odysseus' infant son, Telemachus, from Penelope's arms and sets him before the charging hooves of the team. Odysseus instantly pulls the team to a stop—saving the life of his son. Palamedes has proved that Odysseus is not insane, or he never would have stopped the team in time. He threatens Odysseus with treason—unless he helps Agamemnon track down another missing warrior: the mighty Achilles. Odysseus reluctantly agrees and bids his family farewell.

Palamedes reveals Achilles' last known whereabouts, and Odysseus deduces that Thetis the sea nymph must have put her warrior-son into hiding—as a girl. Disguising himself as a peddler, Odysseus goes from one royal court to another, peddling wares that would appeal to female shoppers. Yet amid the dainty items he places a sword and shield. One day he notices a strong-backed woman eying the weapon instead of the trinkets. Odysseus recognizes Achilles and reveals his identity. The warrior willingly accompanies Palamedes and Odysseus back to the awaiting Greek army.

ESSENTIAL QUESTIONS

- Should people be forced to fight in a war they do not believe in?
- When is it right to lie?
- How important is family?

CONNECTIONS

Achilles at the Court of Lycomedes (1745) This painting by Pompeo Batoni depicts Odysseus' discovery of the disguised Achilles. The scene is a frequent subject for artists. Have the students compare the artist's conception of the scene to their own.

ANTICIPATORY QUESTIONS

- Who was the greatest Greek warrior?
- Who was Odysseus?

- How were marriages arranged in ancient times?
- What is a draft-dodger?
- Do you think all the Greeks will happily go to fight in a war over Helen?

TEACHABLE TERMS

- **Everyman** In fiction an everyman is a character that ordinary people can relate to. Discuss how Odysseus is an everyman and what details make him so.
- **Situational Irony** Achilles' disguise as a woman is an example of situational irony since it presents a striking contrast to what is expected from such a masculine warrior.
- **Culture** In ancient cultures fathers decided whom their daughters were to marry. *Dowries* were monetary sums or goods given by the bride's father to the husband. Discuss this tradition with the students. Is this a flawed system? Explain.
- **Allusion** In a later story Odysseus' friend Mentor will serve as a chaperone and guide (or a literal mentor) to Odysseus' son, Telemachus. Our modern term *mentor* is an allusion (or reference) to this character from mythology.

RECALL QUESTIONS

1. What is Odysseus' solution to King Tyndareus' problem?
2. What does Odysseus do in order to appear mad?
3. How does Palamedes prove that Odysseus is faking his madness?
4. How has Achilles been disguised?
5. How does Odysseus reveal Achilles' identity?

THE TIDES OF WAR

CAST

TYNDAREUS	*King of Sparta*
ODYSSEUS	*Prince of Ithaca*
MENTOR	*Friend of Odysseus*
PENELOPE	*Spartan Princess*
GUARD	*Spartan Guard*
ICARIUS	*Penelope's Father*
PALAMEDES	*Crafty Nobleman*
ACHILLES	*Great Warrior*
DEIDAMIA	*Beautiful Princess*

NARRATOR: Some say the Trojan War began with the dispute between the three most powerful goddesses. Others say it began when Prince Paris of Troy abducted the Greek princess Helen. But for Odysseus it began much earlier—in the kingdom of Sparta.

Odysseus was just a young man—the son of a minor island king. It was his first journey to Sparta. His first journey anywhere really.

The great city pulsed with life—crammed wall to wall with men from every corner of Greece. Princess Helen of Sparta, the most astonishing beauty ever seen, had finally come of age. Now it was the duty of her father, King Tyndareus, to decide exactly whom she should marry. But this was no easy choice. Every king and lord of Greece had shown up in Sparta—each one expecting to claim Helen as his bride. It seemed that Tyndareus' decision could only end in bloodshed, which is exactly why Odysseus had journeyed so far—to see the show. He had brought his friend Mentor along for the ride.

ODYSSEUS: Look at all these prancing fools! Ha! Before this is all over, they will be fighting in the streets over this woman.

NARRATOR: In fact, some fights had already broken out among the suitors in anticipation of the king's decision.

MENTOR: Have you ever seen Helen? They say that the sight of her is enough to put a man in a stupor for days.

ODYSSEUS: She's not the girl for me then. Who wants a woman that will make him a drooling idiot? Give me a homely wife who can spin and cook. Then I'd be a happy man.

MENTOR: Are you serious? I thought you came here to vie for the hand of Helen?

ODYSSEUS: *(defensively)* I never said that.

MENTOR: Riiiight. They say to look upon her is to love her. I say before the end, you will put your name in with the others.

ODYSSEUS: Well, I *am* a prince. Why not? One day I'll be a king just like these peacocks.

MENTOR: Yes, but Ithaca is not much of a kingdom. The rest of these kings have brought jewels for Helen. What could you bring her? Hogs? Plus, I have heard that Menelaus, the very brother of Agamemnon, is here. Ithaca is a pigsty compared to his kingdom—literally.

ODYSSEUS: *(whistles)* The kid brother of Greece's mightiest king, huh? Then I say Helen's father can go ahead and pick his winner. He wouldn't want to offend Agamemnon.

MENTOR: No matter whom he picks, he's going to have a full scale riot on his hands. There's no way to avoid it. Whomever he chooses—even if it is Menelaus—will be at the mercy of all the losers. Men will kill to get their hands on Helen.

ODYSSEUS: Not if the old king plays it right.

MENTOR: What do you mean?

ODYSSEUS: If I were him, I'd—

MENTOR: *You* have a solution? *(laugh)* That's a laugh!

ODYSSEUS: You doubt me? Don't forget. The clever god, Hermes, is one of my ancestors.

MENTOR: Ha! Along with many other liars and thieves.

ODYSSEUS: Better to be the son of a thief than the son of a—

NARRATOR: Odysseus stopped. He spied a girl on the ramparts of the nearby Spartan palace. She was leaning over the stone walls with a look of complete boredom on her face. She absentmindedly tucked a piece of hair behind her ear.

ODYSSEUS: *(breathlessly)* Who is that?

MENTOR: Well, it can't be Helen. She's striking, but no daughter of a god.

ODYSSEUS: She's beautiful!

MENTOR: Yes. She's a fine girl, but I thought you wanted to see Sparta.

ODYSSEUS: Wait here.

MENTOR: Where are you going?

ODYSSEUS: I'm going to find out her name!

MENTOR: What? Are you serious? Odysseus, wait!

NARRATOR: Pushing forward through the crowd, Odysseus made his way toward the side-entrance of the palace.

ODYSSEUS: *(to himself)* They'll never let me in. Security's too tight. I'll need a disguise.

NARRATOR: As he passed a peddler's stand, he slyly pulled loose a length of regal cloth from the displayed wares.

ODYSSEUS: Here we go. A touch of window dressing will do the trick.

NARRATOR: He wrapped the material about his shoulders cloak-like and threw out his chest. With this disguise in place, Odysseus boldly approached the two guards who stood at the palace entrance. As they stepped forward to block his path, Odysseus raised a haughty eyebrow.

GUARD: Stop! Who are you, sir?

ODYSSEUS: *(snotty laugh)* Is this some kind of joke? All of Greece knows who I am!

GUARD: *(sarcastically)* Then I guess I am not a Greek. *(to the other guard)* This must be some fool who thinks he's going to get a peek at Helen.

ODYSSEUS: *(irately)* How dare you insult me like this! I am Menelaus. Perhaps you've heard of me? Agamemnon is my brother.

GUARD: Really? And where are your servants, my lord? And why aren't you using the front entrance to the palace like all the other royal suitors?

ODYSSEUS: Well—I—ummm. I'm traveling incognito?

GUARD: All right, *your majesty*, we're going to take a little trip down to the dungeon.

ODYSSEUS: Wait! What are you doing? Agamemnon shall hear of this! Then heads will roll!

PENELOPE: *(shouting)* Menelaus!

NARRATOR: The sudden female voice caught both Odysseus and the guards by surprise. A girl appeared in the entryway behind the guards. It was the girl from the ramparts.

PENELOPE: Menelaus! I thought that was you. What is going on here?

NARRATOR: Both the guards and Odysseus were looking at the girl in wonder. Odysseus quickly realized she was talking to him.

ODYSSEUS: *(fumbling)* Oh! I— *(self-assured again)* These fools were detaining me! They did not believe I was who I said I was.

PENELOPE: This is the brother to Greece's most powerful king. Do you know what he does to men who insult him?

GUARD: We—uh—well—er…

PENELOPE: He cuts out their tongues! Not that yours is doing you much good now.

GUARD: A thousand apologies, your highness! I thought—

PENELOPE: You thought? You thought? Back to your post! We don't pay you to think!

GUARD: Forgive us, Princess Penelope!

PENELOPE: Now come, Lord Menelaus, and let me show you our palace.

NARRATOR: As the guards scurried back to their posts, Penelope flashed Odysseus a mischievous grin and linked arms with him. He could only stare back at her with admiration. Once they had strolled out of the guards' sight, Odysseus turned to her.

ODYSSEUS: That was amazing! Why did you help me?

PENELOPE: Well, at first I came down just to see you get throttled. I thought you were another one of my cousin Helen's rabid stalkers, so I stopped to watch the guards dispose of you. By the way, you aren't, are you?

ODYSSEUS: I'm an admirer. But not of Helen's.

PENELOPE: But then I found your ever-so-feeble impersonation charming, and I decided to help you out. You're not very good at tricks, are you?

ODYSSEUS: I guess not. I thought I was going to have to spend a night in the dungeon.

PENELOPE: You deserve to—trying to pass for Menelaus. Haven't you ever seen him? He's a huge, red-headed fellow. He looks absolutely nothing like you. But if you want to work on your Menelaus impersonation, I could give you a few pointers.

ODYSSEUS: No, that won't be necessary. I am Odysseus, by the way. *Prince* Odysseus.

PENELOPE: Penelope. So *prince*, huh? Very nice. I think *every* Greek nobleman is here in Sparta now—all drooling over Helen.

NARRATOR: The girl sighed and pushed her hair behind her ear.

ODYSSEUS: I'm not.

PENELOPE: Not what?

ODYSSEUS: Drooling over Helen.

PENELOPE: Then you must have never seen her. When men behold her beauty, they are enraptured. They automatically hand over their heart—not to mention their brain.

ODYSSEUS: There is more to love than beauty.

PENELOPE: I hope so. *(pause)* If not for Helen, then why have you come to Sparta, Odysseus?

ODYSSEUS: I didn't know until now.

PENELOPE: Very well. Keep your secrets. I'll leave you to your business. But if you ever need any help impersonating important Greeks—

ODYSSEUS: I do need your help. I need to find King Tyndareus.

PENELOPE: That's easy. He's in his chambers. He hasn't moved from them for a week. The rumor is he hasn't slept in a week either. He knows how much strife this decision is going to cause.

ODYSSEUS: I think I can help him.

PENELOPE: You?

ODYSSEUS: Show me the way.

NARRATOR: She paused—staring into Odysseus' gleaming eyes.

PENELOPE: You are a strange one, aren't you? *(laugh)* Very well.

NARRATOR: Penelope led him down several hallways—finally stopping before a set of double doors.

PENELOPE: He is within. Good luck.

NARRATOR: Odysseus took the girl's hand into his own and kissed it. The princess Penelope grinned and continued on down the hallway.

ODYSSEUS: *(love-struck)* What a woman!

NARRATOR: Odysseus ducked inside the room. An old man was pacing back and forth in the midst—his grey head bent in thought.

TYNDAREUS: (*old man voice*) Today is the day, and I still haven't chosen! Why me? This is impossible! How can I choose? How will the egos of these kings stand it if I do? They will kill each other—or worse, me. I'm too old to be murdered!

ODYSSEUS: Ahem.

TYNDAREUS: (*shocked*) Ah! Don't sneak up on an old man like that! I'm anxious enough as it is! Who are you? What are you doing here in my chambers?

ODYSSEUS: My name is Odysseus, sir. I am the Prince of Ithaca.

TYNDAREUS: Ithaca? Isn't that that miserable island out in the middle of nowhere? I didn't know it was big enough to have a prince. A bunch of pig-farmers, isn't it?

ODYSSEUS: Are you King Tyndareus?

TYNDAREUS: I am—although I wish to Zeus I weren't. Let me guess. You're here for the hand of my beautiful daughter like every other bloodthirsty king of Greece.

ODYSSEUS: Even if I were here for Helen, I've seen the competition, and I'm outmatched.

TYNDAREUS: That's an understatement! Even Menelaus, the brother of Agamemnon, is here! And that's something!

ODYSSEUS: I'm sure you are wise enough to know your decision could start a war.

TYNDAREUS: Could? I don't see how one can be avoided!

ODYSSEUS: I think I have a solution.

TYNDAREUS: You? If I could laugh, I would. The pig-boy has a solution! That's rich.

ODYSSEUS: Yes, I have a solution, but before I tell you, I would like to make one request.

TYNDAREUS: I knew we would get to this eventually. Very well. What is it that you want?

ODYSSEUS: I met a young woman named Penelope in the palace today. I want to ask her to marry me.

TYNDAREUS: What? So you're really not here for Helen? I mean, Penelope is a nice girl and all—my own niece—but…

ODYSSEUS: Penelope is the bride I desire.

TYNDAREUS: Well, if you're sure. Find a way out of this mess for me, and I will arrange a marriage for you. Penelope's a clever girl, but has few prospects.

ODYSSEUS: Thank you!

TYNDAREUS: Don't thank me yet! I still have to see how a boy born from pig-farmers can solve my problem!

ODYSSEUS: Well, listen. Before you reveal your choice, make all the kings who desire Helen's hand swear an oath that they will fight for the honor of the man you choose—just in case anyone ever tries to steal Helen away from him. Then any man fool enough to challenge the chosen suitor will have to deal with every other king in Greece.

TYNDAREUS: Hmmm. Interesting. You believe these men would swear such an oath—even before the gods?

ODYSSEUS: For a chance at Helen they would do almost anything.

TYNDAREUS: *(overjoyed)* Brilliant, pig-boy! You have a shrewd mind. I believe you have given me the solution to my problem! I thank you!

ODYSSEUS: And Penelope?

TYNDAREUS: She shall be yours, of course. But I will ask you to swear the oath to Helen as well for good measure.

ODYSSEUS: I will gladly! What could it hurt? With these oaths in place, no man would ever attempt to steal Helen.

NARRATOR: The king put Odysseus' plan into action immediately. All the kings and lords gathered and swore to defend Tyndareus' choice. Then the old king revealed his very predictable selection—Menelaus. After all, Menelaus was the brother of Agamemnon, and everyone wanted to stay on Agamemnon's good side. This did not trouble Odysseus. He had gotten what he wanted out of the deal.

King Tyndareus broke the news to his brother, Icarius, that he had promised Penelope in marriage. Icarius was not too happy about the arrangement.

ICARIUS: I can't believe this! You promised Penelope to some penniless pig-farmer!

TYNDAREUS: Well, he is a prince.

ICARIUS: Prince of a pig-sty! What do you think, Penelope? Are you as outraged as I am about this?

PENELOPE: I am not a prissy girl, father. The country might suit me.

ICARIUS: What? Then you mean you will agree to this arrangement?

PENELOPE: Not that I have a choice, my lord, but truthfully, it is not as disagreeable to me as it is to you.

NARRATOR: Even though Icarius begged her not to go, Penelope journeyed to Ithaca to become the wife of Odysseus.

PENELOPE: So, we meet again, Lord Menelaus.

ODYSSEUS: I need some help with my tricks.

PENELOPE: Apparently you don't need my help. I heard that it was your trick that kept Greece from fighting a war over Helen.

ODYSSEUS: That was just a side effect. The real trick was winning your hand.

PENELOPE: *(laughs)* Don't try your tricks on me, Odysseus. You have my hand—and my heart.

NARRATOR: Although Penelope's father predicted sadness for her, the princess loved her husband and her simple life. Every new season seemed to bring them new happiness. The gods blessed Odysseus and Penelope with a son—Telemachus. It seemed that no cloud could ever darken their sun-filled lives.

But then the news came that no one ever expected: Helen had been abducted, and not by any Greek king. A Trojan prince from across the sea had stolen her away. Now Agamemnon called for all the kings of Greece to honor their oath and fight for Menelaus. The Greeks would cross the sea and retrieve his golden bride.

This news caused fear to well up in

Odysseus' heart, and he did what he always did when his mind was troubled. He went to the fields and took up the plow.

ODYSSEUS: Whoa there! Steady now!

NARRATOR: From the edge of the field, Penelope, holding her infant son in her arms, watched her husband struggling against the weight of the plow, driving his oxen in the stifling heat of the day.

PENELOPE: Odysseus!

NARRATOR: Odysseus reined in the oxen and wiped the sweat from his brow.

ODYSSEUS: You shouldn't have the boy out in this heat!

PENELOPE: I know this is troubling news. I hate to see you leave us, but I know you will return home safely.

ODYSSEUS: That's just it, Penelope. I'm not going to war.

PENELOPE: (in shock) Not going? But you swore the oath like the rest of the kings.

ODYSSEUS: I did not swear it for Helen. I swore it for you. War is for warriors. Let them have it.

PENELOPE: They will call you dishonorable.

ODYSSEUS: Honor? Honor is caring for your family, working your land. All I want is to stay here in Ithaca—with you and Telemachus. If I die in a foolish war, he will never know his father.

PENELOPE: They will call you a coward.

ODYSSEUS: Let them.

PENELOPE: Agamemnon will force all the kings to honor their oaths. He will not let you out of yours so easily.

ODYSSEUS: I know that. That's why I've been plowing this morning—clearing my head. Trying to think of a way to escape this war.

PENELOPE: War is dangerous, but it is even more dangerous to oppose Agamemnon. He'll have you killed—or worse. It's madness.

ODYSSEUS: (thoughtfully) Madness! That's it!

PENELOPE: What do you mean?

ODYSSEUS: When I do not report for war, I know they will come for me—just as you have said. But when they arrive, they'll be in for a surprise!

PENELOPE: I don't understand.

ODYSSEUS: They will find that I have gone mad! (happy laugh)

PENELOPE: I think the sun has baked your brain! They would never be fooled by such a trick.

ODYSSEUS: Oh, you think not? We are dealing with morons here, my dear. And you'll be a part of the production as well. You are quite the actress when you want to be.

PENELOPE: (shocked) Odysseus, I have never uttered a deceitful word in my life.

ODYSSEUS: See? That's what I'm talking about. You're a natural.

NARRATOR: Odysseus bit his lip—imagining.

ODYSSEUS: I'll be plowing when they arrive. For a king to plow his own fields is madness to most of those snobs! But instead of two oxen, I'll have an ox yoked to a donkey—pulling against each other. *(laugh)* Yes! It will be perfect!

PENELOPE: Dear, your tricks are not always as convincing as you think they are. Remember how we first met?

ODYSSEUS: Then I'll sow the field with salt!

PENELOPE: If you ruin our cropland, then you really are mad!

ODYSSEUS: Oh, my dear, this is war I am avoiding here. There will always be more cropland. I am not willing to lose my family, my life to a pointless war. Let Menelaus fetch his wife back himself!

NARRATOR: Odysseus moved near the bundle in Penelope's arms.

ODYSSEUS: Did you hear that, my son? *I* will be the one to hear your first words, see your first steps, take you on your first hunt. Your father isn't going anywhere.

NARRATOR: Days later Odysseus received a blustering summons from Agamemnon commanding him to report to the port of Aulis at once.

ODYSSEUS: This is typical of that arrogant fool. Bossing us around like we aren't kings in our own right. Plus, he's acting as if this war is just going to last a matter of weeks. Greece will nip out, grab Helen, and return in time for supper. Foolishness! I've heard of Troy. They have thick walls and are mighty horse lords.

PENELOPE: Agamemnon is not as dimwitted as you think, Odysseus. You must be on your guard, or this trick might not work. And then what would he do to you—to us—if he found out you deceived him?

ODYSSEUS: It will work. Trust me. I have thought of everything.

NARRATOR: When word reached Agamemnon that Odysseus had not reported to Aulis, he dispatched Palamedes, a crafty young nobleman, to retrieve the wayward lord of Ithaca—by any means necessary.

PALAMEDES: Hmmmm. How ironic that the man who engineered the treaty for Helen is now unwilling to honor it. I've heard of Odysseus' cunning tricks before.

NARRATOR: When Palamedes' ship moored at the port of Ithaca, the pale nobleman was greeted by the first act of Odysseus' dramatic production. Mentor, disguised as a servant, was waiting for him at the seaside.

PALAMEDES: You there. Take me to the palace of Odysseus.

MENTOR: *(moaning)* My lord, I will, but it is a sad place these days! My master, Odysseus, has gone mad!

PALAMEDES: What? Gone mad? What do you mean?

MENTOR: You will see! You will see! The gods have cursed his mind.

NARRATOR: As Palamedes passed through the fields of Ithaca, he was greeted by a strange sight. A haggard man—one with scratches running up and down his almost naked body—was driving a plow haphazardly through the field.

MENTOR: See how he yokes an ox to a donkey! Madness! Madness!

PALAMEDES: Hmmm. This is your master?

MENTOR: Yes! May the gods save us! That is Odysseus!

ODYSSEUS: *(crazy voice)* Left! Left, you brute! The harvest will be here soon! Much to do! Much to do!

NARRATOR: Odysseus was slinging something from a pouch hung at his side.

PALAMEDES: What is that he sows the field with?

MENTOR: Salt! Woe is us! Our harvest is ruined! See how our queen weeps her heart out?

NARRATOR: Penelope was there, adding to the scene, clutching Telemachus to her chest with one hand and tearing at her robes with another. Palamedes eyed all of this shrewdly.

PALAMEDES: Hmmmm.

NARRATOR: As Palamedes drew near Penelope, she turned her tear-stained face toward him.

PENELOPE: *(frantically)* Sir, I can tell you must be a noble lord. Please! Please do something! My husband has gone mad!

PALAMEDES: That seems to be an understatement. Would you mind stopping him so that I might speak to him?

PENELOPE: Stop him? We have tried to stop him, but he is like a wild beast!

PALAMEDES: Hmmm. Who is that child you hold in your arms?

PENELOPE: It is the son of Odysseus. Pity him! He has lost his father—to madness!

PALAMEDES: May I see the child?

PENELOPE: Well, I—

PALAMEDES: It will be only for a second.

NARRATOR: Penelope reluctantly handed the child to Palamedes. Odysseus—shrieking now and rolling his eyes back into his head—drove his plow close to where they stood. He spurred the yoked beasts up into a charge. *(snorting of beasts)*

ODYSSEUS: *(gibbering)*

PENELOPE: Another fit! See how he raves like a mad dog!

PALAMEDES: Fear not, madam. I think I can cure your husband's madness.

NARRATOR: With the child still in his arms Palamedes stepped forward—into the path of the stampeding beasts—and laid Telemachus down upon the ground yards before them.

PENELOPE: *(gasping)* Telemachus!

ODYSSEUS: No!

NARRATOR: Odysseus—breaking his act—pulled back fiercely on the reins. The ox and the donkey came to a halt—a mere foot from the infant. Penelope ran forward and snatched up her son.

PENELOPE: What kind of monster are you? You would kill a defenseless child?

PALAMEDES: He is quite safe, my lady. This dramatic production might outwit a nitwit, but not me.

NARRATOR: Palamedes stepped around the sweating beasts and the now-stationary plow. He sneered. Odysseus was kneeling in the dirt—his head in his hands.

PALAMEDES: You know, you *could* have run over the child. Then I would have easily believed you were mad.

NARRATOR: Odysseus remained silent.

PALAMEDES: Hmmm. Still insolent I see. I suppose you know why I have come. Agamemnon will not be pleased when I mention this little episode to him.

ODYSSEUS: What will be done with me?

PALAMEDES: Agamemnon will be merciful toward you—and your family—*if* you cooperate. He has devised a special mission for you—a way for you to make up for this embarrassing display of cowardice. You are not the only warrior who has gone missing. The young Achilles is unaccounted for.

ODYSSEUS: Achilles?

PALAMEDES: Agamemnon cannot fight this war against the Trojans without Greece's finest warrior. We've searched all of Greece though, and the boy is nowhere to be found. We suspect he's been spirited off somewhere by that immortal mother of his, Thetis the sea nymph. Unfortunately, she is better at deception than you are.

ODYSSEUS: What does Achilles have to do with me?

PALAMEDES: Simple. If you help us find him, Agamemnon just might spare your life—and not burn this miserable little kingdom to the ground.

ODYSSEUS: (*grim laugh*) How can a man refuse such a gracious offer?

PALAMEDES: Exactly. Now I suggest you clean yourself up, say goodbye to your wonderfully dramatic family, and avoid any more funny business.

NARRATOR: Odysseus looked up to meet the lord's gaze. His stare burned fiercely.

ODYSSEUS: (*menacingly*) Listen to me now. You may have won today, but someday I will have my reckoning with you—mark my words.

PALAMEDES: Hmmm. I sincerely doubt that. Now make your goodbyes. I will be waiting at my ship.

NARRATOR: Odysseus held his wife and his son in his arms for possibly the last time.

ODYSSEUS: I should have listened to you. My tricks have only gotten me into more trouble.

PENELOPE: Your mind is your weapon. Use it to come home to us—quickly.

ODYSSEUS: Listen. My father is too old to rule. Mentor will be in charge of Ithaca until I return—or until Telemachus comes of age.

PENELOPE: Don't say such things! You will be home soon enough.

ODYSSEUS: You'll tell Telemachus about me, won't you? Tell him what kind of man I was. Only leave this part out.

PENELOPE: Why wouldn't I tell him how much his father risked just to be with him?

ODYSSEUS: Know that I *will* return!

PENELOPE: I will be here waiting.

NARRATOR: Reluctantly, Odysseus joined Palamedes. As the ship pulled out to sea, he could see Penelope waving goodbye from the top of the high hill. A single tear fell from his eye as his homeland slipped away over the line of the sea.

PALAMEDES: Heartbreaking. Much more convincing than your earlier performance.

NARRATOR: Odysseus whirled and punched Palamedes squarely in the jaw. The nobleman sprawled backwards onto the deck. His men rushed forward to restrain Odysseus.

PALAMEDES: Halt! Don't harm him. We need him alive.

NARRATOR: The men raised Palamedes to his feet, and he felt his injured face.

PALAMEDES: Well, you definitely punch much better than you act. Now, if you have that out of your system—

ODYSSEUS: (*angrily*) Let's get one thing straight—I don't work for you or for Agamemnon or any man. I will help you find Achilles, but on my terms!

PALAMEDES: I don't think you're in much of a position to be bargaining.

ODYSSEUS: Oh really? Then tell me, fancy boy, where is Achilles? You have no idea! Are you prepared to go back to Agamemnon empty-handed?

PALAMEDES: (*coldly*) No.

ODYSSEUS: Where was the boy last seen?

PALAMEDES: At the court of his father, Peleus. But that was months ago. He could be anywhere by now.

ODYSSEUS: That's where you're wrong. Achilles has the look of a god about him. He's recognized wherever he goes. Someone would have noticed him by now. He must be in disguise.

PALAMEDES: Ha! How do you disguise a boy who looks like a god? You can't disguise a specimen of manhood like that!

ODYSSEUS: Sure you can.

PALAMEDES: How?

ODYSSEUS: Easy. You disguise him as a woman.

PALAMEDES: What man could pass for a woman?

ODYSSEUS: You'd make the transition easily enough.

PALAMEDES: Hmmm. Achilles would never wear women's clothing. It's dishonorable.

ODYSSEUS: Oh, a man would do many "dishonorable" things when his life is at stake.

PALAMEDES: So you've shown us, but Achilles doesn't care about his life. He's a young warrior, bristling for the chance to prove himself.

ODYSSEUS: That may be, but he has an overprotective, immortal mother who will stop at nothing to save the skin of her darling son. Haven't you heard the rumor about her dipping him in the River Styx?

PALAMEDES: So if you are right—and that's a big *if*—how do we find Achilles among all the women of Greece?

ODYSSEUS: We look in all the households who honor Thetis the sea nymph in their sacrifices. She would only hide her son among her most devout followers.

PALAMEDES: But almost every island kingdom honors Thetis!

ODYSSEUS: Then we have a lot of work to do.

PALAMEDES: Even if we find where he's hiding, how will we pick him out? Inspect every woman of the court? I think their fathers would object.

ODYSSEUS: I can accomplish it with a trick.

PALAMEDES: Hopefully a trick more effective than your last one.

ODYSSEUS: It will be. Now get this hunk of driftwood sailing.

NARRATOR: Odysseus put his plan into motion. The ship of Palamedes sailed to each of the Greek island-kingdoms. Odysseus—disguised as a portly merchant, carrying his wares upon his back—paid a visit to each of the royal palaces. His goods included many dainty items suited for royal ladies.

ODYSSEUS: *(phony accent)* Hello! Hello! Rare perfumes! Ornamental combs! Flowing gowns! Treasures just for the ladies! All right here for rock-bottom prices!

NARRATOR: As he laid out his goods, among all these feminine items, he also placed a well-tempered sword—the kind of sword that a warrior could not resist picking up if his eye happened upon it—and a shield just as keenly made.

At each stop the women fawned over the feminine items but paid no attention to the sword or the shield.

PALAMEDES: Well, you have made a killing off these trinkets you've peddled, but you haven't found Achilles.

ODYSSEUS: Patience is the mark of a clever man. That's probably why you have little of it.

NARRATOR: After weeks, finding no trace of Achilles, Palamedes and Odysseus finally came to the island of Scyros.

PALAMEDES: This is our last stop. I'm going with you this time.

ODYSSEUS: Well, stick to the plan. Don't mess it up!

NARRATOR: The two disguised men made their way to the court of King Lycomedes of Scyros and requested an audience.

ODYSSEUS: Yoo-hoo! Beautiful princesses, I have come to show you goods gathered from the far reaches of the earth! Trinkets to die for! Egyptian knick-knacks! Ethiopian combs!

NARRATOR: A group of royal girls flocked to them and examined the items—cooing and commenting to one another. Among them, Odysseus noticed a large girl—strangely tall and broad-shouldered. Her face was heavily veiled.

ODYSSEUS: (whispering) Psst. The one in the back looks a bit beefy.

PALAMEDES: We have to be sure! We can't just go around accusing royal ladies of being men in disguise!

NARRATOR: The large girl stood in back of the others—ignoring Odysseus' products—but when she caught sight of the sword among the other items, she drew forward and snatched it up.

ODYSSEUS: Oh! A fine choice, *my lady*. That sword was made by the greatest smiths in Greece.

ACHILLES: Hmmm. Good craftsmanship. I mean, uh—(girl voice) Oh, is it?

ODYSSEUS: Sounds like you have a cold, my sweet. I'm surprised you could catch one wearing all those veils.

NARRATOR: The large girl ignored his remarks—moving her finger over the line of the blade, gripping the handle in her hands.

ODYSSEUS: My, my. What a manly grip you have. What does a nice girl like you want with a weapon like that?

ACHILLES: (girl voice) I—uh—will use it to shoo away the flies.

ODYSSEUS: You must have some killer flies here.

ACHILLES: How much?

ODYSSEUS: The price? Let me see here.

NARRATOR: Odysseus turned to Palamedes and nodded. Palamedes drew a horn from underneath his robes and sounded a sudden note upon it. (trumpet sound)

PALAMEDES: (fake shock) To arms! To arms! We are under attack!

(screams of the women)

NARRATOR: The large girl wielded the weapon, jerked away her veils—revealing a handsome, but obviously masculine, face—and crouched low to the ground, expecting an attack.

ACHILLES: What? Who attacks? Where?

NARRATOR: Noticing the complete absence of attackers, Achilles looked around him in confusion. Odysseus pulled off his merchant disguise and beamed proudly.

ODYSSEUS: Well, well, well. So *this* is the great Achilles!

ACHILLES: Who are you? Answer before I slay you!

ODYSSEUS: That won't be necessary. I am Odysseus, and this fool cowering behind me is Palamedes. We have come from King Agamemnon—one of us willingly. You are to report to Aulis at once—for the war at Troy.

NARRATOR: The warrior relaxed, stuck the sword into his waist-sash, and laughed.

ACHILLES: (laugh) Ha-ha! I see. A clever trick! I began to think that no one was ever going to find me here!

PALAMEDES: You sound like you *wanted* to be found.

ACHILLES: Of course! This trick was all my mother's idea. Now that I have been found, I will happily go to the war at Troy.

ODYSSEUS: Happily, huh?

ACHILLES: Naturally. What's the point of being Greece's greatest warrior if you miss out on its greatest war?

ODYSSEUS: Well, you're certainly not lacking in self-esteem.

ACHILLES: Take me to Aulis at once!

PALAMEDES: What about your mother? Won't she be upset?

ACHILLES: She tried to keep me from my destiny and failed. I told her there was nothing you can do to deter fate.

ODYSSEUS: Unfortunately, you are right, my friend.

DEIDAMIA: Achilles?

NARRATOR: The warrior turned. One of the fair-haired princesses was approaching him tenderly.

DEIDAMIA: *(sadly)* You're leaving?

ACHILLES: I'm afraid I must. Duty calls.

DEIDAMIA: What about our child?

NARRATOR: The princess touched her stomach.

PALAMEDES: *(whispering)* Hmmm. Apparently, not everyone was fooled by his disguise!

ACHILLES: Be strong! You must raise him for me. Tell him about his mighty father, and when I return, he shall behold me himself.

NARRATOR: The princess wept as Achilles prepared for his departure.

ACHILLES: I will have my servants gather my things and send word to my fighting men—the Myrmidons.

NARRATOR: Although the weeping princess watched their departure from the palace gate, Achilles did not look back as they left the court of Lycomedes.

ACHILLES: Thank the gods you came when you did. Hiding out among those women was going to be the death of me. All they wanted to do was comb their hair and talk about their feelings! Not even one of them was a challenge at arm wrestling.

NARRATOR: Odysseus rolled his eyes at the young warrior.
   A day of sailing later, their ship entered the port of Aulis. There they saw a thousand ships moored along the coast—their black sails unfurled—ready to depart. The eyes of the warrior Achilles shone as he gazed upon them.

ACHILLES: Gentlemen, this is the greatest sight I have ever seen! All the glory of Greece is laid out before us. This will be the war that will make our names last forever!

NARRATOR: In spite of these majestic words, Odysseus' stomach grew cold. Achilles saw speedy glory within the black sails, but Odysseus only saw long years of slow suffering and death.

ACHILLES: *(shouting)* To Troy!

PALAMEDES: *(shouting)* To Troy!

ODYSSEUS: *(sadly)* To Troy.

DISCUSSION QUESTIONS

- How are women portrayed in this myth?
- Is Helen a good cause to fight a war over? Explain.
- Does Odysseus have a right to try to avoid the war? Explain.
- Even though Odysseus despises being tricked by Palamedes, he agrees to help trick Achilles. What does this show us about his character?
- Would you rather be known for your fighting abilities (like Achilles) or for your tricks (like Odysseus)? Explain.
- How do Odysseus and Achilles treat their children differently? Explain.
- What is Odysseus' greatest asset? Explain.
- Eventually Odysseus will have his revenge on Palamedes for forcing him to the war at Troy. Toward the end of the war, Odysseus convinces Agamemnon that Palamedes is a traitor and has him stoned to death. Does Palamedes deserve this fate? Explain.

WAR AT TROY

TEACHER GUIDE

BACKGROUND

War might have changed since the ancient world, but it's never been pretty. In ancient Greece defeat by an enemy city-state meant total annihilation—death for the able-bodied men, a life of rape and servitude for the women, and slavery for the young.

In spite of their advanced learning, the Greeks still hadn't solved the problem of war. The Greek city-states were locked into eternal combat. Neighbors became enemies, enemies became allies, and allies became enemies once again. In their eyes war was simply a necessary evil, a problem that could never be remedied. The Greek philosopher Aristotle put it bluntly: "We make war that we might live in peace." Even writing 2,500 years ago, he realized that war and peace form a paradox.

The *Iliad*, Homer's epic poem about the Trojan War, was a reference point for the Greeks. Yes, Homer told them, war destroys lives, but it also produces heroes. The heroes of the Trojan War were the epitome of manly virtues—poetic warriors who spoke, fought, loved, wept, took and spared life in the legendary past of Greece. While war brings out the worst in some, it brings out the best in others. As much as he glorified it, Homer never simplified war. Death is the high price paid for glory. And his characters don't die gracefully. They suffer agonizing, horrific deaths.

The *Iliad* shaped how the Greeks thought about war and peace. It gave them their only guide for how a noble man should live and die. Its influence was so great that Alexander the Great, the man who would finally conquer and unite the city-states of Greece, slept with a copy of the poem under his pillow at night.

SUMMARY

Apollo, the god-archer of Olympus, has become angry with the Greeks. In their recent raids of Trojan villages, they have stolen the daughter of one of his priests and given her to Agamemnon, the leader of the Greek armies, as a concubine. In retaliation he has fired poisoned arrows into the Greek camp by the sea, causing a strange sickness among the troops. Calchas the prophet reports all this to Agamemnon, and the warrior Achilles staunchly backs his advice that Agamemnon should give the girl back to her father in order to appease Apollo.

Agamemnon agrees, but angered by Achilles' superior attitude, takes Achilles' concubine (a Trojan girl named Briseis) as his own. When Achilles learns that this has been done, he is furious and swears that neither he nor his fighting men, the Myrmidons, will fight for Agamemnon any longer.

Meanwhile, Thetis, the sea-nymph mother of Achilles, appeals to Zeus. She begs him to cause the Greeks to attack while Achilles has refused to fight. This way the Greeks will be defeated, and her son can return safely home. Zeus agrees and appears in a dream to Agamemnon—telling him to attack.

In Troy the prince Hector has tired after nearly ten years of fighting. He suggests that Paris should defend his own honor and challenge Menelaus, the husband of Helen, to a duel. The winner will win the war. Paris agrees to this.

When Agamemnon musters his troops and rides to the Trojan walls, Hector calls a truce and suggests his man-to-man battle. Menelaus eagerly agrees to this. Paris and Menelaus face off, and the Greek king easily overpowers the Trojan prince. Menelaus is about to drive his sword into Paris' throat when Aphrodite swoops down, saves Paris, and spirits him back safely behind the city walls.

Since Paris has obviously lost, the Greeks demand Helen back. As the Trojans prepare to return Helen to them, Athena causes a Trojan archer to shoot an arrow at Menelaus, wounding him and causing battle to begin once again. The goddesses are pleased with this. They do not want the war to end until Troy has been completely destroyed.

ESSENTIAL QUESTIONS

- When is anger justified?
- Is war full of glory—or terror?
- What causes are worth fighting for?

CONNECTIONS

The *Iliad* (c. 850 B.C.) Homer's epic poem begins with the rage of Achilles, and uses the young warrior as its protagonist. Homer is an excellent storyteller, and many portions of the *Iliad* read quite well. Modern readers might be put off by the "talky" encounters between warriors and frequent listings of genealogies, but in the end, the *Iliad* is the greatest story about war ever told.

ANTICIPATORY QUESTIONS

- What are some of the ways the Trojan War could be resolved?
- How long did the Trojan War last?
- How long would you fight a war before you thought of giving up?
- Which gods will fight for the Greeks?
- Which gods will fight for the Trojans?

TEACHABLE TERMS

- **Author's Purpose** In the *Iliad* Homer does not present either the Greeks or the Trojans as the "bad guys." There are heroes and villains on both sides of the conflicts. Why does he make this choice, and what does it have to say about war?
- **Predict** Ask students what they think will happen in the next part of the story. What event could cause Achilles to re-enter the battle?
- **Metaphor** The Greeks imagined sickness as arrows fired by Apollo, the god of medicine. In this sense the arrows of Apollo on pg. 33 are a metaphor for the plague that is affecting the Greek troops.
- **Armistice** Defined as a ceasing of hostilities between opponents, an armistice between the Greeks and Trojans occurs on pg. 42.
- **Theme** The rage of Achilles is the theme of the *Iliad*. How does the warrior's rage affect the war? How does it affect others than himself?

RECALL QUESTIONS

1. What do the arrows of Apollo cause?
2. Why will Achilles no longer fight for Agamemnon?
3. What solution to the war does Hector propose?
4. Who saves Paris from certain death?
5. What breaks the truce between the Greeks and the Trojans?

WAR AT TROY

CAST

ZEUS	*Ruler of the Gods*
THETIS	*Mother of Achilles*
ACHILLES	*Greatest Greek Warrior*
AGAMEMNON	*Leader of the Greeks*
MENELAUS	*Husband of Helen*
PARIS	*Prince of Troy*
PRIAM	*King of Troy*
HECTOR	*Greatest Prince of Troy*
HERA	*Queen of the Gods*
ATHENA	*Goddess of Wisdom*
HELEN	*Wife of Menelaus*
APHRODITE	*Goddess of Love*
CALCHAS	*Greek Prophet*

NARRATOR: Muse, sing of rage—the rage of Peleus' son, Achilles. The Trojan War had been raging for nine long years. Many Greeks and Trojans had met unflinching deaths on the plains of Troy. Achilles, the mightiest warrior for the Greeks, fought fiercely for King Agamemnon, the leader of the united Greek kings. But there was trouble in the camp.

ACHILLES: *(roaring)* Agamemnon! Agamemnon!

NARRATOR: A plague had struck the Greeks, where they were entrenched on the coast. Men had fallen dead, struck down by the arrows of an unseen god. Calchas the prophet had come to speak to Agamemnon, cowering behind the powerful Achilles for protection, for he feared his news would anger the king. His tidings were simple: Apollo, the Archer of Olympus, was offended—by Agamemnon himself.

CALCHAS: *(frightened)* The Trojan girl, Chryseis! She is the reason for the plague—for the sickness among the men.

ACHILLES: The girl we captured in the countryside, remember? She shares your bed, doesn't she, Agamemnon?

NARRATOR: The king calmly stroked his beard.

AGAMEMNON: Yes. But why is Apollo concerned with her? We've stolen plenty of women. Even Achilles here has one in his tent.

CALCHAS: Chryseis is different! The father you stole her from is a priest to that god.

ACHILLES: Give her back to her father, or Apollo will strike us down.

NARRATOR: The king scowled. He did not enjoy taking orders from warriors and prophets.

AGAMEMNON: Are you sure this is the reason for the sickness among the men?

ACHILLES: *(angrily)* How many more men must die before you listen to reason? The gods have spoken!

AGAMEMNON: *(coldly)* Very well. Return the girl to her father.

NARRATOR: The warrior and the prophet turned to go.

AGAMEMNON: But, Achilles, don't think this is the end of the issue…

NARRATOR: Achilles was so self-less with other men's women, but what about his own? While the army battled on the plains, Agamemnon ordered his guards to retrieve Briseis, the concubine of Achilles, from the warrior's tent. When the swift-footed Achilles returned, wearied from battle, he found his lodge empty.

ACHILLES: *(roaring)* Agamemnon! Agamemnon!

MENELAUS: Brother! Achilles has returned! He has learned what you have done.

AGAMEMNON: Allow him to enter—and let me remind him of his place in this army!

NARRATOR: But Achilles—powerful as he was—needed no permission to enter. He tore past Agamemnon's guards and into the king's presence. The nobles paused in their business to hear the words of the enraged Greek.

ACHILLES: *(snorting)* Where is she?

AGAMEMNON: *(loudly)* Remember whom you are talking to, Achilles! I am the high king! What are you?

ACHILLES: Me? I am the one who will cut your throat if you do not tell me where she is!

AGAMEMNON: She is here in my tent. What does it matter?

ACHILLES: *(growling)* She's mine!

AGAMEMNON: Possessions, possessions. You asked me to give up my prize, and I did. I have taken yours in her place. It's a fair trade. *(pause)* And you would be wise to watch your tone.

ACHILLES: You would be wise to not shake that finger at me—unless you wish to lose it.

AGAMEMNON: Ha! What can *you* do to me?

ACHILLES: *(to the others)* I will fight no more for this man. You have my word. He is a thief and a dog. He is not worthy of Greece. *(spits)* See how well your precious war goes without *me* leading the charges!

NARRATOR: With his honor slighted, Achilles stormed back to his tent. His failure infuriated him. In spite of his power—power given to him by the gods—he could not get what he desired.

Back in his tent, he sat sulking, wiping his eyes over the lost Briseis. It was here that his mother, the silver-footed sea nymph Thetis, found him.

THETIS: *(softly)* Achilles.

ACHILLES: Briseis?

THETIS: No, Dear it's your mother. Thank heavens you got rid of that awful girl.

ACHILLES: Mother! What do you know? Briseis was so beautiful. She was—she was—beautiful—

THETIS: Oh, Achilles. You never were good at words, were you? Why couldn't my son have been a poet, I say to myself. Warriors have such dangerous lives. Poets would always be safe and sound at home.

ACHILLES: Mother, I am strong. I am fierce. This is my destiny.

THETIS: Oh, destiny. If destiny had anything to do with it, dipping you in the River Styx wouldn't have worked the wonders that it has.

ACHILLES: Mother, that has nothing to do with it. Bravery has made me great.

THETIS: Yes, and bravery will get you killed. Now, listen—I've conveniently overheard you and King What's-His-Name arguing.

ACHILLES: I declared I would no longer fight for a man like him!

THETIS: No, I should think not.

ACHILLES: The Greeks will see. Without me, they are nothing. They will come to me and beg me to lead them. With me as their true leader, we'll crush Troy—once and for all!

THETIS: Errr—that's nice, dear. *(excitedly)* I know what would really show Agamemnon you mean business!

ACHILLES: And what would that be?

THETIS: If you went home—back to Greece—right now. That would certainly give him a taste of his own medicine. He would be red with fury. Why I think—

ACHILLES: Mother, I won't run away like a coward.

THETIS: Coward is such a strong word. "Intelligent young man"—that's what I would say.

ACHILLES: No! That's my final answer.

THETIS: *(sadly)* I see—but think about it, my son…

ACHILLES: *(to himself)* I will stay here until Troy has been destroyed.

THETIS: *(to herself, sadly)* And you along with it.

NARRATOR: But Thetis was not so easily defeated. She had done so much trying to save the life of her doomed son. Yet there was still one more card to play.

She flew upward—through the darkness of the night sky—to Olympus. She would go right to the top—to the god in charge. She appeared to the royal Zeus.

THETIS: *(grandly)* Zeus, wide-seeing lord of the sky. It is I, lowly Thetis.

ZEUS: *(kindly)* No need for formalities, Thetis dear. What is it that you want?

THETIS: Great Zeus, it was you who gave me my wonderful son. You said he would be mighty, but now his life is in danger!

ZEUS: He *is* mighty. His life will be glorious—but short. So it goes with mortals.

THETIS: Yes, but here is what I ask. This war has raged for nine long years. My son still stands as the greatest among the Greeks.

ZEUS: How could he not be with such a cunning mother?

THETIS: Thank you, but I wish for a speedy end to this war. Achilles says that he will no longer fight for Agamemnon. If the Greeks were to attack without Achilles, they would be defeated once and for all.

ZEUS: Yes, but they are not stupid enough to attack without their finest warrior.

THETIS: No, not yet. But if you—greatest of gods—appeared to them, telling them to strike—

ZEUS: Ah. But I have sworn not to interfere. My brother, Poseidon, my wife, Hera, and daughter, Athena, all favor the Greeks. My sons, Apollo and Ares, my daughter, Artemis, and my dear sister, Aphrodite, all fight for the Trojans. Someone must stay neutral.

NARRATOR: At this, Thetis dropped her robe. Underneath she was dressed in a gown made from the shells of the sea. They shimmered in the dim light of the Olympian hall. She knew that time had not paled her beauty.

THETIS: (sweetly) Zeus. O, Zeus. You are such a strong, powerful god. Surely, you could do this one, tiny favor.

ZEUS: Well—I—

NARRATOR: She leaned in close to the god—her lips almost touching his.

THETIS: I would be most grateful.

ZEUS: I—I—I need to think—leave me!

THETIS: Yes, Zeus, make your decision. I shall be waiting.

NARRATOR: Once Thetis had disappeared, Zeus sat alone in his throne room. Dare he get involved in this mortal war? Thetis was definitely persuasive, and in his heart, he loved Troy more than any city on the face of the earth. Every other god and goddess had certainly meddled enough in this affair. Why shouldn't he?

ZEUS: I have decided.

NARRATOR: He descended through the atmosphere into the very mind of Agamemnon, where he interrupted a very pleasant dream the Greek commander was having.

ZEUS: (booming) Agamemnon! Agamemnon!

AGAMEMNON: (in shock) Ah! This can't be! Zeus Almighty!

ZEUS: I am speaking to you through a dream, wide-ruling Agamemnon. I come with an important message for you and my Greeks.

AGAMEMNON: Yes, cloud-gatherer!

ZEUS: You must attack immediately. Troy is weak. Strike tomorrow, and you shall win the war.

AGAMEMNON: (shocked) Attack without Achilles? It would be suicide!

ZEUS: (booming) Do I lie? Am I not the lord of the gods? Do not question me, mortal, unless you wish to be a smear upon the sand. This is my message. Do with it what you will.

NARRATOR: And so the glory of Zeus left the mind of Agamemnon. The king awoke and ran from his tent, yelling at the troops.

AGAMEMNON: *(shouting)* To arms! To arms! We attack at dawn!

MENELAUS: *(confused)* Brother! Have you gone mad?

AGAMEMNON: Zeus has come to me in a dream!

MENELAUS: *(sarcastically)* That answers my question.

AGAMEMNON: Silence! *I* command this army. We strike at dawn. Ready the men.

NARRATOR: With the frenzy of Agamemnon spurring them on, the Greeks made ready to attack at daybreak. The king acted like one possessed. He ran around his troops gleefully shouting and throwing his arms toward the sky.

AGAMEMNON: *(shouting)* Glory to Zeus! Glory to Zeus!

NARRATOR: Meanwhile, the actions of the Greeks did not go unnoticed by Trojan spies. They brought their report back to Ilium, where Priam waited in the throne room with his eldest son, Hector.

HECTOR: Father, the spies have reported that the Greeks are preparing for an offensive.

PRIAM: *(feebly)* I see. Many more men will die tomorrow.

HECTOR: We need to end this war. I love my brother, but I grow tired of defending his vanity with the blood of our countrymen.

PRIAM: I have wronged your brother enough, Hector. Because of fear, I sent him away. When he returned, I knew that the gods had reunited us for a reason.

HECTOR: *(angrily)* So that our city could be destroyed?

PRIAM: Our destiny is not our own to decide. We will continue to fight.

HECTOR: *(sigh)* All for a woman.

PRIAM: I would have started such a war for your mother, son. Helen has captured us all in her spell. Men's hearts are mighty things.

HECTOR: Mine is not. It has grown cold with death. Father, what if there were some way to end this war *without* any more senseless bloodshed?

PRIAM: If it were honorable, I would call it a good plan. What is your idea?

HECTOR: We rest the fate of the war on two men—the two whom it most concerns. Menelaus, the husband of Helen has brought all of Greece to our doorstep. He must face off against...

PRIAM: *(shocked)* Paris?

HECTOR: Do not let your love of your son cloud your judgment, Father. What about your love for your people?

PRIAM: Paris is not a fighter. You do not understand. He is not strong and valiant like you.

HECTOR: I can teach him what he needs to know. Menelaus is no Achilles.

PRIAM: I do not like it, but it will be for your brother to decide. Summon him.

NARRATOR: Paris was sent for, and soon, he entered with the lovely-haired Helen walking by his side. When the men-at-arms beheld her, their mouths went slack. Truly, she was the most beautiful creature in the world. This woman alone was worth a thousand years of war.

PRIAM: *(kindly)* Paris, my son. Helen, beautiful Helen.

HECTOR: The Greeks will attack once again tomorrow, Paris.

PARIS: Troy's walls will hold.

HECTOR: *(angrily)* And how do you know that? Perhaps you would care to join us on the field of battle once in a while? Instead of bathing in the sun with your beauty! We are growing short in number—protecting your interests.

PARIS: I am not a coward. But I am no warrior. I would only bring shame on my family.

HECTOR: *(spitefully)* You have done enough of that already.

PRIAM: Hector! *(softly)* Paris, we have an idea of how to end this conflict, but it would require your permission and cooperation.

PARIS: I will do whatever you ask, Father.

HECTOR: Menelaus has come for Helen. Nothing else. I say you two must fight it out. Winner takes the spoils.

HELEN: Nobody need die for me.

HECTOR: Too late. Perhaps you should have thought of that before you so easily left your husband!

PARIS: *(angrily)* Don't you talk to her that way!

PRIAM: My sons! Helen, I beg your forgiveness. Hector feels only for his people. You are our guest, my adopted daughter. Troy has offered you its protection. It was given freely. Feel no guilt.

HELEN: Thank you, but—

PARIS: I will fight him.

HELEN: *(shocked)* Paris!

PARIS: I can do it! It's my fault anyway—this whole mess.

HECTOR: I will teach you. You have much to learn.

PARIS: I can learn quickly.

HECTOR: See that you do. You face him tomorrow.

HELEN: Tomorrow? *(crying)*

PRIAM: Paris, you have made me very proud, my son. You have lived up to the name of Prince of Troy. May the gods smile upon you. You will succeed. I feel it in my heart.

NARRATOR: Hector quickly took Paris to be trained. There was no time to lose. He must learn how to find the chinks in armor, how to wind a large adversary, how to throw a heavy spear—all in one night. Helen was left weeping in the throne room. It was her lot in life to weep. She was made beautiful, yes, but eternally sad. Night wore on, and the morning broke. At the first sight of the sun, the Greek troops began to march across the Trojan plain to the high walls of Troy.

Achilles watched as they scurried like ants across the dirt. His own men, the Myrmidons, had stayed behind. If their leader did not fight, neither would they.

ACHILLES: Look at them. Sheep following a fool! Go! Fail without the great Achilles. I will be here when you return—to hear you begging.

NARRATOR: Priam and Helen watched from the height of the Trojan walls as the great army came finally to a halt far beneath them.

AGAMEMNON: (shouting) Trojans! Beg for mercy! Zeus has smiled upon his Greeks!

NARRATOR: As if in response, the Trojan gates opened, and Hector, Paris, and a troop of men issued slowly forth—holding the banner of truce above their head. Agamemnon and Menelaus came forward to meet them.

AGAMEMNON: (boasting) Ah, so I see you have come to grovel! How pleasing!

HECTOR: (sternly) Hold your tongue, Greek. We have come to suggest a solution to this bloodshed.

AGAMEMNON: A solution is at hand. Zeus has promised *us* victory.

HECTOR: (sarcastically) Yes, I'm sure he has. I do not come to speak to you, but to your brother. Tell me, Menelaus, do you like being the laughing stock of the whole world?

MENELAUS: (angrily) Why you—!

HECTOR: My brother, Paris, here has made a fool of you. He has stolen your pretty wife. Wouldn't you like his insolent head on a platter?

PARIS: (whispering) I don't think he needs any persuading.

MENELAUS: (angrily) Yes! I should have known that was you, you miserable whelp. Hiding behind your walls! We have missed you in the battle! Have you been hiding with the women?

HECTOR: Enough. I've come to give you a chance to exact your revenge on my dear brother.

AGAMEMNON: What do you propose?

HECTOR: A man-to-man battle.

MENELAUS: (excitedly) To the death!

HECTOR: Exactly. Agamemnon, if your eager brother here wins, we will give you what you have come for—Helen of Troy. Or should I say Sparta?

PARIS: (forcefully) Troy.

HECTOR: And if my love-struck brother should win, we keep Helen, and you may all go home. We will even give you enough gold to make your vacation here worthwhile.

AGAMEMNON: Brother, may I speak to you a moment aside?

NARRATOR: Agamemnon and Menelaus withdrew from the others.

AGAMEMNON: Zeus has promised victory. It doesn't matter how—great armies or man-to-man. You must fight this boy.

MENELAUS: Gladly! He has insulted me! His very face is a mockery to me! I will cut it open.

AGAMEMNON: Good. (loudly) Trojan princes, we agree to your terms. My brother is ready. Is yours?

HECTOR: Yes.

NARRATOR: And so the two crowds parted, making way for the combatants. High above on the walls of the city, Helen, crying softly, held the hand of King Priam.

Higher still, other spectators—of the immortal variety—were watching these events with interest as well. Hera and Athena, who both had been furiously trying to bring about the defeat of the Trojans, sat on the chairs of Olympus peering down to earth.

HERA: Ha! The little wispy prince is going to fight the mighty Greek king. Come, Athena, let us watch him be skewered.

ATHENA: He looks like a woman in that armor. Pathetic.

HERA: No wonder he was such a terrible judge of beauty. No manliness in him at all.

NARRATOR: From across the marble hall in which they sat, Aphrodite floated into view. She, too, had come to watch this battle.

ATHENA: (disappointedly) Ugh. Don't look now.

HERA: Aphrodite, how nice. We were just starting to watch your darling Trojan prince be filleted by a hulking Greek.

ATHENA: I bet he cries—begging for mercy before the end.

APHRODITE: (shocked) Paris, no!

NARRATOR: Below them, the battle was beginning.

Athena was right. Paris' armor dwarfed him. He held his sword as if he had never done so before. In fact, he almost hadn't. What did he know of fighting? He had been raised as a shepherd.

Menelaus, a red-headed giant, rippled with power. His great frame held his weapon and shield aloft with majesty. All could see that Paris was no match for him.

AGAMEMNON: (shouting) Fight!

MENELAUS: Hopefully, you have kissed my wife goodbye. This will be the last time you see her.

PARIS: I doubt that.

NARRATOR: Menelaus hurled his spear forth with all his might against Paris' shield. (clang) The shield clattered to the ground. Menelaus roared with laughter.

MENELAUS: Boy, I plan to gouge your eyes out and then send you into Hades blinded.

PARIS: We'll see!

NARRATOR: Menelaus drew his sword and sliced, but Paris was too fast. He swooped beneath it and brought his own sword up against Menelaus' breastplate. (clang)

MENELAUS: I grow tired of this, Trojan. I had hoped to pierce your pretty little head on the first throw.

PARIS: Sorry to keep you waiting.

NARRATOR: Moving swiftly, Paris brought his sword about. It flashed through the air and met Menelaus' with a crash of sound. (*clang*) The force of the blow knocked the sword from Paris' hand, and he fell backward into the dirt.

MENELAUS: (*laughing*) These weapons are for *men*! Not for dainty creatures such as yourself!

HECTOR: (*shouting*) Get up, Paris! Get up!

AGAMEMNON: (*shouting*) Finish him!

NARRATOR: From her viewpoint in the clouds, Aphrodite saw Paris fall. In the flash of an eye, she was gone—flying earthward to save her darling prince.

ATHENA: (*angrily*) Cheat! How dare she interfere! After her!

HERA: (*calmly*) Patience, Athena. This should be interesting. Let us watch the Trojan prince be protected by the goddess of *love*. (*snotty laugh*)

ATHENA: (*laughing*) I never thought of that. How embarrassing to be saved by that creampuff!

NARRATOR: Menelaus reached down into the dust and grabbed Paris by the horse-hair crest of his helmet. He began to drag him. The Greeks started to cheer. (*Greek cheering*)

MENELAUS: Troy! Look at your beautiful *princess*! I drag *her* through the dirt! Have you no *men* to send to fight me?

NARRATOR: He turned to drive his sword through Paris' throat. But Aphrodite was there—invisible to all. She broke the strap on Paris' helmet, and he was free.

APHRODITE: (*shouting*) Run, Paris, run!

MENELAUS: Coward! Have you not shamed your country enough?

HECTOR: (*sadly*) Oh, Paris.

NARRATOR: As Paris ran, Aphrodite shrouded him in a giant cloud. When the smoke cleared, he was gone. He had been taken back safely behind the walls of Troy. Aphrodite's move had been played. Now, it was Hera's turn.

HERA: Athena, let us descend.

NARRATOR: The Greeks were in an uproar. Never before had they seen such a display of cowardice.

AGAMEMNON: Trojans, is this the best you can do? You have forfeited your prize. Bring her forward so that we may go home—in Zeus' victory!

NARRATOR: On the walls of Troy, Priam hung his head in shame. Helen began to sob.

HELEN: (*crying*) Is there nothing that can be done?

PRIAM: I am sorry, my dear. We have agreed to the terms.

NARRATOR: With an invisible gush of wind, Hera and Athena settled to the earth quietly behind Agamemnon and Menelaus.

ATHENA: *(angrily)* This is ridiculous! The war can't be over! Troy is still standing!

HERA: Do not worry. We shall see it burn yet. They will not get off so easily.

MENELAUS: *(shouting)* My wife! My wife! Bring forward my wife!

HERA: That young Trojan archer—with the brown eyes. Do you see him?

ATHENA: I do. Do you have a plan?

HERA: Of course. Go to him. Whisper in his ear. Persuade him to fire his weapon and break this truce. If Helen is returned to Menelaus, we will see this war end too soon!

ATHENA: Lovely. A carefully placed arrow would be the perfect thing to get this battle back to fever pitch. You are full of good ideas.

HERA: Naturally.

NARRATOR: As the Trojans prepared to re-enter the city and present the Greeks with Helen, Athena moved silently behind Pandarus, a young Trojan archer.

ATHENA: *(forcefully)* Pandarus, look at that evil man—Menelaus. He has won unjustly today. He has mocked your country—your king. He will not leave Troy so lightly. He will not stop until he has burned it to the ground—killing your children—taking your wife as his own. End his life now, before he ends yours!

NARRATOR: And Pandarus, barely knowing what he was doing, turned—bow in hand—and fired an arrow into the shoulder of Menelaus.

MENELAUS: *(cry of pain)*

NARRATOR: Pandemonium ensued. Menelaus was wounded but not killed. The Greeks brandished their swords. The Trojans turned—confused—and rushed to meet them. The battle was thick once again. On the walls, Priam groaned.

PRIAM: Well, my dear, it seems that you shall not have to go—but I fear many more Trojans will die.

HELEN: *(sadly)* All for me.

NARRATOR: Though none could see them through the rush of bodies, the clashing of metal, and the dirt of battle, two Olympian forms sauntered as if out for a summer's stroll.

HERA: Not, bad, dear. Not bad.

ATHENA: All in all, I say it's not a bad day's work.

NARRATOR: In the midst of the surrounding chaos, a silvery cloud began to form in front of them.

HERA: Aphrodite, darling, have you delivered your weakling prince?

APHRODITE: *(seething)* Oooh! You two do not play fair!

ATHENA: What do you call swooping down to save your Trojan pet?

APHRODITE: I am not the only god who will be caught up in this! I have powerful allies! Many gods who are close to me!

HERA: Yes, and we have some idea *how* close.

ATHENA: We're terrified. Really.

APHRODITE: *(angrily)* Oooh!

NARRATOR: Aphrodite's cloud disappeared with a cry of disgust.

HERA: She is rather unattractive when she's angry.

ATHENA: True.

HERA: I don't know about you, goddess of war, but I think this conflict has only just begun.

ATHENA: I as well.

HERA: Soon, we will be dancing over ravaging flames. We shall hear their women wailing—lamenting the dead. Smoke will rise from the walls—billows of smoke from the burning of Troy, Aphrodite's precious city. What a day that will be!

ATHENA: Amen.

DISCUSSION QUESTIONS

- How are Paris and Hector typical brothers?
- Judging by Homer's portrayal of the gods, do you think he actually believed in them? Explain.
- What do the other Trojans think of Paris?
- The story of the Trojan War could have ended after the duel of Paris and Menelaus. Would this have been a satisfactory ending? Explain.

THE RAGE OF ACHILLES
TEACHER GUIDE

BACKGROUND

The *Iliad* begins, "Rage—Goddess, sing the rage of Peleus' son Achilles" (trans. Fagles). Homer's theme of Achilles' rage is appropriate as it is Achilles who determines the course of the war. Without him, the Greeks are weak, and when he re-enters the battle after the death of his beloved friend, Patroclus, Achilles is a tornado of fury. In a fit of violent hatred he slays Hector—a foe who has eluded him for ten years—and then dishonorably violates his body.

In addition to excellent storytelling, there's a strong message here: Rage can help you achieve your goals, but it can also cause you to lose your honor. In an extremely moving moment, Achilles agrees to give Hector's body back—not because the gods are angry—but because he has discovered his compassion. This may be the first example of meaningful character development in all of western literature. Amid all the war, all the rage, Achilles has learned what it truly means to be noble.

The epic ends with the funeral of Hector. Achilles knows that his death is soon to follow. The victor will become the victim. Nothing—not even the gods—can stop the turning wheel of fate.

SUMMARY

Even the gods have become embroiled in the conflict of the Trojan War. They fight with one another amid the warring of the Greeks and the Trojans. The Trojan warrior Aeneas is about to be slain by the Greek Diomedes then Aeneas' mother, the goddess Aphrodite, appears. Instead of being intimidated by the goddess, Diomedes drives his spear into her hand. Aphrodite flies directly to Olympus to complain to Zeus, who has grown tired of the gods' bickering. Hera asks for permission for Diomedes to wound her son, Ares, who is fighting on the side of the Trojans. Zeus allows this, and Diomedes hurls his spear into the chest of Ares. Ares, too, flies to Olympus to complain to his father. Zeus has had enough and summons all the gods to Olympus, commanding that they no longer intervene in the battle. They grudgingly agree.

After the other gods have gone, Thetis appears to Zeus and reminds him of his promise: He has agreed to help the Trojans win the war while Achilles is out of the battle. Zeus agrees to aid the Trojans—but only slightly.

The Trojans drive the Greeks back to their encampment on the beach. Hearing the battle so near, Patroclus begs his good friend Achilles to consider fighting, but Achilles refuses. Patroclus then asks to wear Achilles' armor and lead the Myrmidons into battle. Achilles agrees.

Patroclus, disguised as Achilles, strikes fear into the Trojans and drives them back from the Greek camp. Hector duels with Patroclus, slays him, and removes his armor only to discover his true identity. The Trojans retreat back to Troy.

When Achilles hears of Patroclus' death, he is enraged and spurs his chariot toward Troy, yelling for Hector to face him. Hector bids his family farewell and faces Achilles before the Trojan walls. Hector asks Achilles to honor his last request and return his body to his family if he should lose. Achilles refuses. The two duel, and Achilles slays Hector. He ties the prince's body to the back of his chariot, drags it around the walls of Troy several times, and returns to the Greek camp. Zeus, outraged by this, arranges for Hermes to lead King Priam into the Greek camp to reclaim Hector's body. Priam appears in Achilles' tent and begs the warrior to return his son to him—kissing the warrior's bloodstained hand. Achilles is moved to tears by Priam's pleas, and he agrees. The story ends with Achilles observing the funeral pyre of Hector far away on the walls of Troy.

ESSENTIAL QUESTIONS

- Is revenge a good cause to fight for?
- What are the rules of war?
- What is true courage?

CONNECTIONS

Troy **(2004)** Although this film is a flawed attempt at bringing Homer's *Iliad* to the silver screen, it features many scenes that capture the spirit of the Trojan War. The duel scene between Achilles and Hector is particularly well done. **Warning:** This film is rated "R" and contains many scenes of graphic violence and nudity. Scan and preview for scenes you feel to be appropriate for your students.

ANTICIPATORY QUESTIONS

- What could cause Achilles to re-enter the battle?
- Could a mortal wound a god?
- Which characters have not yet faced off in battle?
- If you knew you could not win a fight, would you still fight?

TEACHABLE TERMS

- **Culture**   On pg. 59 Achilles weeps freely after his encounter with the Trojan king, Priam. In Greek culture it was not considered unmanly to weep. Ask students if this is different in their own culture and analyze why or why not.

- **Compare/Contrast**   Have the students compare and contrast the characters of Achilles and Hector. What do they fight for? What do they value?
- **Character Development** By the end of this play, Achilles has changed from the hot-headed warrior he was at the myth's beginning. Ask the students to analyze this change, focusing on the scene on pg. 58 between Achilles and Priam.
- **Predict** Before reading "The Rage of Achilles," have the students predict what will happen in the play based solely on the title. Have them explain their theories.
- **Metaphor** Achilles says, "There are no pacts between wolves and lambs" on pg. 56, comparing Hector to a lamb and himself to a wolf. Have students determine the meaning of these metaphors.

RECALL QUESTIONS

1. Who are the two gods Diomedes wounds?
2. What command does Zeus give all the gods?
3. Why does Achilles re-enter the battle?
4. How does Achilles desecrate Hector's body after winning his duel?
5. What request does Priam make of Achilles?

THE RAGE OF ACHILLES

CAST

ZEUS	*Ruler of the Gods*
ATHENA	*Goddess of Wisdom*
ARES	*God of War*
ARTEMIS	*Goddess of the Moon*
APOLLO	*God of Light*
HERA	*Queen of Heaven*
DIOMEDES	*Mighty Greek Warrior*
AENEAS	*Son of Aphrodite*
APHRODITE	*Goddess of Love*
HECTOR	*Greatest Prince of Troy*
PARIS	*Prince of Troy*
PRIAM	*Old King of Troy*
HELEN	*Wife of Menelaus*
ANDROMACHE	*Wife of Hector*
THETIS	*Mother of Achilles*
ACHILLES	*Greatest Greek Warrior*
PATROCLUS	*Achilles' Best Friend*

NARRATOR: An eagle soared above the plains of Troy. Far below, it could see tiny bodies rushing at one another through the fog of war. Its eyes were the eyes of Zeus.

ZEUS: *(sigh)* This battle will never end, I fear.

NARRATOR: Not only men, but also the gods fought in hand-to-hand combat. The war had become personal, and they warred in the midst of the mortals—god against god. The eye of the eagle focused in.

ATHENA: How dare you, you little worm!

ARTEMIS: Ooof! *(choking)* *(sounds of scuffling)*

NARRATOR: Amid the fray, Athena had taken Artemis' bow from her hands and was lashing her across her face with it. Aphrodite rushed in to rescue her.

APHRODITE: Take this, you cheating cow!

NARRATOR: The goddess of love swung her fist with all her might into the gut of her niece.

ATHENA: Ugh. You call that a punch? Stay out of war! It's no place for hussies like you!

NARRATOR: Blazing like the sun, Apollo swooped in from nowhere, driving his golden chariot.

APOLLO: Ladies! You are goddesses of Olympus! You should not be fighting amongst the mortals!

HERA: Oh, Apollo, pull that stick out of your—

NARRATOR: Hera drove her spear into the spokes of Apollo's chariot wheel, and it shattered immediately. Apollo was thrown violently to the ground!

ARTEMIS: *(to Hera)* Why you old bag! Nobody picks on my brother!

NARRATOR: Artemis cried out and jumped onto Hera's back—taking handfuls of pampered locks between her fingers.

HERA: *(cries in pain)* Hair-pulling! Typical of a weakling!

NARRATOR: Artemis yanked Hera's head back fiercely and reclaimed her bow from the goddess' hands.

ARTEMIS: I'll show you a weakling, you old sow!

NARRATOR: The gods continued to struggle.

ZEUS: *(sigh)* Show me the mortal realm.

NARRATOR: The view blurred and changed. In between the gods, now the humans could be seen—fighting just as fiercely.

Achilles still refused to re-enter the battle, and in his absence, the mighty Greek Diomedes had gained acclaim. By his prowess alone, he had brought down many noble Trojans.

At the moment, he was working on one more. He had cornered Aeneas, the Trojan son of Aphrodite. A cruel smile spread upon his lips.

DIOMEDES: Filthy Trojan! I have slit the throats of many of your countrymen. Now, I have come for yours.

AENEAS: Go home, fool, or I shall send you to Hades.

NARRATOR: Diomedes cried and lunged forward. Aeneas faltered and came under the mercy of the vicious Greek. Diomedes raised his spear to skewer his Trojan enemy. But Aphrodite had seen her darling son at the point of death. She turned from her own Olympian battle to come to his rescue.

APHRODITE: Aeneas!

NARRATOR: She shot forward—between him and the cruel weapon of the Greek—reaching her beautiful arms out to grasp Aeneas and carry him away.

Gazing through the dust of battle, Diomedes blinked. Inches in front of him, he thought he saw a beautiful form appear around Aeneas! He paused with his spear in midair.

DIOMEDES: *(in awe)* A goddess!

NARRATOR: And as the otherworldly arms encircled Aeneas to carry him away, a new thought crossed Diomedes' mind.

DIOMEDES: Why should I fear Olympus? This is war!

NARRATOR: With a cry, he drove the point of his weapon into the soft flesh of Aphrodite's hand.

APHRODITE: Ahhhhhhhhhhhh! My hand! *(cries of pain)*

NARRATOR: She grabbed her wound—dropping Aeneas back into the dirt.

DIOMEDES: *(yelling)* Goddess of love, do not forget Greece! She has stung you!

NARRATOR: Aphrodite flew toward Olympus—holding her injured hand—wailing and moaning as she went.

APHRODITE: (*shrieking*) A stinking mortal! I've been wounded by a stinking mortal!

NARRATOR: Diomedes rushed forward to once again take the Trojan life he had coveted. But Apollo, in his goodness, saw Aeneas where his mother had abandoned him and enveloped him in a golden cloud—transporting him back behind the walls of Troy to safety.

APOLLO: Go, son of Troy. You are no match for this bloodthirsty Greek. I will send Hector his way and see how he fares against a prince.

NARRATOR: Meanwhile, Aphrodite made a noisy entrance into the echoing colonnades of Olympus. There her cries stirred the attention of Zeus. He turned from the eyes of his eagle.

ZEUS: What is this noise, woman?

APHRODITE: (*whining*) Brother, a disgusting Greek stuck his sword into me! How dare he cause a goddess to feel pain! I want to know what you're going to do about it!

ZEUS: (*laughing*) Nothing. Now you know how mortals feel. Perhaps that will teach you not to interfere in their affairs.

APHRODITE: (*hatefully*) Maybe you should get off your high horse and put an end to all this!

ZEUS: (*seriously*) Look at them, Aphrodite. Dying for what they believe in: honor, valor, even love. They all look to us for guidance. What guidance do we give them if we are just as petty as they are?

APHRODITE: (*angrily*) I wouldn't expect *you* to understand!

ZEUS: (*sigh*) Aphrodite, leave me. Return to your battle. You have made your bed. Now you must lie in it.

HERA: Ah, but, husband, she is far better at lying in other people's.

NARRATOR: Hera, her face dirty and clothes torn, appeared in the hallway—glaring at Aphrodite.

HERA: Remove yourself at once, or I will do it for you.

APHRODITE: I was just leaving.

HERA: Good.

NARRATOR: With a final whimper, Aphrodite vanished.

ZEUS: Has there ever been a greater war than this one? The gods even feel the pain of it. What do *you* want?

HERA: This Greek, Diomedes, has proved himself most capable in Achilles' absence. He is fighting Hector, the prince of Troy, as we speak.

ZEUS: So? I grow weary of bloodshed. Let them kill until they have had their fill.

HERA: You're not listening. Alone Hector is no match for Diomedes, but Ares fights alongside the Trojan prince, filling him with the power to hack Greeks down left and right. Our swine-headed son has chosen to side with his hussy, Aphrodite.

ZEUS: And your point? I'm sure *your* hand has been in plenty of Greek victories.

HERA: I do not wish to give Diomedes an advantage necessarily. I just want to even the playing field. Aphrodite has been wounded. Let me cause Diomedes to see beyond his own world and behold the great god of war! Let the god feel the sting of mortal steel!

ZEUS: *(shocked)* Our son? You wish to do this to our son?

HERA: He is no son of ours. He is a tumor. A blight on our glorious mountain. We must cut him out. But he will not die—only taste my anger.

ZEUS: I know you. You will not let me rest until you have had your way. Do as you will. I wish all the gods could feel pain. Then perhaps we would not be so quick to give it to others.

HERA: A very wise decision. I go at once.

ZEUS: *(to himself)* Where will it all end?

NARRATOR: Settling back to Earth, Hera neared where Diomedes and Hector furiously battled. Ares was there behind the Trojan prince, guiding his arm. Diomedes was soon to fail under the onslaught of the dual attack.

ARES: Ah, Mother. Come to see my latest kill?

HERA: *(shouting)* Son, do not be too quick to forget your brain and leave all decisions to the loins! You should not have sided with the harlot of Olympus!

ARES: *(angrily)* Mother, you don't know anything about war! I love to see death—Greek or Trojan it matters not.

HERA: You are no son of mine, you cur. Prepare to know my hatred.

NARRATOR: Waving her arms, Hera pulled back the veil between the mortal and immortal worlds. Into Diomedes' view came the towering form of Ares, red-skinned and clad in black, shining armor. Once again his lust for glory drove his arm, and he hurled his spear—not at Hector—but into the chest of that terrible god. Ares let out a bellow—one that knocked every mortal from their feet and caused every Olympian to freeze in mid-strike.

ARES: *(screams)* Ahhh! Zeus shall hear of this, wench!

NARRATOR: Shooting straight up into the air, Ares cursed his mother, and Hector was left alone amid the fray.

ARES: *(screaming)* Father! Father!

ZEUS: *(exasperated)* What is it now?

ARES: Hera has allowed a mortal to wound me—*me*—the god of war!

ZEUS: Ares, please, don't take yourself so seriously.

ARES: Father, I have put up with this as long as I can. She is *your* wife. You must control her. If you do not have the backbone to stand up to her—then you are not fit to sit on that throne!

ZEUS: *(yelling)* Silence, insolent pup! Don't forget who wields the mighty thunderbolt! It was my generation that defeated the Titans, not you sniveling brats!

NARRATOR: Zeus rose from his throne—his figure growing, filling the room. Ares shrunk back in fear.

ZEUS: I rule the universe! Let all the gods together fix a chain to me! You will not drag down Zeus! I have given you a home! I have given you power! I have given you life! Yet I hear nothing but complaints day after day! I am sick of it! Enough!

NARRATOR: He cupped his hands into a divine megaphone.

ZEUS: *(shouting)* Olympians, return immediately or face my wrath!

NARRATOR: On the battlefield below, all the gods and goddesses stopped in their tracks. They had heard the cry of Zeus. He meant business.

ZEUS: There will be a meeting at once!

NARRATOR: In the blink of an eye, every immortal was in the great hall—nervously tapping their fingers and avoiding eye contact. Only Hera seemed unbothered by Zeus' seething anger and strolled among the others like a lioness.

ZEUS: *(yelling)* This nonsense will stop! My sisters! My brothers! My sons! My daughters! Fighting! Like common men amongst ourselves! We are gods! We should start acting like it! We do not let petty jealousy divide us! From this moment on, I shall direct this war. No one else.

HERA: She started it!

NARRATOR: Hera pointed an accusing finger at Aphrodite.

ZEUS: And *I* am going to end it!

HERA: I hardly think that's fair!

ZEUS: Silence, woman, or you will feel more than sharp words.

NARRATOR: Hera scowled—but stayed silent. Zeus stalked angrily among the gods.

ZEUS: No one is to leave the halls of Olympus. Greece and Troy are dead to you. Your glory is no longer theirs. Your interference is done. *(calming down)* Now, I have said my piece. You may go.

NARRATOR: Sulking, the gods and goddesses milled out of the great hall. Zeus slunk down into his throne and covered his face with his hand. He heard soft footsteps approaching him.

ZEUS: *(half-groaning)* What now?

THETIS: Zeus!

NARRATOR: He slowly looked up. It was Thetis, the immortal mother of Achilles.

ZEUS: Yes, Thetis. What is it?

THETIS: Surely you have not forgotten your promise. The Greeks haven't failed yet. I have seen the future. My son will soon re-enter the battle, if you do not intervene.

ZEUS: I have removed all interferences. No god or goddess will give their support to either side.

THETIS: Here on Olympus maybe. But what about mighty Poseidon? Who will watch him? How do you know that he will not slink out of the sea and aid the Greeks?

ZEUS: Do not try to turn me against my brother Poseidon. I have agreed to help you, and I will. I will give my support to the Trojans—but only slightly. I will not determine the course of this war. It is for men to decide.

THETIS: That is all that I ask. Thank you, Zeus.

ZEUS: (sigh)

NARRATOR: With the support of Zeus and the removal of the Olympians, the tide turned in favor of the Trojans. They drove the Greeks back to their camp beside the hollow ships. Victory was almost at hand. In his lodge, Achilles heard the fight raging just over the top of the hill. He felt soft footsteps in the gloom behind him.

ACHILLES: I see that you have been busy, Mother.

THETIS: Yes, there isn't anything I wouldn't do to save my darling boy.

ACHILLES: Like slaughter a thousand Greeks.

THETIS: Achilles! I only do this because I love you.

ACHILLES: Uh-huh.

THETIS: Now, stay here with your men. I will warn you when the fighting is over. Then, you and your Myrmidons can board your ships and return home.

ACHILLES: Yes, Mother.

NARRATOR: He felt a rustle of wind, and Thetis was gone. Running footsteps beat their way up to the flap of the tent. His dearest friend, Patroclus burst inside—out of breath.

PATROCLUS: Achilles, the Trojans have nearly topped the hill! If they break through the walls, we're finished!

ACHILLES: This is not our fight, Patroclus.

PATROCLUS: You have to do something! How long can your stubbornness hold out? The Myrmidons will follow you into battle! Lead them!

ACHILLES: I will not fight for Agamemnon!

PATROCLUS: Odysseus says that Agamemnon has agreed to give Briseis back to you—and—and gold—if you'll only fight!

ACHILLES: The girl? This isn't about a girl. And gold? He could offer me all the gold in Egypt. I would die before I helped him.

PATROCLUS: (somberly) Then we really are doomed.

ACHILLES: Not we, Patroclus—they.

PATROCLUS: No. We are all Greeks. I, for one, will not sit by and let my brothers be slaughtered. Let me wear your armor. Let me lead the Myrmidons.

NARRATOR: Achilles paused and stared into the eyes of his friend.

ACHILLES: If you think this is your fight, I will give you my blessing. But do not ask me to go against my heart.

PATROCLUS: Thank you!

NARRATOR: The swift-footed warrior placed his hand on Patroclus' noble shoulder.

ACHILLES: We were raised as brothers, Patroclus. I could bear the loss of all others—but not you. I promised father I'd return you safely home. Take my armor. Drive the Trojans back. Save the Greeks—for today. But stay away from stallion-breaking Hector.

NARRATOR: His comrade took up the glistening armor and turned to go.

ACHILLES: Patroclus.

PATROCLUS: Yes?

ACHILLES: Return safely.

NARRATOR: When Patroclus topped the hill, disguised as Achilles, the Myrmidons rose from where they had been sitting idly for days and cheered.

PATROCLUS: (shouting) Men! It is time to fight! Let us see Troy in ruins!

NARRATOR: Thinking that their leader had finally come to his senses, the men grabbed their weapons and charged after him. Achilles was back! The Greeks were sure to conquer now!

When Hector—leading a charge against the Greek battlements—saw the armor of Achilles top the walls, his heart sank. The Myrmidons poured over the walls like ants and began to drive the Trojans back.

HECTOR: Father Zeus protect us.

NARRATOR: Father Zeus viewed this all from above. Something monumental was about to happen. He would need to—

HERA: (soothingly) Husband…

NARRATOR: He turned. Hera was there—but somehow different. She was dressed in a radiant gown—the same gown in which she had once appeared to Paris. Zeus' heart leapt. Somewhere deep down he remembered why he had chosen her as his bride.

HERA: (sing-song voice) Husband, worrying has become your hobby, has it not?

ZEUS: (confused) Yes, it has. No thanks to you and your posse.

HERA: (cutely) I know, I know, darling. That's why I've come. I've come to apologize—for my behavior.

ZEUS: Apologize? That is a bit odd for you.

HERA: But definitely deserved. I was a fool. I let my jealousy get the best of me.

ZEUS: And your blasted temper!

HERA: Oh, yes, a terrible temper. How do you ever put up with me? (sweetly) Come here, husband, let me rub your shoulders.

ZEUS: Well, that would be nice.

HERA: (soothingly) Greeks—Trojans—forget about them. I have. Just relax.

NARRATOR: She began to hum softly—weaving her spell.

HERA: Sleep, Zeus, sleep. Forget the world. Forget Troy.

ZEUS: Well—I—certainly—am—feeling—a bit—sleepy— (snoring)

HERA: (hatefully) Ha! Dumb oaf.

NARRATOR: She left his side and ran quickly through the deserted halls of Olympus. Reaching the east edge of the palace, she leaned over, looking down to the ocean far below.

HERA: *(yelling)* Brother Poseidon! I have put the great Zeus to sleep! I have worked my spell! Now, let's make these Trojans bleed!

NARRATOR: Poseidon heard her cry and from beneath the sea his mighty hands surged forth. The Greeks felt his power move through them. Not only had the fearsome Achilles returned, but now, the gods once again favored them. The Trojan troops were driven back even further from the beaches.

Patroclus, disguised as Achilles, pushed forward, cutting Trojan heads from Trojan bodies. Many fled before him, but one stood his ground—the brave Hector. The prince of Troy loomed through the clouds of dust and came face to face with the mighty opponent he had not yet faced.

HECTOR: At last, Achilles, we two meet. It is here that this war will be decided—with our blood.

PATROCLUS: Correction—your blood!

NARRATOR: Patroclus let out a war cry and rushed forward. Wearing Achilles' armor had perhaps given him too much confidence. It was a clumsy attack, and Patroclus exposed his weakness.

Hector sidestepped Patroclus effortlessly and brought his spear up beneath his opponent's golden shield. The Greek felt the Trojan's spear enter his stomach. The force of his run drove it in deeper. Hector jerked loose his spear, and Patroclus fell to the ground—lifeless. Hector knelt and removed the dead man's helmet.

HECTOR: What? This is an imposter! What is the meaning of this?

NARRATOR: There was no reply as the spirit of Patroclus slipped from his body and sank into the Underworld.

Slumbering loudly on his throne, Zeus had missed this fateful battle. Aphrodite, who had been furiously pacing about the palace, suddenly appeared in the doorway of the great hall.

APHRODITE: *(screaming)* Zeus! What are you doing?

ZEUS: *(waking up)* Huh, what?

APHRODITE: Sleeping? The fate of the known world is at stake, and you're sleeping?

ZEUS: Sleeping? But I— *(roaring)* Heeeeera!

NARRATOR: Below on the battlefield, Hector had removed the golden armor of Achilles from Patroclus. This was his to wear not. The Trojan prince fell back to where his men had retreated—below the walls of Troy.

In camp, Achilles learned of what had befallen his friend. Blinded by tears of anger, he jumped into his chariot—sword in hand—and whipped the horses into a frenzy. He was out for blood! He would slaughter the man who had slain Patroclus!

ACHILLES: *(screaming)* Hector! Hector!

NARRATOR: Achilles tore down the plains toward Troy. The land was a blur beside him as he sped, but in the smeared flashes of color, he saw his mother flying alongside him.

THETIS: *(frantically)* Achilles! No! All that I have worked for! Don't risk your life for this man!

ACHILLES: *(crazy)* He has killed Patroclus, Mother! I will kill him and everyone he loves!

THETIS: Son! He may kill *you!*

ACHILLES: I will not die. It will be his flesh that the birds will feast on.

THETIS: (*crying*) Son, you have no armor! Please, this is madness.

ACHILLES: I will fight him with my fists if I have to, Mother. (*screaming*) Hector!

THETIS: (*frantically*) There! In your chariot, I had hoped not to use it. I had Hephaestus make you almighty armor in his forge! It will protect you! Please, promise you will take it!

ACHILLES: I don't need magic to protect me! I'm not a weakling! I am Achilles! (*screaming*) Hector!

THETIS: (*softly*) Please, son, for your mother—

ACHILLES: (*quietly*) I will, Mother, but your meddling is done. My fate is my fate. Whatever will be, will be.

THETIS: But, Achilles—

ACHILLES: Goodbye, Mother. (*yelling*) Hector! Hector!

NARRATOR: His chariot was now in sight of the Trojan walls. Hector stood inside Troy's open gates watching the trail of dust make its way across the plain—his face grim.

HECTOR: This man will be the death of me.

NARRATOR: Hector's wife, Andromache, came to stand with him one last time. In her white arms she held their infant son, Astyanax.

ANDROMACHE: (*crying*) Be careful, my husband. I have heard stories of this Greek's—brutality.

HECTOR: (*soothingly*) Hush now.

ANDROMACHE: What will I do? What will our son do if you should die?

HECTOR: Troy will always live on—no matter what happens to me. He is our future. Astyanax, did you hear that? You are our future.

NARRATOR: He took his son and kissed his head. Then he took his wife and kissed her one final time.

HECTOR: Now, I must go. Troy will not fall this day.

ANDROMACHE: (*crying*) See that *you* do not.

ACHILLES: (*bellowing*) Hector! Hector!

NARRATOR: Without looking back, Hector stepped through the gates of Troy. They closed behind him as Achilles' chariot skidded to a stop yards before him.

In the distance, large groups of Greeks could be seen making their way toward the city. They were coming to see the fight.

Achilles jumped quickly out of the chariot and started to buckle on his shining armor.

ACHILLES: (*violently*) Hector! You and I! No one else. You have killed my friend. Now, I return the favor!

HECTOR: I only did what I had to do. You would have done no less.

ACHILLES: Do not speak to me, you piece of filth!

HECTOR: I will fight you, but I ask one thing—

ACHILLES: Do not ask me for anything! I give murderers no favors! Wolves make no pacts with lambs!

HECTOR: Are you not an honorable man? If I die in this battle, give my body back to my family, so that I may have a godly burial.

ACHILLES: You deserve nothing! What do you know of honor? Whose armor do you wear now, you vomiting dog?

HECTOR: Yours—but I see that you have gotten a fine replacement—from the gods no doubt.

ACHILLES: Enough! I will cut your body to pieces, and it shall lie in the sun until the birds pick it clean.

HECTOR: So be it.

NARRATOR: The two faced off under the heat of the blazing Trojan sun.

Swift-footed Achilles began to dance, crouching and springing. The long fight had been building up within him. Hector stood his ground, strong and regal, worthy of a Trojan prince. They started to circle one another.

From the walls, Paris watched with shame.

PARIS: This is all because of me.

HELEN: No—me.

ACHILLES: Time to die, Trojan.

NARRATOR: Achilles darted forward—spinning as he came. His spear hummed as it cut the air. (clang) Hector blocked the blow, but it had been close.

HECTOR: (sarcastically) Perhaps I would be a better warrior if I had god-given armor.

ACHILLES: Perhaps I will use your guts as a sash.

NARRATOR: Achilles charged again, but this time, Hector brought up his spear. Achilles faltered for a moment, but changed direction and gripped the spear—ripping it from Hector's grasp.

HECTOR: (grunt) Not to worry. I have other ways of defending myself.

NARRATOR: Hector pulled out his sword. He steadied himself—waiting for the next advance.

ACHILLES: Skewered by his own spear—how fitting!

NARRATOR: Achilles pummeled forward once again—sword in one hand and spear in another. Hector blocked the sword with his shield, but the spear—the spear Achilles drove deep into the soft flesh at his neck.

HECTOR: (cries out) (choking)

ANDROMACHE: Noooooo!

NARRATOR: Hector fell on the battlefield. The world stood still for a moment. Achilles knelt over the body and pushed the spear in deeper for good measure. A black pool of blood started to spread out over the sands. Wailing was heard from the walls of Troy.

PARIS: (strangely) Hector! I must save him—

ANDROMACHE: *(weeping)* Too late. You had your chance!

PARIS: I—I—Hector.

ANDROMACHE: Don't say his name. You are not worthy enough to speak it. He has died for your stupidity. Now, leave him be.

NARRATOR: The triumphant Greek spectators cheered and, rushing forward from the ring they had formed, began to kick the lifeless body and drive their own swords into its flesh.

ACHILLES: Trojans! See what I have done to your dishonorable prince! Who is next? I will kill you all for the grief that you have given me.

NARRATOR: From his high viewpoint, Priam clutched his chest. His most beloved son now lay in the dirt.

PRIAM: *(weeping)* My son—gods above—give me back my son.

NARRATOR: But Hector was gone. In his madness, Achilles shooed away the soldiers, rolled the corpse over and spat in its face. Taking the point of his sword, he drove it through the dead man's feet. Through these holes he fed leather straps, and he lashed them to his chariot.

ACHILLES: Now see how the Greeks honor fools!

NARRATOR: He spurred his horses forward. The chariot rocked into motion—the body of Hector being dragged behind. Achilles started to scream.

ACHILLES: *(screaming)* Fear me, Trojans, the mighty Achilles! See your dead Hector! See how his skin rips from his body! How low is your precious prince now?

NARRATOR: Around the walls of Troy, he tore. Andromache turned away in grief. Paris could not look away. Priam buried his head in his hands.

ACHILLES: Watch the worms infest him! The dogs eat his organs! You will see him rot before you! Troy! Troy! Time to smell the stench of your leader!

NARRATOR: From Olympus, Zeus watched with disapproval. The champion of his favorite city was being dragged through the dirt like a dead animal.

ZEUS: *(booming)* Thetis! Thetis!

NARRATOR: Thetis appeared in a shimmering wave of color.

THETIS: *(innocently)* Yes, Zeus?

ZEUS: Your son—is shaming Greece.

THETIS: *(groveling)* Oh, Zeus, please. I told him not to go. He won't listen.

ZEUS: You must make him listen, or he will anger me.

THETIS: Yes, Zeus.

ZEUS: Destroying the body of the Trojan prince is shameful. He must give the body back to the father or face the consequences.

THETIS: But, Zeus, he's so hard-headed. He never listens.

ZEUS: You will make him listen, or he shall be destroyed.

THETIS: I will.

NARRATOR: The sun began to set on the grisly scene. Achilles had pulled the body until it was almost unrecognizable—round and round the city—and finally, he had stopped. With one final battle cry, he turned his back on the Trojan walls and headed back to his camp—the body kicking up dust behind him.

That night, Zeus sent the rainbow-goddess Iris to the old king Priam. She informed him that he must claim the body of his dead son. Zeus would ensure that no harm would come to him.

PRIAM: Honor will once again come to my household.

NARRATOR: Hermes himself guided Priam through the night, undetected into the Greek camp. As a younger man, Priam's anger would have cried out for the death of this Greek warrior, but he was tired of death. He only wanted his son. In the blackness of night, he slipped into Achilles' tent.

ACHILLES: Who's there?

PRIAM: An old man—an old father.

ACHILLES: You! How did you get here?

PRIAM: Please, do not sound an alarm. I come in peace.

ACHILLES: No one could sneak in here.

PRIAM: The gods have sent me. No man deserves the punishment you have dealt my son.

ACHILLES: You do not know what your son has done.

PRIAM: Yes, he has killed many. But, tell me, Achilles, how many have you killed?

ACHILLES: It's not the same!

PRIAM: How many friends? How many husbands? How many sons?

ACHILLES: I will not hear this! I will call the guards!

PRIAM: No, you will not, because surely you remember *your* old father, and you know how he would feel if he were to lose you as I have lost my son.

ACHILLES: No.

PRIAM: As I held Hector, he held you in his arms on the day of your birth. Sons are precious things. *My* son is a precious thing. Please, let me take him and bury him. Give him one last shred of honor. You have proved your point.

NARRATOR: Achilles was silent for a moment. The old king knelt to the ground, and took the warrior's bloodstained hand and kissed it.

PRIAM: *(slowly)* There. I have done what no father has ever done before. I have kissed the hand of the murderer of my own son.

NARRATOR: Achilles pulled his hands from the grip of the old man and brought them to his face. Hot tears welled up—for his own father—for Patroclus—for the father who knelt before him. When he cleared his own eyes, he saw tears upon Priam's cheeks as well.

ACHILLES: I will give you your son.

NARRATOR: He took the old man by the hand.

ACHILLES: Had we met under different circumstances, we might have been friends, old king. I will hold back the Greeks until you have mourned your son.

PRIAM: Twelve days is all we ask. To wash him, bury him, and celebrate his life.

ACHILLES: Then, I am your enemy once again, but tonight, I give you leave.

PRIAM: Thank you—my son.

NARRATOR: Priam was gone. Achilles sat silently in his tent. He began to weep once again. He did not know why. For Patroclus? For Hector? For himself?

Many days later when he entered the morning air, Achilles could see the silhouetted walls of Troy far away. Smoke billowed up between the rosy fingers of the dawn. It was the funeral pyre of Hector— burning on the city walls. Troy's greatest prince was fading away—his death preceding the death of his great city.

ACHILLES: Goodbye, Hector. We shall see each other again soon, I think. We were both built too glorious to be long in this world. Years from now, people will remember us— in stories, in song. Greek and Trojan children alike will say, "Tell us of the great city of Troy." Our names and deeds will live not just for a time—but for an eternity.

NARRATOR: As the great Achilles watched from afar, the Trojans buried Hector, breaker of horses.

DISCUSSION QUESTIONS

- What is tragic about Hector's death?
- Homer's epic poem the *Iliad* begins with the events of "War at Troy" and ends after the death of Hector. Why do you think Homer chose only to tell this brief portion of the ten-year Trojan War?
- Why is it almost impossible for the gods to truly understand war?
- If you had the choice between a long, uninteresting life and a brief life filled with fame, which would you choose? Explain.

THE MAROONED PRINCE
TEACHER GUIDE

BACKGROUND

Pscyhologically complex, the myth of Prince Philoctetes and his abandonment upon the island of Lemnos became the basis for one of the ancient Greek playwright Sophocles' most famous works. Wounds, both physical and mental, are its theme. Philoctetes has been physically wounded by a snake, and it is a wound that causes him daily disability and pain. But he has also been mentally wounded. Abandoned by his comrades and left alone in his suffering, Philoctetes has become less than a man.

Also present is the theme of duty versus morality. Odysseus, presented here as callous and manipulative, encourages Pyrrhus, the innocent young son of Achilles, to deceive Philoctetes. Pyrrhus struggles with these orders, pitting his sense of duty against his conscience. Ultimately, he decides to go against his mentor and deal with Philoctetes honorably.

The issues that the play explores are important for young people to encounter. In life is there clear-cut good and evil? Or is there (as Odysseus asserts) only what is good *for you*?

SUMMARY

Heracles (Hercules) and his death form the first part of this play in a flashback. A young prince named Philoctetes is the only one brave enough to light the funeral pyre of the famous hero (suffering to the point of death because of a poisoned robe). The hero bestows his bow and arrow upon the young prince before he dies and ascends to Mount Olympus, where is transformed into a god.

The story moves years forward to the Trojan War when Philoctetes is headed to Troy with his fellow Greeks. As the Greeks stop upon the island of Lemnos, the prince is bitten by a snake, which is actually Hera in disguise. (She is angry for the prince's help to her enemy, Heracles.) Hera appears to the prince and tells him that the snakebite will be a wound that will never heal. Odysseus convinces the other Greeks to leave the wounded prince behind on the island—and he is left alone on the island for ten years.

Between the action of the last play and this play, the warrior Achilles dies. (In the supplemental materials there are two worksheets that tell different versions of Achilles' death.) After the death of Achilles, the Greeks learn from Helenus, a captured Trojan prophet, that they will only take Troy after the son of Achilles joins the battle and the bow and arrows of Heracles are used in battle. Odysseus sails back to Greece and discovers Achilles' son. Pyrrhus is the boy's name, and he is abnormally developed for one his age. Odysseus convinces Pyrrhus to join the war at Troy. He tells Pyrrhus that he must help him trick Prince Philoctetes into coming along as well. The prince has been trapped on Lemnos alone for ten years and blames Odysseus for this. Odysseus gives the boy several lies to tell the wounded prince that will trick him into coming onto their ship. Then they will force him to return with them to Troy.

Pyrrhus goes ashore and discovers the prince, who is tortured daily by his horrible wound and lives like an animal. Pyrrhus feels pity for Philoctetes and despises that he must lie to him. The prince graciously allows Pyrrhus to hold his bow and arrows. Just then an attack comes upon the prince, and as he writhes upon the ground in agony, Pyrrhus considers running away with the weapon. His conscience keeps him from doing this. After the prince's fit passes, Pyrrhus decides to tell the truth. He tells the prince that he must come to Troy peacefully. The prince begins to howl. He has been betrayed, and his betrayer now holds his bow and arrows. He swears he will never go to Troy and begs the boy to return his weapon to him. Pyrrhus is about to comply when Odysseus appears and commands him to stop. Philoctetes recognizes Odysseus and realizes he is behind the boy's lies. Each man commands Pyrrhus to give the bow to him. Pyrrhus decides to return the bow to Philoctetes. The prince raises the weapon and is about to kill Odysseus, but Pyrrhus begs him to stop. Just then the sky overhead grows dark, and Heracles (now an Olympian god) commands Philoctetes to return to the war at Troy, using his bow to bring about the destruction of Troy. His mind immediately changed by this command, Philoctetes agrees to journey to Troy with Pyrrhus and Odysseus.

ESSENTIAL QUESTIONS

- Is it right to commit immoral acts for a good cause?
- Is there such a thing as *right* or *wrong*?
- Is it ever right to deceive someone?

CONNECTIONS

Philoctetes by Sophocles (409 B.C.) Much of "The Marooned Prince" is inspired by the ancient Greek tragedy *Philoctetes*. The play is one of Sophocles' most famous works and deals with the issue of duty versus morality.

ANTICIPATORY QUESTIONS

- Have you ever faced a difficult decision? Explain.
- Has someone you trusted ever turned out to be untrustworthy? Explain.
- Have you ever known anyone who was crippled? Explain.

TEACHABLE TERMS

- **Character Development** While Odysseus was portrayed as sympathetic in other myths, here he appears manipulative and self-centered. Have your students analyze how Odysseus has changed throughout the course of the war.
- **Flashback** The story behind the bow and arrows of Heracles and Philoctetes' abandonment on the island of Lemnos are flashbacks to a time before the Trojan War began.
- **Inner Conflict** Pyrrhus' dilemma determining the appropriate course of action is an example of inner conflict.
- **Deus Ex Machina** Latin for "god out of a machine," this term refers to an ending that seems too convenient or artificial. Have your students discuss the appearance of Heracles at the end of this story. Is this ending true to the story's characters? Or is this the only way the author could have gotten Philoctetes, who was previously completely against going to Troy, to change his mind?

RECALL QUESTIONS

1. How did Philoctetes receive the bow and arrows of Heracles?
2. Why did the Greeks leave Philoctetes behind on an island?
3. What prophecy does Helenus tell the Greek leaders?
4. Why does Odysseus need Pyrrhus to help him retrieve Philoctetes?
5. Which god appears at the end of the play?

THE MAROONED PRINCE

CAST

ODYSSEUS	*King of Ithaca*
PYRRHUS	*Son of Achilles*
PHILOCTETES	*Marooned Prince*
HERA	*Queen of the Gods*
HERACLES	*Greatest Mortal Hero*
AGAMEMNON	*Leader of the Greek Armies*
CALCHAS	*Greek Prophet*

NARRATOR: The great hero Heracles had finally been defeated. In his life he had slain vicious lions, boars, and even the many-headed monster, the Hydra, but he was at last brought to destruction by a woman. His wife—inspired by the goddess Hera—had given him a magically poisoned robe, and when he placed it over his powerful shoulders, it grafted onto his skin and engulfed his body with poisonous flames.

HERACLES: Argh! No! *(cries of pain)*

NARRATOR: Hera laughed as the hero burned alive.

HERA: Taste my anger, Heracles! At long last, I have defeated you. Now your pain will drive you mad, and you will become a monster—just like those you've fought against your entire life!

NARRATOR: As Hera had planned, the torment was not enough to kill Heracles outright. The hero rampaged beast-like throughout the countryside, causing havoc wherever he went, trying to free himself from the torture of the flaming robe. At last, Heracles realized he was defeated and cried out for someone—anyone—to end his life.

HERACLES: Argh! *(cries of pain)* Will no one help me? Kill me! Put me out of my misery! If you don't, I'll become a murderous monster!

NARRATOR: In spite of this request, no one dared draw a sword against the great hero for fear of Hera's retribution. On the mountain of Oeta Heracles at last made an altar-mound of branches and—his mind lost in a frenzy—lay down upon it. The whole countryside had gathered to watch.

HERACLES: *(in pain)* Isn't anyone brave enough to light this fire? Can't you see my pain?

NARRATOR: No one took pity on him, until a boy—a little prince named Philoctetes—stepped forward.

PHILOCTETES: *(young voice)* I will.

HERACLES: Thank you. *(loudly)* Behold! This boy is braver than all you men!

NARRATOR: The boy touched a torch to the dry branches of Heracles' funeral pyre. As the fire spread, the hero continued to speak majestically.

HERACLES: My mighty bow and infallible arrows lie upon the ground. Give them to this boy. He will be a great warrior! I have seen it!

NARRATOR: The flames consumed Heracles. As his body burned, a golden, mist-like form rose from the flames—a shimmering vision of how the hero had once appeared, strong and whole. It was his spirit rising up from his mortal body.

HERA: Wha—? What is happening?

NARRATOR: As it ascended, the spirit of Heracles spoke.

HERACLES: Hera, my step-mother. Long have you been my enemy. You thought at last you had defeated me! But my father, Zeus, has seen my mighty works on earth and has decreed that I will rise to Olympus to become one of the immortal gods.

HERA: *(screaming)* No! No!

NARRATOR: The golden spirit of Heracles locked eyes with the little prince, Philoctetes.

HERACLES: Listen, brave boy! Use my bow well. The heroes of old are passing away. Remember our great deeds and all that we stood for. Fight for what is right, what is true. Fight against the monsters of this world, but make sure that you do not become a monster yourself. Now I leave the world to you—and the next generation of mighty men.

NARRATOR: The spirit of Heracles reached the gray cloud-covering of the sky. There was

a flash of lightning, and the great hero was gone from the earth.

Fueled by Heracles' command, the prince Philoctetes spent the next ten years of his life training to be worthy of the hero's mighty weapon. When he had reached the age of manhood, the conflict at Troy at last gave him the chance to prove he was a great warrior. A thousand Greek ships set sail for Troy, and Philoctetes eagerly left his own kingdom behind to win glory in the Great War. But when the Greek fleet moored by the barren island of Lemnos and Philoctetes went ashore to fetch water, a serpent slithered forth from the scraggly bushes and sank its fangs into his ankle.

PHILOCTETES: *(cry of pain)* Ah!

NARRATOR: Philoctetes fell to the ground, grasping his wound. As the snake recoiled, he noticed that it had bizarre, fluorescent markings. In fact, it was painted more like a peacock than a serpent.

HERA: *(far-away laughing)* Ha-ha!

NARRATOR: To Philoctetes' astonishment, the snake floated up into the air, its form writhing and stretching until it took on the form of a goddess.

HERA: Ha-ha! S-s-sucker! How do you like my s-s-sting? I call that trick "the serpent of revenge!" *(evil laugh)*

PHILOCTETES: *(in shock)* Goddess Hera? Revenge? What have I ever done to you?

HERA: Have you forgotten about Heracles? You allowed that miserable step-son of mine to leave this world! He was supposed to transform into a monster of rage! Now he's a god—the toast of Olympus! I can't even walk through *my own home* anymore without seeing his smug face! And, of course, Zeus couldn't be happier! *(cry of disgust)*

PHILOCTETES: But that was years ago! Why bring this punishment against me now?

HERA: Eh. I've been busy. This whole war business has practically eaten up all my time. But I *never* forget a wrong against me!

NARRATOR: A searing pain shot through Philoctetes' body.

PHILOCTETES: *(cry of pain)* Ah!

HERA: Yes, you will think, "Ah!" My venom will cause the nastiest wound known to man. Your ankle will swell to the size of a tree trunk. It will blister over, and when those blisters break, they will spill foul-smelling pus everywhere! It will reek for miles and miles!

PHILOCTETES: *(in shock)* That's disgusting!

HERA: That's the idea. In fact, the rest of the Greeks will be so disgusted, they will leave you behind on this miserable island.

PHILOCTETES: Ha! You underestimate them. We are war-comrades. They would never leave me behind over a little stench.

HERA: They haven't ever smelled a stench like this before!

PHILOCTETES: *(cry of pain)*

NARRATOR: And so began the symptoms that Hera had described. The prince would suffer from them for many years. Hera watched his agony with glee—holding a hand before her nose to ward off the putrid odor that began to fill the air.

HERA: *(covered nose)* Heracles might have given you his bow and arrows, but they will do you little good stranded here on this island for eternity. *(evil laugh)* Whew! What a stench! Enjoy my little curse!

NARRATOR: With that the goddess disappeared.

When Philoctetes' comrades found him lying in the bushes, they were at first horrified at the sight of his ankle and then nauseated by the smell of it. Dragging the wounded prince with one arm and covering their noses with the other, the soldiers took him before Agamemnon, the leader of the Greek army, to see what should be done.

AGAMEMNON: Gods above! What is that smell? What has happened?

NARRATOR: Philoctetes told his story, and then he watched in silence as his fate was decided.

AGAMEMNON: Well, we must load him aboard a ship—preferably a ship downwind from the others.

NARRATOR: Odysseus stepped forward. He was a man renowned among the Greek lords because of his crafty mind.

ODYSSEUS: Ahem. Your majesty, might I interject? This man has obviously been cursed by the gods. Why should we risk taking him with us?

AGAMEMNON: We need all the able-bodied men we can get for this war!

ODYSSEUS: Able-bodied? Look at him! He can barely walk.

AGAMEMNON: Well, he is a comrade—a prince of Greece. We have to take him with us—wounded or not. It's our duty.

ODYSSEUS: Duty? It's your duty to watch out for the rest of us, too! Who could stand to be on the same ship as he is? We'll die of the stink! Besides, what if this wound turns out to be more than just a wound? What if it turns into a plague—a sickness that spreads to us all? Then by the time we reach Troy, we'll all be limping half-men like he is.

AGAMEMNON: You don't think—?

ODYSSEUS: I *do* think, Lord Agamemnon. That's why I say leave him behind.

PHILOCTETES: I can't believe this!

NARRATOR: No official decision was passed. Philoctetes fought excruciating pain all through the night—howling like a beast—but at last fell into an exhausted slumber. When Philoctetes awoke, he was still on the barren island, but the ships of his countrymen were gone.

PHILOCTETES: *(devastated)* I would have never believed it if I hadn't seen it with my own eyes. They have abandoned me. Curse them! Curse them!

NARRATOR: Time ran its course, and nine years passed. A tiny cave became Philoctetes' home. He could barely walk because of the wound, and his fabled bow became his livelihood. He shot down birds to fill his stomach. In the winters he ground stone against stone until a spark sprang up to save his life.

Meanwhile, Philoctetes' former comrades fought their war at Troy. The ninth year of the campaign brought the death of Hector, which was soon followed by the death of Achilles—pierced through the heel by the arrow of Paris. Death begat death, yet it seemed the war would never end.

The Greek kings turned to Calchas the prophet for guidance, but he could only shrug his shoulders.

CALCHAS: The gods have not given me the answer to that riddle. But they have shown me who does have the answer. Helenus—the prophet son of Priam—knows how to end this war once and for all.

AGAMEMNON: But he's a Trojan! How are we supposed to find out from him?

ODYSSEUS: Simple, my king. We ask him.

AGAMEMNON: Is that supposed to be some kind of joke?

ODYSSEUS: Of course not. I will go into Troy—in a disguise, of course—and bring you this Helenus.

AGAMEMNON: What makes you think he's going to betray his country? He's the son of the Trojan king!

ODYSSEUS: Oh, he will talk. There are methods of *persuasion* that no man can resist.

NARRATION: Odysseus did as promised. He infiltrated Troy, abducted the prophet-prince, and brought him back to the Greek camp. Helenus was a small man—far from the stature of his brother, Hector.

ODYSSEUS: The prophet has given me his words. He was an easy enough nut to crack. There are two things that must happen before Troy will fall.

AGAMEMNON: Yes? Yes?

ODYSSEUS: The first is that the son of Achilles must join the battle.

AGAMEMNON: What? Achilles has no son! The prophet is lying to you.

ODYSSEUS: Trust me, your majesty. I know a lie when I see one, and this is no lie. Achilles does have a son—one sired upon a daughter of King Lycomedes during his time of hiding on the island of Scyros.

AGAMEMNON: The boy would not yet be ten years of age!

ODYSSEUS: But the blood of Achilles flows through his veins, your worship. I think we will find a man-child living in Scyros—one with the power to bring down Troy.

AGAMEMNON: You said there were two things. What is the second?

ODYSSEUS: The bow and arrows of Heracles must be used against Troy.

AGAMEMNON: The bow and arrows of Heracles? Why does that sound familiar?

ODYSSEUS: Because they are carried by Prince Philoctetes—the man we abandoned on Lemnos.

AGAMEMNON: Then your task is before you! Return to Scyros and find this son of Achilles, and on your way back, stop off at Lemnos. Tell that Prince What's-his-name it's time to serve his country. We shall see Troy fall yet!

ODYSSEUS: (sarcastically) My lord, you have such an excellent way of over-simplifying everything.

AGAMEMNON: Thank you!

NARRATOR: Odysseus took a ship of men and sailed to Scyros. It was easy enough to find the son of Achilles. His mother had named him Pyrrhus "red-head." He had red-gold hair—just like his father's—still unshorn like a boy's, hanging long to his shoulders. In build he looked twice his age.

ODYSSEUS: You must be the son of Achilles! You resemble him in every way!

PYRRHUS: I do? Then you must know my father.

ODYSSEUS: I *knew* your father. He fell in battle before the walls of Troy—slain by the cowardly prince, Paris.

NARRATOR: The boy let this news sink in for a moment.

PYRRHUS: I want to feel sadness. I really do. But I never knew him, you see. When you do not know your father, it's like living with the blood of a stranger running through your veins.

NARRATOR: These words caused Odysseus to falter for a moment. He thought of his own son—growing up in Ithaca without a father.

PYRRHUS: I try to look at myself and guess what he must be like. They say that he was an honorable man. Is that true?

ODYSSEUS: Naturally. He was always one to follow orders—never questioning. A true patriot. Pyrrhus, I can tell you are a brave boy, and your grandfather has told me that you are already a skilled athlete. I've come to take you with me—back to Troy.

PYRRHUS: (eagerly) To fight?

ODYSSEUS: Of course. There is a prophecy about you, you know.

PYRRHUS: About me?

ODYSSEUS: The gods have declared that Troy will not fall until the son of Achilles joins the battle.

PYRRHUS: Then let us leave at once!

NARRATOR: It had been simple for the trickster to convince Pyrrhus to come to Troy. His true challenge would be Philoctetes. As they sailed toward Lemnos, Odysseus mulled a plan over in his head.

ODYSSEUS: Of course! Why didn't I think of it sooner? I will use the boy.

NARRATOR: Odysseus explained the situation to his young protégé.

PYRRHUS: (disappointed) Then the prophecy was not only about me? We must bring Philoctetes to Troy as well?

ODYSSEUS: Yes. And I will need your help.

NARRATOR: As the ship moored in the shallows near the island, Odysseus jumped overboard and motioned for Pyrrhus to follow.

ODYSSEUS: Come, boy! The crew will head up the coast a bit and wait for my signal to return. This island is rocky Lemnos—a land untrodden and lonely. This is where I abandoned him all those years ago.

NARRATOR: The boy looked around him and squinted into the bright midday light.

PYRRHUS: There is nothing here. Maybe he is dead. Didn't you say it's been nearly ten years?

ODYSSEUS: Oh, there is enough here to keep a man alive. A man can live on roots if need be.

PYRRHUS: Animals live on roots—not men.

ODYSSEUS: A man can become an animal quicker than you think.

PYRRHUS: Being alone on this island would be a cruel fate for any creature.

ODYSSEUS: I can hear the disapproval in your voice, but I tell you honestly, I had no choice. I was commanded to leave him, by my kings, Agamemnon and Menelaus.

NARRATOR: At the mention of the two great Greek kings, Pyrrhus' back straightened, and all doubt seemed to leave his face.

PYRRHUS: Then you had no choice!

ODYSSEUS: Now, be quiet. If he hears us, it will ruin our plan to reclaim him. Remember: your orders are to serve me—to spy on him.

NARRATOR: The two made their way up the nearest slope as stealthily as they could. Above them in the side of the hill, they saw a cave.

ODYSSEUS: (whispering) Perhaps he lives in that cave? Now, go. I'll hide here. You go and see if he is sleeping inside.

NARRATOR: The boy nodded obediently and ran lightly—silently—up the hill of rocks, sneaking close to the cave-mouth and peering inside.

PYRRHUS: It's empty!

ODYSSEUS: Does it look lived-in?

PYRRHUS: There's a pallet of trampled leaves—some sort of bed.

ODYSSEUS: Then he still lives! And what else do you see? Is there anything else inside the cave?

PYRRHUS: Rags are drying in the sun, full of pieces of skin and pus from his sores. There is a horrible stench about them!

ODYSSEUS: That's nothing compared to the source! Do you see a weapon? A bow and arrows?

PYRRHUS: No.

ODYSSEUS: *(under his breath)* Of course, not. That would be too easy. *(aloud)* His wound is still fresh, and he can only travel as far as he can drag himself. He can't be far off then. He is probably out hunting a meal. We will wait for his return.

NARRATOR: The young man picked his way back down the hill to Odysseus' side.

ODYSSEUS: We must prepare for the prince's return. I have not told you about the mighty weapon he possesses—the bow of Heracles.

NARRATOR: At the mention of Heracles, the boy's eyes lit up.

PYRRHUS: Heracles! *The* Heracles? Philoctetes carries this weapon?

ODYSSEUS: Why do you think I shrink and hide? According to legend, those arrows never miss their mark. Plus, I am not Philoctetes' favorite person, you know. It was I who led him ashore and abandoned him here—with a trick.

PYRRHUS: What must I do when he returns?

ODYSSEUS: You are physically strong, Pyrrhus, but for this mission you must use strength of the mind. Entangle Philoctetes with clever words. Let me give you a piece of my wisdom: With a lie is always best to mix in a portion of truth. It's easier to swallow that way. When he asks you your name, tell him, "I am Achilles' son." There is no lie in that. But I have also crafted a clever story, full of twists of turns, that will cause him to drop his guard. And when his guard is down, he will be ours! Now listen closely.

NARRATOR: And so Odysseus fed his words to Pyrrhus.

PYRRHUS: Must I use so many lies?

ODYSSEUS: Remember, the end justifies the means. Just a few shameless deeds, and afterward you'll be called one of the most virtuous of men.

PYRRHUS: Why not tell him the truth? We can win him over by persuading him.

ODYSSEUS: Persuasion is impossible. He will never forgive the Greeks for what we have done to him. Remember you cannot succeed without his bow.

PYRRHUS: *(sudden idea)* I know! What if I fight Philoctetes, capture him, and make him our hostage? At least that would be a straight fight. It seems cruel and dishonorable to trick a cripple. Honest failure is better than treacherous victory—to me anyway.

ODYSSEUS: *(laugh)* You *are* the son of Achilles! Who else would suggest fighting against the arrows of Heracles that cannot miss? But, no, listen: When I was young like you, I held my tongue and let my hand do the work. But slowly I learned it is words that win—and not deeds.

PYRRHUS: *(grudgingly)* Then what are your orders? Apart from telling lies that is.

ODYSSEUS: I order you to capture him—to take him with trickery.

PYRRHUS: If there is no other way, then I guess I must do what you ask.

ODYSSEUS: Stay here at the cave and wait for him. I will go back to the ship. If I think you're in trouble, I will come to you for back-up, but think on your feet! Lure him to the ship any way that you can! Either that or steal the bow. May Hermes give you craftiness and Athena give you wisdom!

NARRATOR: As Odysseus disappeared down the hillside, the young man seated himself before the cave of the marooned prince and awaited his return. He stared at the man's meager belongings—his rancid wrappings.

PYRRHUS: What a wretch. He must drag himself out to hunt. He must be out now, trying to bring down mangy birds with his arrows.

PHILOCTETES: *(far-away groan)*

PYRRHUS: He approaches!

NARRATOR: A pathetic form appeared over the top of the hillside. Pyrrhus had never seen a man so shrunken and emaciated, yet from his frame he could tell he had once been a powerful man. Rather than walking upright, Philoctetes crutched from rock to rock. When he spied Pyrrhus, his bleary eyes opened wide.

PHILOCTETES: *(shouting)* Wait! Don't move!

PYRRHUS: *(happily)* Greetings!

PHILOCTETES: Do not move! I will come down to you.

NARRATOR: The prince moved down the hillside at a surprising speed. Pyrrhus noticed an enormous bow and quiver slung over the man's knobby shoulders. A pair of sickly birds was gripped in his hand.

PHILOCTETES: *(eagerly)* You are a Greek? Your clothes are Greek, and you speak the tongue of my homeland. Please! Tell me that you are Greek.

PYRRHUS: I am a Greek and a friend.

PHILOCTETES: A friend? You are too kind! You must understand, I have been here alone—without another soul to talk to—for so long. Where are my manners? Please! Sit! Sit! Are you hungry? I can cook these up!

NARRATOR: He held up the two birds.

PYRRHUS: No, I am not hungry.

PHILOCTETES: You must tell me who you are and what lucky wind has brought you to me!

NARRATOR: So Pyrrhus began his lies mixed with truth.

PYRRHUS: I am from the island of Scyros, and I am sailing back there. I am called Pyrrhus, the son of—

PHILOCTETES: Achilles! Of course. How did I not see it before? But wait. Where did you say you are sailing from?

PYRRHUS: I sail from Troy.

PHILOCTETES: You are sailing *away* from Troy? Is the war over?

PYRRHUS: No, it is not—unfortunately. Did *you* fight in the war? Is that where you got that wound?

NARRATOR: The question caused the prince to pause.

PHILOCTETES: Then you have not recognized me?

PYRRHUS: No. Should I?

PHILOCTETES: Perhaps that is the biggest insult. I thought at least some news of my fate would have reached Greece. Betrayed by my countrymen and my existence wiped out. Curse them!

PYRRHUS: I am sorry.

PHILOCTETES: It is not your fault, my boy. It is my own vanity, too, for, you see, I was once famous in all of Greece—as the bearer of the bow of Heracles.

PYRRHUS: That is a mighty weapon!

PHILOCTETES: Yes. It is the only thing that has kept me alive these many years.

PYRRHUS: Has no one ever stopped here before? Like I have?

PHILOCTETES: I have had visitors over the years—sure. They all stare at me with that same expression you use on me now—pity. But when they see my pain and smell my sore, they leave me behind. I only hope that the gods curse the men who did this to me— Agamemnon, Menelaus, and, the most of all, Odysseus!

NARRATOR: This was the line that Pyrrhus had been waiting for—the line that Odysseus had told him to expect. He felt his next series of lies rising within him like vomit.

PYRRHUS: Those are names that I curse, too!

PHILOCTETES: What do you mean? Have you been wronged by these men?

PYRRHUS: That is why I am sailing home. When I reached the war at Troy, I learned that my father was dead.

PHILOCTETES: Wait! Achilles? Dead? Surely this is not true.

PYRRHUS: Yes, I'm afraid so. My father was slain as he battled before the walls of Troy.

PHILOCTETES: How can the gods allow this? A good man like Achilles is dead, yet reptiles and villains like Odysseus still live! Are the gods themselves evil? They obviously favor evil men! *(sadly)* These are heavy tidings!

PYRRHUS: They were for me as well. The man I had journeyed so far to meet was no longer upon the earth. The only thing I requested from the Greeks was that I be given his armor—as a memento.

PHILOCTETES: And?

NARRATOR: Pyrrhus fidgeted nervously. He was unaccustomed to this lying.

PYRRHUS: Odysseus himself wore it and would not give it over to me. Neither would Agamemnon and Menelaus when I asked them for justice. So, right then and there, I swore that I would not fight for such men—and now I am sailing home.

PHILOCTETES: My boy! Your story almost breaks my heart—to see an honorable young man treated in such a way. But I can tell you this: You are a true son of Achilles to stand up to such black-hearted men! Your father would have been proud of you!

NARRATOR: These words caused Pyrrhus to blush.

PYRRHUS: I would not be too sure. But there is more. I have not told you everything. While I was in Troy, the Greeks heard a prophecy that Troy would never be taken unless Philoctetes came and joined the war.

NARRATOR: The crippled warrior pulled himself closer to the boy—his face like a madman's.

PHILOCTETES: Tell me, boy. Tell me what those vultures said when they heard these words!

PYRRHUS: Odysseus declared that he would bring you to Troy—either by persuasion or force. That is why I tell you—to warn you.

PHILOCTETES: Oh, he said that, did he? Why the smug fool! I would sooner go into Hades than aid those gutless curs! I would sooner befriend the snake that gave me this wound! He may be a clever spinner of lies, but he is not clever enough to fool me again! May the gods curse him for his arrogance!

PYRRHUS: I wanted to give you that warning before I departed.

PHILOCTETES: *(panicked)* You are leaving? Now? So soon?

PYRRHUS: I must catch the tide.

PHILOCTETES: Please, young master, I beg of you in the name of your father, take me with you! You can stow me away wherever you wish. I'll sleep in the hold of the ship if I have to—wherever the smell of me will be least offensive to you. But please take me back to Greece! Do not leave me here marooned like so many others have. Please! I beg you. I beg you.

PYRRHUS: There is no need to beg, sir. I will happily comply. It would be a dishonor to leave a noble warrior like you marooned here.

PHILOCTETES: My boy! You have made me the happiest man alive!

NARRATOR: Philoctetes grabbed the young man's hands in thanks, but Pyrrhus shied away and glanced awkwardly aside. He imagined the prince's face when they would reach the ship—only to see Odysseus aboard and a troop of men waiting to bind him.

PYRRHUS: Let's be on our way. Fetch what you want to take with you from the cave.

PHILOCTETES: I have only a few meager possessions. A jar filled with an herb to ease my pain. A few extra arrows that I keep hidden away.

NARRATOR: Philoctetes pulled the magnificent bow and quiver from his shoulders.

PYRRHUS: Is that your famous bow?

PHILOCTETES: Yes. I never set it down. I keep it with me at all times.

PYRRHUS: (eagerly) May I hold it? I mean—only if you will allow me to.

PHILOCTETES: May you hold it? Of course, you can, my boy! You have given me back my life! You have given me the chance to once again see my home! Take it! Take it!

NARRATOR: The boy took the massive bow into his hands, and he felt its power move through him. Carved upon it were representations of each of Heracles' twelve labors. Philoctetes trustingly turned to his cave. Just then his body began to quiver, and he fell down upon the ground.

PHILOCTETES: Argh! (yells of pain)

PYRRHUS: What is it? What is happening?

PHILOCTETES: The pain is coming! Argh!

NARRATOR: The prince's face became contorted and red with pain. He writhed and grasped blindly at his swollen ankle. The wound throbbed and began to secret a foul substance. A stifling smell filled the air.

PHILOCTETES: (in pain) Argh! My foot! Cut it off! Please! If you have a sword, cut—it—off! I beg you.

PYRRHUS: (frightened) This is madness! Are you all right?

PHILOCTETES: (psychotically) Don't touch me! Whatever you do—don't touch me! Argh!

NARRATOR: Pyrrhus backed away in horror—the bow still clutched tightly in his hand. He could not tear his eyes away from the writhing prince, but suddenly his mind told him that this was his chance. In his hand he held the bows and arrows he had come for. Their owner lay helpless upon the ground. He remembered Odysseus' words: trick him and run.

PHILOCTETES: (in pain) Argh! Odysseus!

NARRATOR: At the sound of Odysseus' name, the boy jumped—half-expecting to see Odysseus standing next to him.

PHILOCTETES: (in pain) Odysseus, how I wish—it—was—you—who—felt—this—pain! Argh!

NARRATOR: The urge to run returned, but for some reason, Pyrrhus remained rooted to the spot.

PHILOCTETES: (relieved) It is passing. It is passing. I thought it never would. Come, boy. Lift me to my feet.

PYRRHUS: I can't.

PHILOCTETES: Don't be afraid. Help me up.

PYRRHUS: I—I—can't keep it from you any longer.

PHILOCTETES: Keep what?

PYRRHUS: You cannot sail home. You must come with me—back to Troy.

PHILOCTETES: *(in confusion)* Wha—what are you saying?

PYRRHUS: You must fight! You must fight the Trojans and help us win this war!

NARRATOR: Philoctetes' look of confusion settled into realization.

PHILOCTETES: *(angrily)* I see it all now. You are one of them, and I am betrayed! I should have known! I thought I had found a friend, but I see only a stranger before me. Give me back my bow!

PYRRHUS: I can't do that.

PHILOCTETES: Gods above, will you now deny me my bow?

NARRATOR: The prince dug his fingers into the dirt and began to crawl toward Pyrrhus. The boy backed away in horror.

PHILOCTETES: Give it to me, boy! It's not just a weapon. It's my life! Without it I will die here upon this miserable island! How can you steal from me the very last shred of my dignity?

PYRRHUS: It is my duty to take this bow—if you will not come willingly. It is not my choice.

PHILOCTETES: There is always a choice, boy. Now give me my bow—before you lose your soul entirely.

NARRATOR: Pyrrhus turned his back upon the prostrate man.

PHILOCTETES: Rocks! Caves! Cliffs! Hear me now! I speak to you now because no one else will listen. You have been my only friends these many years! Now here stands the son of Achilles, Greece's greatest warrior. He holds the holy bow of earth's greatest hero but does the most cowardly deed a man has ever done—stealing life from a corpse—stealing life from a cripple!

PYRRHUS: *(to himself)* Why did I ever leave my home? Who knew the world was so horrible?

NARRATOR: Pyrrhus turned back to the prince, and Philoctetes' face lit up with hope.

PHILOCTETES: I knew it! You are not evil. You have learned terrible tricks from evil men, but leave evil to them. Let us sail away! Return my bow to me!

NARRATOR: Pyrrhus stared at the weapon in his hand. He took a step forward, but before he took another, Pyrrhus heard the commanding voice of Odysseus behind him.

ODYSSEUS: *(yelling)* Traitor! Coward!

PHILOCTETES: No! No! It can't be! It can't be!

ODYSSEUS: Do not take another step, Pyrrhus. You are falling prey to a deranged man—a man who cares nothing about his country! Don't listen to a word he says!

PHILOCTETES: *(shrieking)* Give me my bow, Pyrrhus! Let me strike this demon down once and for all!

ODYSSEUS: Ah, Philoctetes. I see you are looking—and smelling—as healthy as ever.

PHILOCTETES: I should have known you were behind this trick! Who else could stoop so low?

ODYSSEUS: Says the man squirming upon the ground. Give it up, Philoctetes. My men are on their way. We're going to drag you to Troy—whether you like it or not.

PHILOCTETES: I still have my sea-cliffs. I'll throw myself into the sea before I go with you.

ODYSSEUS: Still overdramatic, I see. Very well. The prophecy did not involve you, anyway. Just your marvelous bow. And since we seem to have that in our possession…

PHILOCTETES: Who will wield it? You?

ODYSSEUS: I will certainly do a better job than a cripple.

PHILOCTETES: How can you live with yourself? How can you pray to the gods when you commit such evil acts?

ODYSSEUS: Good and evil? There is only winning and losing. You have lost, and I have won. Now, come, Pyrrhus. Let's leave this wretch to the crows.

NARRATOR: The boy did not move.

ODYSSEUS: Pyrrhus! (*pause*) That was not a suggestion. That was an *order!*

PYRRHUS: I have had enough of your *orders.* I was wrong to obey any of them.

ODYSSEUS: What foolishness is this?

PYRRHUS: I told lies—and you were right. They got me what I wanted. But it doesn't feel right, and it never will.

ODYSSEUS: (*slowly*) Now, boy, don't do anything foolish.

PYRRHUS: I am giving this bow back to its rightful owner.

ODYSSEUS: And what makes you think I will let you?

PYRRHUS: How can you stop me when I hold this weapon? They are the arrows that never miss, and I will use them against you if I have to.

NARRATOR: The face of Odysseus suddenly became a mask of anger.

ODYSSEUS: (*sudden anger*) Do you have any idea what is like to endure ten *long* years of war? To be absent from your home—from your children? To fill your life with killing and pain? Soon you will, boy! And then you will do anything—anything—to end it. Now is your chance to end it—for all of us—yet you are going to throw it away! Just like a fool!

PYRRHUS: I may be foolish, but what I do is right.

NARRATOR: Pyrrhus stepped forward and placed the bow and quiver into the eager hands of Philoctetes.

ODYSSEUS: Traitor!

NARRATOR: Odysseus ripped his sword lose from his sheath, but Philoctetes—even in his weakness—still had speed. He knew his weapon better than anything else in the world. He had the bow bent and an arrow notched into its string before Odysseus had taken three steps. Odysseus stopped his charge.

PHILOCTETES: (*chuckling*) How sweet it is! I have waited for this for ten years—ten long, excruciating years! And now I will get to see you die.

PYRRHUS: No, my friend.

NARRATOR: Pyrrhus stepped between Philoctetes and his target.

PHILOCTETES: *(angrily)* Move out of the way!

ODYSSEUS: Stupid boy! You should have let him kill me! Now the lunatic will kill you, too!

PYRRHUS: No! There will be no bloodshed here. Philoctetes, I promised you that I would take you home to Greece, and that is what I will do. Odysseus will be allowed to leave—alive, but empty-handed.

ODYSSEUS: I will not leave until I have what I came for! I will go through anyone I have to, but I will get to it—or die trying.

PHILOCTETES: Step aside, boy! Let me end this war-hungry monster's life!

PYRRHUS: Silence, both of you! Philoctetes, your anger has made you a savage! You must put it away. What Odysseus did to you was wrong, but war makes men do evil things! And that is why we must end it—together!

PHILOCTETES: I will never go to Troy! I will not fight for those men! Not even if the gods themselves commanded it.

NARRATOR: At these words the sky above them grew dark, and a mass of swirling clouds appeared. *(thunder noises)* Lightning flashed overhead, and all three men fell to their faces.

HERACLES: *(booming)* Hear me! Hear me! It is I, Heracles!

NARRATOR: The massive form of a bearded man appeared within the clouds and stared down at the prone mortals.

PHILOCTETES: *(frightened)* Heracles! You have come back!

HERACLES: I come from Olympus to declare the desires of my father, Zeus. Philoctetes, you must put away your grudge. Your destiny is to go to Troy.

PHILOCTETES: But all my suffering! All these long years of suffering!

HERACLES: Olympus will put an end to your suffering. There is a skilled healer among the Greeks at Troy. The gods will give him the knowledge to heal your wound.

PHILOCTETES: Thank you! Oh, thank you!

HERACLES: But afterward you must fight! This war must end. Even we immortals tire of it. You will slay Prince Paris with my divine arrows and bring even more glory and honor to my name.

PHILOCTETES: I will! It was you who gave me the bow, and I will use it as you command.

HERACLES: And, you, son of Achilles.

NARRATOR: The boy looked up into the face of the god.

HERACLES: You must fight as well, and you will bring about the downfall of Troy. But stick close to this prince. Listen to his council. Although this wound has poisoned his mind and his body for ten years, his strength and wisdom will return. Mark his words well. Together you will bring down Troy.

NARRATOR: The clouds and the face within them began to fade away.

HERACLES: I command you all to fight nobly, and when Troy has fallen, remain holy. Do not desecrate her.

PHILOCTETES: We will obey, holy one.

HERACLES: Do not delay then. The time is right, and the tides are calling.

NARRATOR: The god-storm dissipated, and the bright of the day returned. The three men rose speechless from the sight they had just beheld and made ready to sail for Troy.

As he prepared to board the ship that would take him to Troy, Philoctetes turned back for one last look at his island home.

PHILOCTETES: Farewell, Lemnos. I have hated you for ten long years. I never thought I would be able to leave you behind. Now I go to Troy—to be healed of my wound—to gain glory. Farewell forever.

DISCUSSION QUESTIONS

- Should orders be followed at all times? Explain.
- Pyrrhus' struggle over his actions is a great example of inner conflict. When have you had an inner or moral conflict over something?
- Did Pyrrhus do the right thing? Explain.
- Was it right for Odysseus to abandon Philoctetes on the island? Explain.
- What do you think motivates Odysseus? Explain.
- How has Philoctetes' constant suffering affected his mind? Explain.
- Does Philoctetes have a right to kill Odysseus? Explain.
- What do you think is the theme of this story? Explain.

THE FALL OF TROY
TEACHER GUIDE

BACKGROUND

The true tragedy of the Trojan War lies in its conclusion. The trick of the Trojan Horse leads to a bloody and brutal massacre. Seemingly driven mad by ten years of war, the Greeks become bloodthirsty barbarians—raping women and murdering children. Every war must have a loser, but the Trojan War has two. The Trojans lose their lives and their homes. The Greeks lose their humanity.

The Trojan War connects with a maxim frequently taught to children, "It's not whether you win or lose; it's how you play the game."

No trick is more famous—or maybe "infamous"—than the Trojan Horse. The Greeks, whose ancestors used this deception to finally rout their Trojan enemies, were even a bit embarrassed by it. They called it a cowardly act and mourned that their ancestors had so mercilessly laid waste to the beautiful city of Troy.

Today even those who believe in a historical Trojan War, consider the Trojan Horse to be a mythical addition. They see it as a silly folktale trick. But in ancient times city walls were often breached in creative ways.

Heavily fortified walls could lead to months of siege warfare and much bloodshed. Typically, the easiest way around the walls was to bribe someone on the inside to open the front gate. Another option was digging under the walls. Some attackers are even on record as crawling up a fortress' sewer system to gain a surprise entrance through the toilet.

SUMMARY

Prince Philoctetes, his wound healed, has joined the Trojan War. What now troubles him is a change he has seen come over Pyrrhus, the young son of Achilles. War has agreed with him in a frightening way—he seems to love killing. Philoctetes tells Agamemnon and Odysseus about his concerns, but they are not receptive. It is Pyrrhus' job to kill, they say, so he *should* enjoy it.

A distance grows up between Philoctetes and the young warrior. Pyrrhus accuses the prince of cowardice—why did he come to Troy if he was not going to use his legendary bow and arrows? In response to this Philoctetes challenges the Trojan prince Paris to a duel. As prophesied, Paris dies by the bow and arrows of Heracles, wielded by Philoctetes.

Afterward, Odysseus hatches the clever trick of the Trojan Horse. Philoctetes opposes this idea since it is cowardly, but, nevertheless, the plan is put into motion. The Greeks construct a giant wooden horse in secret, and pretending to sail away, they leave it standing on the beach for the Trojans to discover. A Greek named Sinon is also left behind to help trick the Trojans.

When the horse is found, Priam and his son Laocoön come to examine it. Sinon, captured by the Trojans, tells Priam that the Greeks made the horse as an offering to Poseidon, constructing it so large that the Trojans could not bring it within their city walls. This would steal Poseidon's blessing away from the Greeks, he says. Laocoön states that he does not trust the horse and throws his spear at it. Immediately, two sea serpents come from the waves and drag him to his death. This seems to prove that the blessing of the gods is attached to the horse. Priam orders the city gate dismantled and the horse brought inside the city walls.

The Trojans celebrate what they think is a victory over the Greeks with a wild celebration. The men hidden within the horse wait until the Trojans have fallen asleep and sneak out from the horse. The Greek army, which has secretly sailed back, storms into Troy and begins to massacre its citizens.

Through the carnage Philoctetes keeps an eye on the bloodthirsty Pyrrhus, following him into the royal palace. Before the prince can stop him, Pyrrhus slays Priam and drags away Andromache and Hecuba to be his slaves.

Prince Philoctetes realizes that there is nothing he can do to stop the slaughter of the Trojans. He witnesses the murder of Astyanax, Hector's infant son. Then the prince symbolically burns his bow, signifying that he is done with war and mankind. He vows to sail from Troy and never return to Greece—instead seeking a new home on the shores of Italy.

ESSENTIAL QUESTIONS

- Is everything "fair in love and war"?
- Can humans lose their humanity?
- Is war "a necessary evil"?
- Do innocent people die in wars?

ANTICIPATORY QUESTIONS

- Have you ever heard the saying, "It's not whether you win or lose. It's how you play the game"? Is this true?
- What happens to the losers in wars?
- Is winning through a trick cheating?
- Can traumatic events alter someone's personality?

CONNECTIONS

The Trojan Women (1971) This film version of Euripides' famous tragedy shows how the aftermath of the Trojan War affects the women of Troy—Hecuba, Andromache, Cassandra, and Helen. (This film is not rated and may contain inappropriate content.)

TEACHABLE TERMS

- **Round Character** How has the character of Pyrrhus changed over the course of the last two plays? Discuss the difference between round characters (those that undergo a change) and static characters (those that do not change).
- **Symbol** Pyrrhus' new name Neoptolemus ("new war") is symbolic of his new purpose in the conflict. Have the students discuss how the leaders of the Greek armies are using the boy as a weapon.
- **Theme** The Trojan War ends with a series of cold-hearted events. The Greeks, who chronicled these events, were even ashamed of them. Have the students examine what the tale has to say about war and the effects of war.
- **Antagonist** Since the protagonist of this play is Philoctetes, ask the students who or what the antagonist would be. Have them back up their answer with proof. Answers might range from "Odysseus" to "human brutality."

RECALL QUESTIONS

1. What person does Prince Philoctetes kill in a duel?
2. What person has become mentally unbalanced since he came to the Trojan War?
3. What is Odysseus' idea for ending the Trojan War?
4. What happens when Laocoön hurls his spear at the Trojan Horse?
5. What is the job of Sinon the Greek in the plot of the Trojan Horse?

THE FALL OF TROY

CAST

PHILOCTETES	*Famous Archer*
PYRRHUS	*Son of Achilles*
PARIS	*Prince of Troy*
PRIAM	*King of Troy*
HELEN	*Stolen Queen*
ODYSSEUS	*Tricky Greek King*
AGAMEMNON	*Leader of the Greeks*
MENELAUS	*Agamemnon's Brother*
LAOCOÖN	*Son of Priam*
TROJAN	*Trojan Warrior*
GREEK	*Greek Soldier*
SINON	*Sneaky Greek*
CASSANDRA	*Trojan Princess*

NARRATOR: Since Prince Philoctetes had come to Troy, he had become a new man. An expert healer in the Greek camp had healed his wound, his body had regained its strength, and his skill with the bow had returned. Yet while Philoctetes had changed back into his former self, his young friend Pyrrhus, the son of Achilles, had struggled with the brutality of war.

One day soon after their arrival at Troy, Pyrrhus returned from battle ashen-faced and shaking.

PHILOCTETES: Pyrrhus, we have routed the Trojans! They thought they could take our camp, but they had another thing coming! Ha!

NARRATOR: The boy threw his sword disgustedly to the ground.

PHILOCTETES: What's the matter?

PYRRHUS: *(strangely)* I killed today. It was my first.

PHILOCTETES: It's a gruesome milestone for every man.

PYRRHUS: But I hated it. I completely hated it.

PHILOCTETES: No one loves to kill.

PYRRHUS: I had expected not to love it. But I never expected the revulsion I felt—for myself. *(faltering voice)* He—he was young. It was—a messy death.

NARRATOR: Tears appeared in the young boy's eyes.

PHILOCTETES: It's over now. Put it out of your mind.

PYRRHUS: *(angrily)* I can't. Don't you see? I can't. I saw the life leave his eyes! He died because of me! I will never forget it! It will haunt me the rest of my days!

NARRATOR: From that day on the boy's innocence seemed to be lost, and he went about the Greek camp like one in a trance. Concerned about his well-being, Philoctetes went to speak to Agamemnon and Menelaus. Much to the prince's chagrin, Odysseus, too, was lurking in the darkness of the tent.

PHILOCTETES: My lords, I am worried about the boy, Pyrrhus. He is troubled.

AGAMEMNON: Achilles' son? Troubled how?

PHILOCTETES: He killed for the first time last week. Since that time, I've heard him sobbing in his tent each night.

ODYSSEUS: Tell him to toughen up. We all must deal with war in our own way. He'll get over it. It's his destiny to kill. The sooner he accepts it, the better.

PHILOCTETES: I didn't think *you* would understand, Odysseus. But for those of us with a conscience, it's a bit more difficult to deal with such horrors.

AGAMEMNON: The boy is prophesied to bring about the destruction of Troy. He *must* kill.

ODYSSEUS: I don't believe this. I travel all the way back to Greece to find this boy, and now he's not going to fight? All over a few tears?

MENELAUS: Achilles had no problem killing!

PHILOCTETES: This boy is not his father! Think of the pressure he feels! The entire army has hinged their hope upon him.

ODYSSEUS: Feelings are insignificant in war. He was born to kill. He was brought here to kill. So kill he shall.

PHILOCTETES: All I am saying is that the boy is not well. Let him take a rest from battle until he is ready to fight again.

AGAMEMNON: Very well. We will keep the boy from battle until he is ready to return.

NARRATOR: Philoctetes felt that what he had done would help Pyrrhus, but when the boy learned that he was withheld from battle, he approached the prince angrily.

PYRRHUS: *(angrily)* I can't believe it! You went behind my back and ratted me out! Now I am forced to sit on the sidelines like a fool! I am shamed!

PHILOCTETES: It is not shameful to admit that you do not like to kill. Only bloodthirsty beasts enjoy killing.

PYRRHUS: My father would be so ashamed of me!

PHILOCTETES: Your father? You only know your father through other men. He was not a butcher. It was not below him to feel remorse—to shed tears.

PYRRHUS: Yes, but look where he is now! I will not make the same mistake he made.

NARRATOR: After this, a distance grew up between Philoctetes and his young friend. Pyrrhus soon returned to the battlefield and won many astounding victories. At least on the outside, killing no longer seemed to bother him. The good-natured boy who had taken pity on Philoctetes at Lemnos seemed to fade away—and a monster took his place.

PHILOCTETES: I heard you raided a Trojan temple—singlehandedly.

PYRRHUS: *(pleased)* Yes, it was a good kill.

PHILOCTETES: I also heard there were women and children there.

PYRRHUS: *(coldly)* Enemies are enemies.

PHILOCTETES: A cold outlook. *(pause)* I haven't seen you in the camp once in these past weeks. What do you do with yourself these days—apart from slaughtering women and children?

PYRRHUS: *(snidely)* I've been around. Mainly in Agamemnon's tent—planning strategy with the kings and Odysseus.

PHILOCTETES: Odysseus? I remember that you once did not trust that trickster.

PYRRHUS: What? Are you jealous that they're asking me to their secret meetings and not you?

PHILOCTETES: I hate to say it, but you have changed, Pyrrhus.

PYRRHUS: *(sudden anger)* Don't call me that childish nickname! Odysseus has given me a new name: Neoptolemus. It means "new war," and that's how I want to be known. My father fought the old war, and I fight the new one.

PHILOCTETES: New war? How fitting. Don't you see? They are just using you.

PYRRHUS: Using me? Ha! Using me how? To destroy Trojans. What's good for them is good for me. I hate all Trojans. I want to see them all die.

PHILOCTETES: I see. They've taken away your humanity and turned you into a killing beast.

PYRRHUS: It's what I'm good at. It's my purpose in life. I've accepted that.

PHILOCTETES: Killing is evil. I pray you do not love it.

PYRRHUS: *You* obviously don't love it. Since you came here, you haven't done a blasted thing with that bow of yours. Where are the deaths that Heracles promised? Where is the death of Paris?

PHILOCTETES: I haven't yet met Paris in a battle, but when I do—

PYRRHUS: Spoken like a true coward. You're no better than he is—hiding on the back lines. I don't know what *we* ever saw in you. We should have left you on that island—to rot.

NARRATOR: Although Philoctetes tried to shield himself against them, the words of Pyrrhus wounded him. War had ruined this boy, and so the war must be ended before it could ruin any others. Philoctetes prepared himself for battle.

The next morning, when the rosy fingers of the dawn first entered the sky, Philoctetes was already standing alone before the towering gates of Troy.

PHILOCTETES: *(yelling)* Prince Paris! Come forth! Paris!

NARRATOR: The alarm was sounded upon the walls, and soon Paris himself appeared upon the ramparts.

PARIS: Greek, what do you want? Surely you are not here to fight. Haven't you heard? It was *my* bow that brought down Achilles!

PHILOCTETES: You might have slain the mighty Achilles, but I say you are still a coward!

(angry shouts from the Trojans)

PARIS: I would watch your tongue! I will kill *you* just like I killed him!

PHILOCTETES: You mean by shooting me in the back?

PARIS: (angrily) Why you—!

PHILOCTETES: Achilles battled with the spear, but you ended his life with an arrow. You did not match him honorably. Now, Paris, come and face me, for I fight with the bow and arrows of Heracles. From one prince to another, I issue this challenge.

PARIS: This will prove nothing. It's a trick. I refuse your challenge.

NARRATOR: Priam, the elderly king of Troy, stood by his son's side.

PRIAM: Son, a challenge cannot be so easily refused.

PARIS: Father, you would have me fight this man?

PRIAM: Of course, Paris! He has called your bravery into question! You are the slayer of Achilles! What do you have to fear?

PARIS: Very well.

NARRATOR: Paris began to bolt on his armor, and his beloved Helen came to his side.

PARIS: Nothing to fear, my love. I will teach this crowing fool a lesson and return to you.

HELEN: See that you do! I have heard of the mighty bow of Heracles.

PARIS: So have I. But it is not Heracles who wields it now. It is a mortal man—one I will vanquish.

NARRATOR: At last the gates of Troy swung open to reveal Paris—prepared for battle. Philoctetes awaited him on the plain, his own bow at-the-ready.

PHILOCTETES: Have you made your peace with death, dishonorable prince?

PARIS: I could ask you the same question. *My* arrows are guided by Apollo.

PHILOCTETES: Justice guides mine. Achilles was my friend once—a great Greek. I fight in his name. I revenge his murder.

PARIS: Your precious Achilles murdered my brother.

PHILOCTETES: Then I guess we are even. Wrong for wrong. It will be for the gods to decide.

NARRATOR: Philoctetes pulled five arrows forth from his quiver and drove them into the hard ground.

PHILOCTETES: I battle with only five arrows, and I doubt I will need them all.

PARIS: Ha! You are so sure of yourself, aren't you? Ahhhh!

NARRATOR: With a cry, Paris notched his first arrow into his bow. Philoctetes snatched up his first arrow and loosed it. It flew to the side of Paris and stuck into the Trojan gates. *(shoom)*

PHILOCTETES: Blast!

NARRATOR: Paris released his first shaft. *(twang)* Philoctetes rolled to the side, and he felt the arrow pass close by to his ear. *(shoom)*

PARIS: *(yelling)* One more shot, Greek! That's all I will need.

NARRATOR: Paris began to run toward the Prince, drawing forth his second missile. *(shoom)* Philoctetes grabbed up his second and sent it flying. *(twang)* It caught Paris between the knuckles of his bow-hand, and the Trojan dropped his weapon into the dirt.

PARIS: *(cry of pain)* Ah!

NARRATOR: The Prince of Troy, a shaft now piercing his bow-hand, drew his sword. *(shing)* Philoctetes sent his third shaft flying, *(twang)* and before it hit home, the fourth. *(twang)* The first arrow sank into Paris' ankle and the second caught him in the eye.

PARIS: *(dying grunt)* Uh!

HELEN: Nooooo! *(weeping)*

NARRATOR: As Paris fell to the ground, Philoctetes rose. One of his arrows was still driven into the ground before him.

PHILOCTETES: Only four arrows, Troy! I have brought down your prince! Achilles is revenged!

HELEN: *(weeping)* Paris! My Paris! How can I live without him?

NARRATOR: Philoctetes remounted his chariot, and without giving Troy a second look, drove back to the Greek camp.

The troops let up a cheer when they saw the prince returning. *(Greek cheering)* Agamemnon welcomed the prince in his royal tent.

AGAMEMNON: Well done, prince!

PHILOCTETES: Yes, the prophecy of Heracles has come true. Give the glory to him. His bow was the weapon that brought down Paris of Troy.

PYRRHUS: *(eagerly)* Tell us how he fell, prince! Give us every detail.

NARRATOR: Philoctetes stared coldly at the young warrior.

PHILOCTETES: Real men do not savor bloodshed.

AGAMEMNON: Maybe now the Trojans will finally surrender since their lover-boy prince is dead.

MENELAUS: Ha! If I know my cheating cow of a wife, she'll take up with the next prince that comes along!

ODYSSEUS: Menelaus is right, I think. There are reports that the remaining Trojan princes are already fighting over which will inherit Helen from Paris.

AGAMEMNON: How much longer must this go on?

ODYSSEUS: Sirs, it seems to me that there is another way that we can win this war. Our noble young Neoptolemus has shown us that no matter how much the Trojans bleed, we have not yet reached their heart. It's time we try a different tactic.

NARRATOR: Philoctetes eyed Odysseus coldly.

PHILOCTETES: I can't wait to hear what *you're* going to suggest! I'm sure it's dishonorable.

ODYSSEUS: Tell me, prince. What honor is there in continuing this war until every last one of us is dead?

AGAMEMNON: What is your idea?

ODYSSEUS: We'll have Epeios the craftsman build an enormous structure that will appear to be a tribute to the gods. Yet inside the structure, we will hide our best fighting men. Then we sail down the coast—pretending to retreat.

PHILOCTETES: A trick! Of course. I would expect nothing less from you.

ODYSSEUS: This *trick* will save a thousand Greek lives! As I was saying, the Trojans will take the structure inside the city walls—so that it will bless them instead of us.

PHILOCTETES: *(laugh)* And what if they don't? What if they decide to burn our tribute instead? Then our best men will be dead. The Trojans are not fools!

ODYSSEUS: Why did *we* Greeks go to such lengths to steal the sacred statue of Athena from the Trojans? Men will do strange things to gain the favor of the gods. Now I guarantee that this will work! Once the structure is

inside the city walls, the men will creep out and open the city gates. Then it will be—

PYRRHUS: *(happily)* A bloodbath.

PHILOCTETES: It's dishonorable!

ODYSSEUS: What is this fool babbling about? This is war!

AGAMEMNON: Now, gentlemen, please. What do you think, Menelaus?

MENELAUS: I think I will do *anything* to get my wife back—so I can *kill her* with my very own hands!

ODYSSEUS: See what a noble cause we fight for? Let's end this—now.

NARRATOR: There was silence within the tent.

AGAMEMNON: Please leave us, prince. We must deliberate about this.

PHILOCTETES: I see. I am good enough to bring down Paris, but not to offer my counsel. Well, I will give it anyway. If Troy is taken in such a way, it will only bring a curse upon Greece.

AGAMEMNON: Thank you for your words. Goodbye.

NARRATOR: So the plan was put into motion. Odysseus enlisted the greatest craftsmen among the Greek troops and in secret a giant structure was built—one that took on the form of a horse. Odysseus directed every facet of its construction.

ODYSSEUS: They'll assume our tribute is to Poseidon in return for our safe voyage home. That god created the horse, you know.

PYRRHUS: Perfect! You've thought of everything!

NARRATOR: The men who would hide within the horse-like structure were selected.

AGAMEMNON: The bow and arrows of Heracles must be within the city when the trap is sprung.

NARRATOR: The kings look expectantly toward Philoctetes. There was a pause.

PHILOCTETES: I will go—but only to make sure our cause does not grow too bloody. When I heard Heracles speaking out of the heavens—

PYRRHUS: You were obviously drunk.

(snickers from the Greeks)

PHILOCTETES: You were there, too. And so was Odysseus. We all heard him. He said for us to remain holy as we conquer Troy. I have seen what we Greeks are capable of. I don't want to see innocent women and children harmed in this action.

PYRRHUS: It's war! No one is innocent in war!

ODYSSEUS: Exactly!

PHILOCTETES: Pyrrhus, *you* may not think so, but your father thought differently.

PYRRHUS: You speak of Achilles as if he were dead, but he stands before you! I am Achilles reborn! I am Neoptolemus, and I will make Troy bleed!

(cheers from the Greeks)

NARRATOR: A week later the Greek encampment that had stood on the Trojan beach for ten years now lay in smoking ruin. The Greeks and their ships were gone. In their place there stood a three-story-high wooden structure that had been pieced together from rough logs with mud and pitch. A barrel-like belly, supported on four stout legs and topped by a rising head, formed the crude shape of a horse. A perplexed party of Trojan noblemen stood in its shadow.

PRIAM: *(overjoyed)* I can't believe it! They have finally given up. They have finally gone. I knew the gods would give us victory.

NARRATOR: Among the gathered men stood Laocoön, one of Priam's dwindling number of sons.

LAOCOÖN: How can we be sure that they have left? The Greeks are tricky.

PRIAM: Bah! Nonsense. Who would go to this much trouble for a trick? No. They are gone. I can feel it.

LAOCOÖN: Then why is this *thing* here?

PRIAM: The Greeks are not barbarians, my son. They serve the same gods we do. They have made this structure as an offering for a safe voyage home.

LAOCOÖN: But look at its midsection. There is enough room in there to hide a troop of men. The Greeks have slaughtered our people and raped our homeland for ten years. Why would they pack up and leave so quickly?

PRIAM: I say that this horse is a gift to the gods. There can be no evil in such a thing.

NARRATOR: A cry rose from down the beach. Two soldiers were dragging a haggard-looking man between them. He was wailing piteously.

SINON: *(screaming)* No! Spare me, noble Trojans! Spare me!

PRIAM: Who is this then? *(mockingly)* Perhaps you *are* right, Laocoön. The Greeks have not fled. There is *one* left. *(chuckle)*

NARRATOR: The sniveling man crawled to Priam's robe and kissed it between his hands.

SINON: Oh, Trojan king! I have been wronged! Severely wronged!

LAOCOÖN: What are you babbling about?

SINON: My countrymen have fled—given up! Oh, this long, long war has broken their will.

PRIAM: When did they leave?

SINON: Yesterday, my lord.

LAOCOÖN: And why were you left behind?

SINON: The Fates have cursed me—that's why! It was all the fault of Calchas the prophet, that lying rat! He said a human sacrifice was needed, and that it should be me. What have I done? I'm only a poor farmer! A farmer who will never see his family again! *(weeping)*

LAOCOÖN: Why were the Greeks so quick to leave without a warning?

SINON: I have been sworn to secrecy! The gods will strike me down if I break my oath!

LAOCOÖN: Answer me, or *I* will strike you down.

SINON: Since the mighty Achilles passed beneath the earth, our army has been doomed. Agamemnon and Menelaus quarreled like spoiled children. The men threatened to mutiny. So they decided to give it up, and they left me to be tortured by the enemy! *(weeping)*

LAOCOÖN: *(hatefully)* Ridiculous man.

PRIAM: What is the meaning of this tribute then? Tell us, and we will spare your life.

SINON: O, merciful king! We toiled many days on the horse. It was another scheme of Calchas the prophet. He told the kings that Poseidon would be honored by such an offering, and our journey home would be a safe one.

LAOCOÖN: Seems a bit large for an offering.

SINON: Here is the craftiness of that man! He told the kings to build it so tall that you noble lords could never fit it inside your glorious walls. If it ever found its way into your city, he said Poseidon would bless you instead of us, and the voyage home would be doomed.

LAOCOÖN: I don't believe you.

SINON: Why would I lie? You have saved me. I only repay my debt with this information.

PRIAM: Laocoön, my son. Do not be so suspicious. Think of how this war has tired even us. The Greeks have been camped upon this beach for ten years. Is it so hard to believe they have gone home?

NARRATOR: Laocoön said no more, but his mouth tensed with anger, and he gripped his spear tightly.

PRIAM: Greek, thank you for this information. You have served us well.

LAOCOÖN: No, Father! It is a trick! I can feel it. I fear the Greeks even when they bring gifts! And I do not trust this monstrosity!

NARRATOR: He turned and flung his spear toward the towering horse. It stuck into a plank of the wooden beast's belly. *(thwack) (hissing shriek)*

LAOCOÖN: *(shocked)* What?

SINON: Look! Look!

NARRATOR: In the same instant that the spear struck the horse, the nearby shallows of the sea began to foam. Two serpentine forms rose from the brine. *(hissing)*

LAOCOÖN: By the gods!

SINON: Ah! *(screaming)*

NARRATOR: The twin sea serpents at once fell upon Laocoön and dragged him screaming back into the tide.

LAOCOÖN: No! Ah! *(hideous screaming)*

NARRATOR: The guards rushed forward into the waves, swords drawn, but the body of Laocoön was already lost.

PRIAM: *(weakly)* No. No. No. Another son. Lost. I can take no more of this.

SINON: You saw him! He attacked the horse! It's like I said. Poseidon favors this tribute.

NARRATOR: No one dared argue against the Greek offering now. The gods had made a violent statement of their loyalty.

PRIAM: The Greeks have taken my Hector— my Paris. I will lose no more of my sons! Get this horse within our walls at any cost. Let the Greeks be cursed by the sea and die like the dogs that they are.

NARRATOR: The ailing king was led away, and the remaining men attended the task of moving the giant structure. Logs were placed beneath it, and it was rolled triumphantly into the city.

Within the structure, the hidden men smiled to themselves. Their plan had worked.

That night as the royal family lamented their latest loss, the rest of Troy rejoiced. The Greeks had been defeated. In the middle of the city square, the giant horse towered over the proceedings. Almost every Trojan was drunk and dancing to the glory of Poseidon. *(loud, drunken cheering from the Trojans)*

Only one person could sense the true nature of the horse—the Trojan princess, Cassandra.

CASSANDRA: Fools! Why do you celebrate? Put away your wine and pick up your swords! The Greeks are within the horse.

TROJAN: There she goes again! Crazy Cassandra. *(laugh)* More wine!

CASSANDRA: *(insanely)* They're going to attack us! Massacre us in our beds! Believe me! Please!

NARRATOR: At last some drunken men grabbed her by either arm, threw her within the temple of Athena, and barred the door.

TROJAN: Stay in there! Maybe Athena will teach you some wisdom! Ha!

NARRATOR: It was not too long before the festival expired as most of the city had fallen into a drunken slumber. The men within the horse heard the commotion die down.

Sinon the Greek had been brought back to Troy as the Trojans' special guest. Now, with his hosts incoherent, Sinon shimmied up the horse's leg and triggered the trap door that had been cleverly hidden within the beast's belly.

SINON: *(hissing)* The city sleeps! It is ours for the taking!

NARRATOR: The dark forms of the hidden Greek soldiers silently dropped down from the trapdoor. Pyrrhus ran to the city ramparts and, lighting a torch, signaled to the rest of the Greek troops, which had returned and were waiting across the plain.

PYRRHUS: *(laugh)* Troy, awake! Your doom is here!

TROJAN: What? *(shouting)* Awake! Awake! The Greeks are upon us!

(sounds of confusion and fighting)

NARRATOR: What followed was a massacre. The full Greek army plowed straight through the dismembered gates. The sleeping Trojans were taken unaware and slaughtered—many without the chance to return a blow. It was only a matter of minutes before Troy was in flames.

GREEK: *(shouting)* Die, Trojan!

TROJAN: *(choking, dying sounds)* Ah!

NARRATOR: Shaking off their initial disorientation, the Trojans regrouped. Some Trojans—in their ingenuity—took up Greek armor from the fallen bodies and disguised themselves—standing in the Greek ranks until they saw an opportunity to ambush their enemies.

GREEK: Come on, brother! Let's charge the citadel! Let's see these Trojans die!

TROJAN: You first!

GREEK: What? *(dying sound)*

NARRATOR: Amid the commotion and the rush of bodies, Philoctetes noted the position of Pyrrhus.

PHILOCTETES: Pyrrhus, where are you going?

PYRRHUS: I'm off to the royal palace! I am going to finish what I started!

NARRATOR: Philoctetes followed Pyrrhus through the carnage. As they neared the palace, they saw that it was barricaded. Menelaus was there, leading a battering-ram assault against its jeweled doors.

MENELAUS: Batter down these doors, men! I have a date with my wife tonight! A date to die for!

(crumbling sound)

NARRATOR: Philoctetes looked up. A tower upon the roof above them was tottering— being pushed over by the Trojans.

PHILOCTETES: Look out! The tower!

NARRATOR: But it was too late. The heavy stones came crashing down, crushing the men who battered against the doors. (crashing sounds and dying moans)

PYRRHUS: Grrrrr. C'mon, men! Regroup! Regroup!

NARRATOR: Pyrrhus himself seized one end of the battering ram and pulled it toward the palace doors again.

PYRRHUS: Now is not the time to stop! Follow me! I am Achilles reborn! Troy is on its knees.

NARRATOR: Men rushed to Pyrrhus' side, and the onslaught was renewed against the doors. At last they broke inward.

Within, a host of Trojans awaited the Greeks and battled them in the cramped palace hallways. Pyrrhus led a bloody charge forward. Philoctetes fired his bow time and time again—dropping Trojans left and right. Somewhere in the fighting, he lost sight of Pyrrhus.

PHILOCTETES: Pyrrhus! Pyrrhus!

NARRATOR: A dread of what the boy would do had seized Philoctetes. He left the battle—running through the long hallways, searching for the boy-warrior, but encountering no one.

PYRRHUS: (distantly) Ha! At last we meet!

NARRATOR: Philoctetes heard Pyrrhus' rabid cries ahead of him. The hallway opened into a chamber, and there in the midst was Pyrrhus, his sword dripping blood.

PYRRHUS: Philoctetes! Welcome! Look whom I have found here! Aren't they beautiful? The crowned heads of Troy! They were trying to escape!

NARRATOR: A huge god-shrine filled half the room. Hecuba and Andromache, the queen and princess of Troy, clung desperately to it. The old king, Priam, sat in a stupor upon the altar.

PHILOCTETES: (quietly) Pyrrhus, come away from this place. Let them escape. Now is the time for mercy.

PYRRHUS: (crazily) I told you not to call me that name! Here is where I will gain my fame—with *his* death.

NARRATOR: He pointed his sword toward Priam.

PYRRHUS: Old king, face me! I want to be the one who can boast about slaying the king of Troy.

PRIAM: (feebly) Very well.

NARRATOR: Priam rose and began to buckle on his royal armor.

PHILOCTETES: Pyrrhus! No!

PYRRHUS: I told you not to call me that! I am Achilles! Achilles!

NARRATOR: A wave of recognition passed over the old king's face, and he pointed a finger at Pyrrhus.

PRIAM: So you are the son of Achilles? I knew your father. *He* was not above showing mercy.

PYRRHUS: *(angrily)* Mercy only brought him death! There should be no mercy in war. Only kill or be killed!

PRIAM: *(grim laugh)* Then I was mistaken. You are no son of Achilles. How could a cruel butcher like you come from such a noble man like him?

PYRRHUS: *(psychotically)* I'll send you to Hades, and you can ask him yourself!

NARRATOR: Before Philoctetes could react, Pyrrhus ran forward and plunged his sword into the old king's side.

PRIAM: *(dying gasp)* Ah!

PHILOCTETES: Pyrrhus! Nooo!

NARRATOR: Hecuba fell sobbing upon the slain body of the king. Pyrrhus watched this with glee.

PHILOCTETES: What have you done?

PYRRHUS: I have done what Achilles should have done before. Troy is dead. Now get out of my way, or I will send you down to Hades as well.

NARRATOR: Pyrrhus moved toward the terrified queen and princess. Philoctetes drew his bow and aimed his arrow-tip toward Pyrrhus.

PHILOCTETES: Stop!

NARRATOR: An amused smile played across Pyrrhus' lips.

PYRRHUS: What are going to do? Kill me? Fine! Let's see it! Do it! Then you'd be no better than I am. You'll just be proving my point! We're all monsters, Philoctetes. The sooner you accept it, the better.

PHILOCTETES: You are mad. The whole world is mad.

PYRRHUS: That may be, prince. But how will *you* change that? The engine of war is raging. Its wheels are already in motion. There is no way to stop it! *(pause)* Now, kill me, so it can consume you, too.

PHILOCTETES: No. I will have no part of it.

NARRATOR: Philoctetes lowered his bow.

PYRRHUS: Ha! I knew it! *(spitting)* You coward! I will see you in Hades!

NARRATOR: Pyrrhus grabbed the two weeping women and dragged them away. As Andromache faded into the shadows, Philoctetes noticed that she clung desperately to a bundle at her chest—her son, the son of Hector.

His insides numb, Philoctetes wandered the darkened palace hallways and at last made his way out into the open air. From his high vantage point, the night's carnage spread out below him. Smoke and noise filled the air—women wailing, children crying, men dying.

Standing there as if in a trance, Philoctetes could not tell how much time passed—perhaps minutes or hours. It did not matter. Greece and Troy were both dying this day, and there was nothing he could do to stop it. At last the sounds of death began to grow fainter.

Philoctetes looked up. Another light was growing. It was not the ravaging flames of the city, but the morning breaking far away.

PHILOCTETES: How strange. Even on such a bloody day as this, the sun still rises.

NARRATOR: It illuminated the bodies of the slain—lying in the streets of Troy as thickly as cobblestones. The gutters ran blood.

Philoctetes spied Pyrrhus mounting the broken city walls. In his grip he held a young child, displaying it to the cheering Greeks below. Philoctetes instinctively knew who it was.

PHILOCTETES: They tell themselves that it is right to kill a child. They say, only a fool kills the father and spares the son.

NARRATOR: As he spoke these words, he saw Pyrrhus drop the child over the side of the walls. A cheer went up from the Greek troops below. *(Greek cheer)*

PHILOCTETES: So passes Greece.

NARRATOR: Philoctetes disappeared back into the darkness of the palace hallways, back to where he had seen the king of Troy murdered. He walked to the bloodstained Trojan altar—an altar to the deaf and blind gods. Philoctetes tenderly placed the bow and arrows of Heracles upon it.

PHILOCTETES: Heracles, once you warned me that men can become monsters. You gave me this mighty gift, but even with all its power, it could not save us from ourselves. I now return it to you.

NARRATOR: He picked up a fallen torch and kindled his offering.

PHILOCTETES: Troy has fallen. And with it, mankind. Now I, too, will pass from this world.

NARRATOR: While the other Greeks lingered in Troy to loot and pillage, Philoctetes boarded a ship and sailed from those cursed shores. He did not return to Greece—the land that he had once called home. Instead he set a new course, out across the sea toward a new home, a new world— perhaps a world kinder than the one he had left behind.

DISCUSSION QUESTIONS

- Do you think it was right for the Greeks to win their victory through a trick? Explain.
- Almost all the Greeks will have great difficulty reaching their homes again. Some will even meet with death on their return journey. For some, like Odysseus, it will take them many years to reach their home. Do they deserve these fates? Explain.
- The murder of Astyanax, Hector's son, is one of the most heartbreaking parts of the entire Trojan War. Why do you think he was murdered?
- Should war be ruthless or humane? Explain.
- Should Philoctetes have killed Pyrrhus? Would his death have changed anything? Explain.
- Philoctetes says that Greece fell along with Troy? What does he mean?

SEARCHING FOR ODYSSEUS
TEACHER GUIDE

BACKGROUND

Just a baby when his father leaves for Troy, Telemachus struggles with many questions: Who is his father? Where is his father? Will he ever return? What impact does he have on his life? Should he seek him out? These are sentiments that many teenagers today can relate to. Some deal with Telemachus' exact situation—an absent parent. But even those who have a relationship with both parents still struggle from time to time with their parents' impact on their identities. They search for their parents (or at least their humanity). In the end they can discover, like Telemachus, they respect their parents more than they thought possible.

Telemachus' portion of the *Odyssey*, nothing more than a few protracted conversations, is not the most exciting part of the epic tale. Apart from Athena's transformations and some comedy relief from the incredibly happy, but also drugged, Helen and Menelaus, it may seem bland. At its heart it's the story of a young man searching for a father, a man who many consider to be dead. Before his journey, Telemachus scorns the father who "abandoned" him. On his mini-adventure he hears the many merits of his father from the noblest lips in Greece. He learns to respect the father he's never met and is, therefore, prepared for his return.

SUMMARY

Growing up, Telemachus has always been perplexed by the absence of his father. He asks his mother many questions about Odysseus, and together they await his return. After the fall of Troy, Odysseus does not return with the other heroes of the war. After a few years, others assume that Odysseus has died or has abandoned his homeland, but Penelope remains convinced that he will return. Suitors from the surrounding area begin to arrive at Ithaca, all asking to take Odysseus' place as Penelope's husband. Most of these are greedy and corrupt men who only want to control Ithaca. Penelope delays making a decision between them, and in an effort to pressure her, they abuse her hospitality and take up residence within the palace of Ithaca.

Penelope further stalls the suitors by asking for them to wait while she weaves a burial shroud for her father-in-law, Laertes. The suitors agree, but using one of Penelope's maids as a spy, they learn that she has been weaving everyday and pulling her work loose every night, so the shroud is no nearer to completion. They demand that she choose a suitor at once.

Athena appears to Telemachus disguised as his father's old friend, Mentor, and tells him to sail away and seek out news from the other kings of Greece concerning his father. Telemachus complies. He sails to Pylos and speaks to Nestor, who can tell him nothing more than tales of his father's greatness. He then visits Menelaus and Helen in Sparta, where the two appear to be incredibly happy. They tell him that they have heard news of Odysseus from Proteus, a shape-shifting creature. Odysseus has been trapped on the island of Calypso the sea nymph for several years. Telemachus wonders why someone as crafty as Odysseus hasn't figured out a way to escape and return home.

Athena appears to Telemachus again, this time in her true goddess form, and tells him that Zeus has sent Hermes to Calypso, ordering Odysseus' release. She tells Telemachus to return to Ithaca and seek out his father, who will meet him in the hut of Eumaeus the swineherd.

ESSENTIAL QUESTIONS

- Are parents important to one's identity?
- Is it important to respect your parents?

ANTICIPATORY QUESTIONS

- Who was Odysseus' son?
- How many years was Odysseus away from his home?
- Why did Odysseus try to avoid the Trojan War?
- Would you want to be the son of Odysseus?
- Would you be proud if Odysseus were your father?

CONNECTIONS

Big Fish (2003) In this film directed by Tim Burton, a young man must come to grips with his larger-than-life father, who is dying of a terminal illness. Like Odysseus, the father is a colorful character, who tells far-fetched tales of adventures and travels that he has had in his past. The son dismisses these stories as fantasies and desires to know his "real" father. Throughout the film, he considers his father to be a liar and a cheat, until he finally understands that the man and his stories are one. Like Telemachus, the son in this film is searching for his father's true identity by listening to fantastic tales of his past. This film is rated PG-13 and may contain some scenes inappropriate for younger viewers.

TEACHABLE TERMS

- **Contrast** Telemachus is contrasted with another young nobleman, Pisistratus, who also has a famous father. Have the students compare and contrast the two young men.
- **Point-of-view** This portion of the story is told from Telemachus' point-of-view. Have the students theorize how it would have been different if it had been told from Penelope's point-of-view.
- **Comedy Relief** The dialogue between Menelaus and Helen on pg. 105-107 is supposed to add some comic relief to the story. Ask the students to determine why this part of the story is humorous.
- **In Medias Res** Latin for "in the middle of things," this literary technique begins a story in the middle (or even at the conclusion of its events) and then tells the earlier part of the story via flashbacks. The *Odyssey* is told in this manner. Ask the students why they think Homer began his story at this point.

RECALL QUESTIONS

1. Why do noblemen take up residence at Ithaca?
2. What trick does Penelope play on them?
3. What is one of the disguises that Athena uses?
4. Who is Proteus?
5. Where has Odysseus been for the last several years?

SEARCHING FOR ODYSSEUS

CAST

TELEMACHUS	*Son of Odysseus*
PENELOPE	*Wife of Odysseus*
MENTOR	*Trusted Friend of Odysseus*
ANTINOUS	*Suitor to Penelope*
EURYMACHUS	*Suitor to Penelope*
HANDMAID	*Deceptive Servant*
EURYCLEIA	*Old Nurse*
MENELAUS	*King of Sparta*
HELEN	*Queen of Sparta*
ATHENA	*Goddess of Wisdom*
NESTOR	*Wise, Old King of Pylos*
PISISTRATUS	*Son of Nestor*

NARRATOR: Odysseus left for the Great War at Troy long before Telemachus could remember. As a boy, he often asked his mother for details about the father who had been away so long at war.

TELEMACHUS: What is my father like? Is he strong?

PENELOPE: He is strong, but not the strongest.

TELEMACHUS: Is he fast?

PENELOPE: He is fast, but not the fastest.

TELEMACHUS: Then what is he?

PENELOPE: He is the smartest—the craftiest. If there is a man who can find his way home from Troy safely, it is your father. Athena has always loved his shifty mind. She will guide him home to us.

NARRATOR: Growing up this gave Telemachus hope, and when he was ten years old, the news of Greek victory reached Ithaca. Troy had fallen.

TELEMACHUS: The war is over! That means father will return soon.

PENELOPE: Yes, my son.

NARRATOR: But as the tides brought home many Greek ships, filled with fathers and husbands, none came for them.

PENELOPE: Do not give up hope! Continue to watch the seas. Above all things, your father is faithful.

NARRATOR: As weeks turned into months and yawned into years, Telemachus grew up, and his innocence started to melt away. He began to doubt that Odysseus would ever come home, and he prepared to become king in his place.

Penelope never showed her own despair in front of Telemachus, though he could see it in the rims of her eyes.

PENELOPE: I worry about you, my son. Why don't you make friends? Why don't you chase the girls as other young boys do? Go and drink deep from life! These are your carefree days.

TELEMACHUS: Carefree? One day soon I will be the ruler of this island. We must face reality, Mother. Odysseus is not coming home.

PENELOPE: *(shocked)* He is *father* to you!

TELEMACHUS: Father? I never even knew the man. He's a stranger to me.

PENELOPE: He knows *you*. He will return to us. No matter what.

TELEMACHUS: And what if he is dead?

PENELOPE: He is not dead. I can feel it.

TELEMACHUS: If he is not in Hades, where is he? If I knew he were dead, at least my heart would not be filled with questions.

PENELOPE: He is faithful. He is faithful.

TELEMACHUS: Are you telling me that? Or yourself?

NARRATOR: When Odysseus had departed for Troy, he had left his friend Mentor in charge of Ithaca until Telemachus came of age. Penelope asked Mentor to speak to Telemachus and ease his troubled mind.

MENTOR: Your mother says you are doubting your father. That's dangerous business. I've doubted him many times myself, but he has always come through.

TELEMACHUS: You call him my father, but who on this earth truly knows who his father is?

MENTOR: *(laugh)* I remember having this very conversation with Odysseus when he was about your age. He could not believe that feeble old Laertes was truly his father. It's a phase all young men go through.

NARRATOR: Mentor placed a reassuring hand upon the boy's shoulder.

MENTOR: Odysseus *is* your father, and he will return home to you.

NARRATOR: Soon enough there came a distraction from Telemachus and Penelope's long wait of grief. Vultures descended. A pack of nobles from the surrounding islands—one-hundred and eight to be exact—came knocking on Ithaca's gates. They were suitors for Penelope's hand, but, in truth, they only lusted for the crown she represented.

ANTINOUS: Odysseus is dead, my lady! It is time you marry again.

PENELOPE: Not dead, good sir. Only delayed. Since my husband is still living, I cannot remarry. But I welcome you to stay here and await his return here at Ithaca in our humble hall.

NARRATOR: The suitors smiled at Penelope's hospitable offer. In this invitation they saw a way to break her.

ANTINOUS: We will wait here until we get what we want. Our rudeness will snap this delicate queen soon enough.

EURYMACHUS: What if she still refuses?

ANTINOUS: Then we live here—with free food and drink—until she decides to choose between us.

EURYMACHUS: What about the boy? He could be dangerous.

ANTINOUS: He's a frightened brat. He will do nothing to stop us.

NARRATOR: The suitors moved into the royal halls, ate up the food, guzzled the wine, and romanced the serving wenches. A year came and went. Still no Odysseus.

TELEMACHUS: Mother, how long can this go on? Let me run these men out of Ithaca.

PENELOPE: They are our guests. The gods command us to be hospitable.

TELEMACHUS: Yes, but these men are not guests. They're pigs! They're abusing us!

PENELOPE: What can you do to them? You are still a boy, and they are dangerous men. I cannot lose you, too.

NARRATOR: Had his mother finally admitted that she had lost Odysseus? Even though she managed to evade the suitors' advances, each day without Odysseus eroded away a bit of her resolve—like a wave impacting upon the beach.

The suitors—under the leadership of two thugs, Antinous and Eurymachus—had made a game of depleting Penelope's resources, but still they tired of her tricks and refusals.

ANTINOUS: The king of Ithaca is dead! Choose a new king from among us!

NARRATOR: Telemachus was nearing manhood. The suitors knew, as the rightful heir, he was growing dangerous. Penelope sensed this was their last offer of "peace" before they risked open war.

PENELOPE: I will choose—

EURYMACHUS: Yes! Finally!

PENELOPE: (*continuing*) As soon as I have woven a burial shroud for my father-in-law, Laertes.

EURYMACHUS: What?

PENELOPE: The years lie heavily upon him. I must finish his shroud before death seizes him. Surely you understand.

NARRATOR: Antinous eyed her suspiciously.

ANTINOUS: (*shrewdly*) Fine! Weave for the old coot. How long can a bit of weaving take?

EURYMACHUS: Hopefully not longer than the wine holds out! (*laugh*)

NARRATOR: This was Penelope's final diversion—her last-ditch effort to hold out for Odysseus. Penelope took to her loom. In her weaving, she put the image of the sea, and Odysseus' ship tossed upon it. Even in all her despair, a thread of hope still survived.

In secret the suitors consulted with Penelope's handmaidens, who had become their lovers and spies.

ANTINOUS: Well, is she actually weaving?

HANDMAID: Yes, she arises before dawn and weaves for the entire day, but still she seems to make no progress.

EURYMACHUS: It must be some kind of trick.

ANTINOUS: Watch her closely. She will make a mistake, and when she does, we will have the perfect reason to force her into choosing among us.

NARRATOR: Only Eurycleia, the elderly nurse of Telemachus and Odysseus before him, was trusted with the truth of Penelope's plan. Each morning the queen arose before dawn and pulled loose the previous day's threads, and through this the suitors' ambitions were thwarted for yet another day.

TELEMACHUS: What will happen when your weaving is completed? Will you really marry one of those—those—pigs?

PENELOPE: To keep you safe, my son, I would do anything. But your father will return first though.

TELEMACHUS: We can't hold out for a dream! These pigs have turned our noble home into a brothel. We still have friends in our own household, don't we? Let me drive these suitors from our home!

PENELOPE: Friends? Telemachus, we have no friends. Only a few here at Ithaca remain loyal to us. All the others have been bribed or frightened into corruption.

TELEMACHUS: Then I will go to get help elsewhere!

PENELOPE: Yes, go! But do not return until your father has come home and made Ithaca safe again.

TELEMACHUS: If I don't make Ithaca safe, no one will. I will go and return with an army. Odysseus had many friends among the other kings of Greece, right? Surely there will be one who will help us.

NARRATOR: Telemachus moved to put his plan into action, but a goddess found him first.

An old sailor came to the Ithacan hall, his head bare and his beard a grizzled mess. His skin was burnt and flaking from endless hours in the sun. This was his outward appearance at least. His eyes were gray like a cloudy morning. Mentes was Athena in disguise, and the goddess found her way to the angry prince.

ATHENA: *(old man voice)* Young lord, I am an old sailor, Mentes, a friend of Lord Odysseus for many years. I seek the hospitality of your hall.

TELEMACHUS: You came at the wrong time, old man. This hall has given all the hospitality it can. My mother has been made a prisoner in her own home.

NARRATOR: Telemachus filled the disguised Athena in on the entire situation—how the suitors had crawled out of every surrounding hole-in-the-wall island and converged on Ithaca.

ATHENA: *(angrily)* I've known Odysseus forever! He wouldn't dare stand for this!

TELEMACHUS: Odysseus is not here, old man. His bones lie out there in the waves somewhere.

ATHENA: *(strangely)* No! No! I know that he is alive. It must be some prophecy that the gods have placed in my brain, but I know that he is alive. Someone—or something—holds him captive across the wine-dark sea. But he will return.

NARRATOR: Telemachus stared into the old man's gray goddess eyes.

TELEMACHUS: Whatever you say.

ATHENA: *(happily)* So you are Telemachus! My, how you have grown! I see much of your father in you.

TELEMACHUS: *(bitter laugh)* My friends call me lucky—to be the son of such a famous father. I say the lucky ones are those who see their father grow old in the midst of his possessions. I must be the most *un*lucky son who ever lived.

ATHENA: *(angrily)* Unlucky? Whose blood flows through your veins? Your father would not give up so easily! You are no longer a whining boy! You're a man! Send these suitors packing! Gather them together and *command* them to leave!

TELEMACHUS: They will only refuse. I know it.

ATHENA: Of course, but that will only be your first move. After you have delivered your ultimatum, take a crew of trusted sailors and seek elsewhere for news of your father.

TELEMACHUS: And just leave my mother behind?

ATHENA: Yes, Telemachus.

TELEMACHUS: Where should I go?

ATHENA: At Pylos seek out King Nestor. He was one of your father's greatest friends. Then travel to Sparta and speak with King Menelaus. Between the two of them, you just might hear word of your storm-tossed father.

TELEMACHUS: Tell me, what gives you such clairvoyance?

NARRATOR: The gray eyes flashed, and the shape of the sailor melted away. The goddess Athena winged herself away, transformed into a high-flying owl. *(hooting of an owl)*

TELEMACHUS: *(in shock)* A goddess? Then maybe she speaks the truth. Could Odysseus still live?

NARRATOR: Telemachus returned to the common hall, where the suitors had set up their never-ending feast. It stunk like over-spiced food and unmixed wine.

TELEMACHUS: *(angrily)* Suitors! Neighbors! Men of the surrounding isles! I am Telemachus, the son of Odysseus, ruler of Ithaca.

NARRATOR: The drunken slobs turned. Some hung limply in the arms of Penelope's handmaidens. Some of them disrespectfully continued their feasting.

TELEMACHUS: Too long have you haunted my mother's hall. I command that you leave this palace. If Odysseus is dead, *I* am his heir, and Ithaca is mine!

NARRATOR: Antinous and Eurymachus began to howl with laughter.

EURYMACHUS: *(drunkenly)* And if we don't, what's a limp-wristed creampuff like you going to do about it?

ANTINOUS: *(fake respect)* We follow the will of the *gods*, boy! You have no authority here!

EURYMACHUS: Yeah! *(hiccup)*

TELEMACHUS: *(violently)* The gods? For your rudeness here, I pray that the gods strike you down!

NARRATOR: This sobered them a bit. They had never heard such strong words from the boy.

TELEMACHUS: My mother is an honorable woman, and you—

ANTINOUS: (*growling*) Your mother is a harlot, boy! A deceiver! Don't you know what she's been up to?

EURYMACHUS: (*yelling*) Tricked us! Tricked us all!

(*shouts of approval from the suitors*)

ANTINOUS: She's had no intention of completing that shroud she's been weaving. Every night she's been pulling loose her day's work.

EURYMACHUS: The lying wench!

ANTINOUS: Her very own maids ratted her out. Even *they* were appalled by her deceit. Now she's caught! And she *will* marry one of us. Her excuses are done.

NARRATOR: Telemachus could only sneer as they returned to their revelry. His part had been played. He had taken his stand and proved powerless. It was time for him to begin his journey.

Old Eurycleia was the only one Telemachus told of his plan. She poured unmixed wine into jars, sewed up bags of barley for his voyage, and kissed him upon the forehead before he left.

EURYCLEIA: Be careful, boy. Your father would be proud of your bravery.

TELEMACHUS: Would he?

EURYCLEIA: Of course. It took all the bravery he had to leave you and your mother behind.

TELEMACHUS: Will you console mother after I'm gone? Make her understand why I'm going.

EURYCLEIA: Your mother is stronger than you think, boy. These brutes will not break her. She is as solid as an oak!

NARRATOR: Telemachus found a ship and a crew already waiting for him at the Ithacan port. (It was Athena's doing, he later discovered.) To his surprise, Mentor stood beside the craft.

TELEMACHUS: Mentor?

ATHENA: (*man voice*) I have come to help you on your voyage.

TELEMACHUS: But how—?

NARRATOR: Telemachus noticed Mentor's sea-gray eyes and smiled to himself.

ATHENA: (*man voice*) Few sons are the equals of their fathers. Many fall short. Too few surpass them. But in you, Telemachus, I see Odysseus' cunning.

NARRATOR: Telemachus took to sea, with Athena-Mentor at his side. They steered a course toward Pylos, home of Nestor, oldest and wisest king of Greece.

TELEMACHUS: Mentor, a wise friend told me that Odysseus might be out there somewhere—held captive over the sea by some force. But what force could keep a man like him from his family? Maybe he just prefers the adventure of the open sea to home and hearth.

ATHENA: Then you do not know your father as I know him.

NARRATOR: They found Nestor in his palace, and Telemachus thought he must be one of the deathless gods. The man had reigned over his people for three generations of men and still his eyes blazed with youthful glory. A banquet was in progress, and he welcomed them to it, even without formal introductions.

ATHENA: *(whispering)* When the time is right ask Nestor your question. Remember: He is far too wise to lie.

TELEMACHUS: *(whispering)* What should I say? I've never spoken in front of a king!

ATHENA: Your father would find the words. *You* must do the same.

TELEMACHUS: But I'm *not* Odysseus. Why does everyone keep assuming—

NESTOR: *(addressing Telemachus)* Tell me, young traveler, what brings you to sandy Pylos?

TELEMACHUS: *(grandly)* Noble Nestor, I have heard many tales of your wisdom—a man who has lorded over many men. I see in this hall many of your noble sons. I'm sure your heart swells with pride when you behold them. I have come to your hall seeking not a son, but a father. Odysseus—I believe you know him well.

NESTOR: Never before have I heard a young man speak in such a way! So much grace! I believe I see your father in you, my boy. Are you not the son of Odysseus?

TELEMACHUS: You have guessed it, my lord.

NARRATOR: Telemachus told Nestor of the suitors and the plight of his mother. Nestor fumed with indignation, yet when the conversation turned to Odysseus, he could offer Telemachus little news.

NESTOR: Odysseus was one of my dearest friends. After the fall of Troy, the Greek kings departed those shores in separate groups. One left swiftly behind the flagship of Menelaus, while the other tarried behind with Agamemnon. I was in the first group, and the last time I saw your father was on the beaches of Troy.

TELEMACHUS: Can you tell me no more?

NESTOR: King Menelaus is whom you should seek. Perhaps he has heard more news than I. He roamed the seas for seven years.

TELEMACHUS: Why?

NESTOR: We departed Troy without the blessing of the gods! So hasty were we to return home with the spoils of the Trojans! In anger, the gods cursed Menelaus. He wandered a full seven years upon the sea with his golden bride, Helen. Agamemnon, who stayed behind to make all the proper sacrifices, received a swift trip home to Mycenae. Unfortunately, only death waited for him there.

TELEMACHUS: Agamemnon is dead?

NESTOR: Struck down by his wife's lover. I thought all of Greece had heard of the murder of its greatest king! His queen took his cousin as her lover shortly after his departure for Troy, and together they hatched a plan to seize his throne.

TELEMACHUS: What would drive a wife to do such a thing?

ATHENA: The murder of a loving daughter.

NESTOR: Your friend speaks truth. The sacrifice of Iphigenia had driven her mother mad. With Menelaus lost at sea, it fell to the son of Agamemnon to avenge his father's murder. He did so. He put the lover and his very own mother to the sword. It took determination! You, my boy, should strive to be such a son!

NARRATOR: The old man's eyes became soft.

NESTOR: I remember your father before the Great War. I've never seen a man more content. He loved his Ithaca and his Penelope. He spoke of you often and vowed to return to you someday. If any man would wish to return home, it would be he. I hope he still lives.

NARRATOR: Although Telemachus did not will them, tears beaded in the corners of his eyes.

ATHENA: (*grandly*) Then the course is clear: Go to Menelaus. He will give you the information you seek. Farewell!

NARRATOR: The gray-eyed Mentor rose, and his robe melted into a covering of feathers. Athena once again winged herself away in the form of an owl! (*hooting*)

NESTOR: (*in shock*) By the gods! You are truly favored to have a goddess as your companion! (*laughing*) Telemachus, tonight you will sleep here at the palace. Tomorrow I will have my son Pisistratus take you by chariot to Sparta.

NARRATOR: Pisistratus was a nice enough fellow—the kind of young man who gains his identity from his status and heritage. He wanted to know everything about Odysseus.

PISISTRATUS: What do you think first gave your father the idea for the Trojan Horse?

TELEMACHUS: I do not know.

PISISTRATUS: I wonder how he became so tricky. Can you imagine what it would be like to have the bards sing about you in your own lifetime?

TELEMACHUS: No, I cannot.

PISISTRATUS: Do you think they will sing songs about us one day? The son of Achilles is just as famous as his father. Do you think we will live up to our fathers?

TELEMACHUS: I can't say.

NARRATOR: Telemachus spent most of the chariot ride to Sparta in silence. He honestly had no answers for Pisistratus.

As Nestor's palace at Pylos had dwarfed the hall of Ithaca, Lacedaemon, the fortress of Menelaus, dwarfed Pylos. Crowds of people thronged through the streets. (*cheering of a crowd*) Pisistratus stated the obvious:

PISISTRATUS: Must be some kind of celebration.

NARRATOR: The two young princes were admitted to the palace where an enormous feast was being held. Because of their noble bearing and some haughty words from Pisistratus, they were admitted into the royal banquet hall without question. There they beheld the red-haired king himself, Menelaus.

MENELAUS: *(happily)* Hello! The guards told me two boys had arrived that looked like the gods themselves! They weren't exaggerating!

PISISTRATUS: What is this happy occasion?

MENELAUS: *(laughing)* Today, my daughter has been wed! Have a seat! Feast with us!

NARRATOR: Menelaus whisked them to a seat among the revelers, promising to soon return. He was beside himself with duties on such a special day.

PISISTRATUS: Father told me of this marriage. Hermione, the daughter of Menelaus and Helen, was given to Neoptolemus, the son of Achilles. A good match, I say.

TELEMACHUS: Any daughter of Helen must be a jewel among women.

PISISTRATUS: Eh. I saw her once. She's fair enough, I guess. Father will make a better match for me, I'm sure.

NARRATOR: The noon feast began to give way to the evening feast, and at last Menelaus appeared at their side—winded and somewhat drunk.

MENELAUS: A wedding! There's nothing like it! Now tell me, lads, where do you hail from?

PISISTRATUS: I am Pisistratus, the son of Nestor and this is Telemachus, son of—

MENELAUS: *(in shock)* Odysseus! Of course! How did I not see it before?

NARRATOR: Pisistratus looked away in annoyance. Odysseus' name always seemed to get a bigger reaction than his father's.

MENELAUS: *(to a servant)* Fetch the queen, Helen! She will wish to speak with our special guests.

NARRATOR: Menelaus eyed Telemachus like a beggar who had found a pearl.

MENELAUS: My boy, what a pleasure to meet the son of Odysseus! I have never met a finer man than your father!

TELEMACHUS: That is why I have come to you. I hope one day to meet him myself.

MENELAUS: Oh yes. *I* had my own troubles reaching home, which I shall tell you shortly—but first allow me to introduce my wife. Perhaps you have heard of her?

PISISTRATUS: Of course! Helen of Troy!

NARRATOR: Menelaus glared at Pisistratus.

MENELAUS: *(growling)* Helen of *Sparta*!

PISISTRATUS: Err. That's what I meant!

NARRATOR: As many men claim, after setting eyes on Helen, it is impossible to describe exactly how she looked. Long after their encounter with her, Telemachus had to hear Pisistratus stammer over himself trying to describe her features, contradicting himself until he finally resorted to one word: *beautiful*.

HELEN: Yes, my dear. Helen of *Sparta*. How nice it sounds! I've tried to forget Troy—that horrible place! I curse Aphrodite daily for forcing me there.

MENELAUS: *(grumbling)* It's hard to force the willing.

HELEN: *(ignoring him)* Who are these fine-looking young guests?

MENELAUS: These, my angel, are mighty princes. The son of Nestor and the son of Odysseus.

NARRATOR: Her eyes locked onto those of Telemachus. The prince immediately felt that certain feeling that most men did when they beheld Helen: a kind of worthlessness. They instantly realized how unworthy they were of such a woman. Of course, this just made them want her all the more.

HELEN: I remember your father well, my boy. Before the fall of the Troy, he snuck into the city disguised as an old beggar man—to spring some trap I assume. As the daughter of a god, I could see through his disguise, but I raised no alarm. No, when I saw him and his great Greek mind at work, I grew homesick.

MENELAUS: *(angrily)* Had you finally tired of your Trojan prince?

NARRATOR: Helen gracefully ignored Menelaus' comment and passed him a golden cup.

HELEN: Here, darling. Drink this. *(pause)* I know what you boys are thinking: Yes, I, Helen the one who started a war for her own shameless lust. Even though I was such a harlot, I missed Greece. Aphrodite's spell held me for ten long years, but at last its magic grew thin. I yearned to sail back home—be reunited with the husband and the daughter I had left behind.

NARRATOR: She took her husband's hand.

HELEN: Thanks to Odysseus, I saw reason. Because of him, I returned home.

MENELAUS: *(grumbling)* That and the Trojans lost the war. I had planned to kill her with my own hands, you know!

HELEN: *(through gritted teeth)* Darling! Drink up! We have guests.

NARRATOR: Menelaus took a drink, and his features softened.

MENELAUS: But when I cornered her in the Trojan palace and I saw her beautiful body once again, I knew I could not bring myself to kill her as I planned.

HELEN: Awww. He says the sweetest things.

TELEMACHUS: But Odysseus has still not returned to Ithaca, my lady.

HELEN: No? How unfortunate. Wait a minute. My darling king, didn't we hear news of him?

MENELAUS: We did, my queen. After we left Troy, the winds of the gods blew us far off course, all the way to the shores of Egypt. We were trapped there for many years. We knew that some god was holding us there until we repented—

HELEN: Ahem. Tell him of Proteus, dear.

MENELAUS: *(gritting his teeth)* I was just coming to that, my dove. Proteus, the Old Man of the Sea, a creature who has the ability to assume the shape of any creature, suns himself daily on the Egyptian beaches. I knew he would be able to tell us how to return to Sparta.

HELEN: Tell them about the wrestling match. That is the best part.

MENELAUS: *(angrily)* I am about to! *(calming)* I knew in order to get Proteus to tell me what I wished, I would have to wrestle him.

HELEN: While we're young, dear.

MENELAUS: I knew Proteus would change from form to form, trying to loosen my grip. If I held on to the bitter end, I could ask him any question, and he would be forced to answer.

HELEN: These boys don't have all day. Anyway, my noble husband hid himself behind a rock, and when the Old Man of the Sea came out of the depths, he jumped upon him, and the two wrestled fiercely.

NARRATOR: Menelaus stared at his wife with a look of thinly veiled hatred.

HELEN: It was no easy contest! Proteus transformed himself into a lion, a serpent, a leopard, and a pig!

PISISTRATUS: *(excited)* Fantastic!

HELEN: Can you imagine a grown man wrestling a pig? *(laughs)* Proteus even assumed the shape of a swift-flowing stream! Isn't that right, dear?

MENELAUS: It almost drowned me to hold on!

HELEN: Then Proteus grew into a tall tree! But he could not defeat my husband! There was Menelaus—clinging fiercely to his highest branches! He almost fell to his death.

MENELAUS: *(suddenly angry)* That would have broken your heart, wouldn't it? Then you would have run back to your Trojan boyfriends!

NARRATOR: Helen reached over, took Menelaus' cup, and refilled it from a pitcher at her side. The king took a swig, softened, and continued his story.

MENELAUS: *(happy sigh)* That's better. But I held on. That was his final form, and his shape-shifting stopped! Then I asked my questions of him. He told me the path to get home, how to make amends with the gods I had offended. I asked after my brother, Agamemnon, and Proteus told me of his death.

PISISTRATUS: We heard of Agamemnon's murder.

MENELAUS: Women! You put your trust in them, and they just rip your heart out! Isn't that right, *dear*?

NARRATOR: Helen furiously summoned a servant.

HELEN: Refill this pitcher at once! *(laughs)* Where were we? Oh, yes. Proteus also mentioned another Greek king who was lost at sea: your father.

TELEMACHUS: What did he tell you?

HELEN: Proteus said that your father had been a prisoner for many years—on the island of Calypso the sea nymph.

MENELAUS: That's just like a woman, isn't it? Mark my words, boys, stay away from them! They'll trap you for sure.

NARRATOR: The servant returned with a fresh pitcher of wine. Helen quickly sprinkled a powdery substance into it and refilled her husband's glass.

HELEN: Not to worry. It is only a potion that helps you forget the pains of the past. Would you boys care for a sip?

NARRATOR: Telemachus and Pisistratus declined.

HELEN: Better, dear?

MENELAUS: (sigh) Better.

HELEN: Good luck finding your father.

NARRATOR: That night in Menelaus' palace Telemachus fought sleep. All these years—all these waiting years, he had thought Odysseus must be dead. But in reality he was the prisoner of a nymph? It seemed too far-fetched to believe. For all his cunning, Odysseus could not escape from a nymph? Or maybe he didn't want to escape. Perhaps he had found a mate he loved more than his wife and son.

They stayed in Sparta for a week. Pisistratus loved rubbing elbows with the likes of Menelaus and Helen, but Telemachus was restless. Menelaus' news held little hope for him and his mother.

One morning, Telemachus awoke, and a gray-eyed woman was standing over him. She wore glistening armor, and an owl perched on her shoulder. Finally, the goddess and he were past disguises.

ATHENA: (booming) Telemachus, return to Ithaca at once. I have beseeched Zeus to free your father. Hermes has gone to the isle of the sea nymph Calypso and commanded her to release him. Your father is on his way home even as we speak.

TELEMACHUS: I can't believe it!

ATHENA: Return to Ithaca, but do not go to the palace. Seek out the hut of Eumaeus the swine-herder. Your father will be there.

TELEMACHUS: I will go.

NARRATOR: The boy paused.

TELEMACHUS: Lady Athena, I openly admit that you are wiser than I—but I must ask one question. What was the point of this quest? Why this wild-goose chase across the sea? Why didn't you just tell me what I needed to know?

NARRATOR: The goddess smiled sweetly.

ATHENA: Oh, Telemachus. Nothing in this life is ever simple. Your whole life you've lived with an empty space where a father should fit. Now your father is coming home. *Odysseus* is coming home. Don't you wish to know this noble man that the mightiest kings of earth praise? Don't you wish to know the man who brought Troy to its knees? The man who could make fickle Helen dream of home? Don't you wish to see the man that other men see in you?

NARRATOR: Telemachus paused thoughtfully.

TELEMACHUS: (thoughtfully) I never realized it until now, but I do.

ATHENA: Then your quest is complete. Hurry home. Your father is waiting there for you!

DISCUSSION QUESTIONS

- What does Telemachus learn on his journey?
- How is Telemachus like his father? How does Telemachus seem different than his father?
- Is Penelope a good wife? Explain.
- Why do you think Odysseus has been on the island of Calypso the sea nymph so long?

ON CALYPSO'S ISLE
TEACHER GUIDE

BACKGROUND

In ancient Greece it was the *Iliad*, not the *Odyssey*, that earned a central place in society as the text that defined what it meant to be Greek. Great men quoted its lines, treated its characters as real historical figures, and lived their lives according to its values. In contrast the Greeks viewed the *Odyssey* as an entertaining fantasy, but not the same instruction manual for being a man that the *Iliad* was.

Over the centuries both poems have remained popular, but in the modern world the *Odyssey* has nudged its way ahead of the *Iliad*. It may be that people's tastes have changed over time. The *Iliad* is all about war and death and glory; the *Odyssey* is about journeys, home, friendships, and family. Another possible reason for this preference change is the charm of Odysseus, an everyman character on a mission most can empathize with. He's not on quest to slay a monster, conquer a kingdom, or find a treasure; he is a tired, middle-aged man who just wants to return home to his family.

The *Odyssey* begins *in medias res* ("in the middle of things"). Telemachus' journey to find news of his father comes first, and then the story shifts to the island of Calypso the sea nymph. Calypso means "concealer," and she has kept Odysseus prisoner on her island for seven years. From her island Odysseus sails and shipwrecks in the land of the Phaeacians, where he is invited to tell the tale of his journey. Then, in flashback, he narrates previous adventures he has had (prior to Calypso) such as encounters with the Cyclops, Circe the witch, the Sirens, the Lotus

Eaters, Scylla and Charybdis, etc. This makes for a somewhat confusing narrative. For example, the reader learns that Poseidon hates Odysseus before finding out why: Odysseus had previously blinded his Cyclops son Polyphemus.

Because of the *Odyssey's* jumbled structure, the five plays that deal with the *Odyssey* in this book are interchangeable. For example, if you want to follow the design of the *Odyssey*, you would read them in the order they appear in this book. But if you would rather, for the sake of clarity, put them in chronological order, they would go in this order:

- "In the Cave of the Cyclops"
- "Circe the Witch"
- "On Calypso's Isle"
- "Searching for Odysseus"
- "Return to Ithaca"

SUMMARY

Calypso the sea nymph has kept Odysseus prisoner on her island for seven years. Although the goddess is beautiful and she promises him eternal life, Odysseus misses his home and his family. He spends each night with Calypso but spends each day weeping on the beach.

At last Athena decides to intervene and goes to her father, Zeus. Zeus agrees that Odysseus needs to be freed, and he dispatches Hermes to break the bad news to Calypso. The sea nymph is infuriated. She asks why the male gods can take mortal lovers, but she can't. In the end, she relents and agrees to release Odysseus.

Odysseus is overjoyed by this news and begins to build himself a raft. When it is completed, he bids the heartbroken nymph goodbye and sets out for his home.

As soon as Odysseus is out to sea, Poseidon, who hates the Greek because he has blinded his son, destroys his raft with a storm. Odysseus barely survives and washes up on the beaches of a strange land. A group of girls are doing their laundry on the beach when they discover the naked Odysseus. Among them is the princess Nausicaa, who takes the traveler to her father, the King of the Phaeacians. The Phaeacians have magical ships that can take Odysseus home to Ithaca, but first they ask him to stay in their hall and tell them the story of his travels. Odysseus begins his tale.

ESSENTIAL QUESTIONS

- What brings a person happiness in life?
- Is there more to love than just attraction?
- What motivates a person to persevere in spite of many obstacles?

ANTICIPATORY QUESTIONS

- Where did Athena tell Telemachus his father has been for the last seven years?
- Is it right to hold someone captive against his or her will?
- What would happen if Odysseus never made it home?
- Would you take a gift of immortality if it means an eternity of sadness?
- What is a sea nymph?

CONNECTIONS

O Brother, Where Art Thou? (2000) This film directed by the Coen brothers has many parallels to the *Odyssey*. The protagonist's full name is Ulysses Everett McGill (Ulysses is the Latin name for Odysseus). He is returning to his home in order to stop his wife (named Penny) from marrying a new suitor. Along the way he is lured astray by three Siren-like temptresses, assaulted by a one-eyed Bible salesman, and nearly drowned by a flood. Having students view this film in order to

pick out the similarities between its events and the *Odyssey* is a great assignment. This film is rated PG-13 for language and mild violence.

TEACHABLE TERMS

- **Complex Character** Repeatedly Odysseus is shown to have conflicting character traits. He is a family man, but he agrees to massacre innocent Trojans. He loves his wife, yet he has affairs with Calypso and Circe on his journey. Do these conflicting traits make him more realistic as a character? Explain.
- **Theme** Even though Odysseus is offered immortality and the chance to spend eternity with a beautiful woman, he is still unhappy. Have your students discuss what message this is presenting.
- **Sexism** Calypso's speech on pg. 116 may be the oldest complaint of sexism in literature. She wonders why the gods can take lovers by force, but when goddesses do, they are forced to release them? Ask the students whether or not she has a case.
- **Protagonist** In the first part of the *Odyssey*, Telemachus was the protagonist (or main character). Now the story has shifted to Odysseus. Have your students identify this shift in protagonist.

RECALL QUESTIONS

1. Who goes to Zeus and asks him to free Odysseus?
2. Calypso offers Odysseus eternal life if he will do what?
3. Which god hates Odysseus?
4. In the court of King Alcinous what makes Odysseus weep?
5. The Phaeacians have magical what?

ON CALYPSO'S ISLE

CAST

ODYSSEUS	*Wily Adventurer*
CALYPSO	*Amorous Sea Nymph*
NYMPH	*Servant to Calypso*
ATHENA	*Goddess of War and Wisdom*
POSEIDON	*Ruler of the Seas and Oceans*
ZEUS	*Ruler of the Gods*
HERMES	*Messenger God*
ALCINOUS	*King of Phaeacia*
NAUSICAA	*Daughter of Alcinous*
GIRL	*Handmaiden to Nausicaa*

NARRATOR: It had been seven long years for Odysseus—a prisoner on the island of Calypso the lovely-braided sea nymph and her sister-nymphs. After Odysseus had washed up on her shores—clinging to the blasted remnants of his ship—Calypso had claimed him as her mate, promising him a share in her eternal life as long as he remained her lover. Each night they spent together in her glittering cave, but each day Odysseus found himself looking out over the sea—dreaming of Ithaca and his beloved Penelope.

NYMPH: Mistress, the *man* is weeping again.

CALYPSO: *(sigh)* He's still pining for his home and his mortal family. It's a phase. He'll forget them eventually.

NYMPH: It has already been seven years, and his sadness seems to have only grown.

CALYPSO: Don't tell me that you're feeling sorry for him?

NYMPH: Of course not. I'm only saying that desperate men try desperate tactics. He might try to escape.

CALYPSO: How could he escape? You, my servants, keep him under constant surveillance. He is surrounded by miles of sea. And besides, why would he want to leave? He gets to spend each night in my arms and each day attended by my lovely nymphs. Plus, I have offered him eternal life. What greater gift can you give to a mortal?

NYMPH: All I am saying is that the man is not happy.

CALYPSO: I am happy, and that is all that matters.

NARRATOR: Despite her harsh words, Calypso cared deeply for her mortal lover. Every trick she had tried to win over Odysseus' heart had failed. She knew—if given the chance to escape—he would take it.

CALYPSO: Odysseus, dear, are you not happy with me here?

ODYSSEUS: You have been very kind to me through the years. But I cannot lie: I desire to see my home again—my family.

CALYPSO: *(irritated)* Go ahead and say what you mean. You miss *her*—your mortal wife.

NARRATOR: Odysseus remained silent.

CALYPSO: What does she have that I do not? Are her eyes lovelier than mine? Is her skin more youthful and radiant? Does she have all the contours of a goddess?

ODYSSEUS: No. Her beauty cannot compare to yours. But beauty is not the only thing that stirs the heart.

CALYPSO: *(mocking laugh)* So you desire this mortal woman, who will wither and die, over me, who will remain beautiful forever?

ODYSSEUS: I do. *(pause)* And I will ask again: Will you let me go to her?

CALYPSO: *(fake sadness)* I am afraid not, my dear. It is for your own good. You are not thinking clearly. Give me another year, and I will have changed your mind. By then your home will be but a distant memory.

ODYSSEUS: *(passionately)* You've said that for the last *seven* years! Can't you see? I will never forget my home!

CALYPSO: These memories will fade—in time. Now let us retire.

NARRATOR: It seemed that Odysseus would be trapped on the island of Ogygia forever. His clever mind could see no way out. Athena, his patron goddess, had apparently abandoned him—left him at the mercy of the amorous nymph. But, unbeknownst to him, Athena had not forgotten her beloved hero.

ATHENA: *(angrily)* Enough is enough! Calypso has had her chance to win him over. She's had her fun! Now she's just keeping him from reaching his home. Something must be done!

NARRATOR: The goddess went before Zeus, her royal father.

ATHENA: Mighty Zeus, I come asking a favor.

ZEUS: Athena, my favorite daughter! You know I will grant you anything—if it's in my power.

ATHENA: This favor has to do with Odysseus.

ZEUS: I'm not surprised. He has become your pet project, hasn't he?

ATHENA: I have made it my mission to see him safely home.

ZEUS: Well, that is tricky business, isn't it? Many of the Greeks offended the gods during the war at Troy. For their crimes they must not reach their homes without a few trials.

ATHENA: Odysseus has already been at sea for nearly nine years! For seven of those years, Calypso the Concealer has held him prisoner in her little love nest!

ZEUS: There are worse ways to spend seven years.

ATHENA: Father, hasn't he suffered enough?

POSEIDON: I can answer that question for you.

NARRATOR: The god Poseidon—his beard matted with seaweed and brine—appeared beside his Olympian brother.

ZEUS: Brother, we were having a private conversation.

POSEIDON: That miserable mortal's life concerns me, too. He blinded my son.

ZEUS: No one cares about your son. He's a brute who got what he deserved. Imagine eating his guests! How barbaric!

POSEIDON: I will punish whomever I want! And I want Odysseus to pay for what he's done!

NARRATOR: Athena glared at her uncle.

ATHENA: Haven't you had your revenge? The saying is "An eye for an eye," but you want his life for what he did!

POSEIDON: And I will have it! Odysseus must cross the sea to return to his home. So set the mortal free, and I can destroy him once and for all! I'll have him right where I want him. Not even you can stop me, Athena.

NARRATOR: Athena seethed in anger.

ATHENA: Odysseus is wily. He will find some way to survive.

POSEIDON: Unless he grows a pair of gills, he is doomed!

ZEUS: (obliviously) Good. Good. Sounds like we are agreed. Hermes! Hermes!

NARRATOR: Winging his way into the throne room, Hermes the messenger god alighted before Zeus and bowed grandiosely.

HERMES: (pompously) Yes, master? I live to serve! My life is but an insignificant speck compared to your awesome—

ZEUS: (irritated) Hermes, knock it off!

HERMES: Yes, supreme ruler of heaven and earth!

ZEUS: I need you to go to the island of Calypso the sea nymph—

HERMES: Ooh, gladly. If you're going to see some nymph, she's definitely the one to see. Isn't she the one with the—

NARRATOR: Hermes' hands shaped curves in midair.

ATHENA: (angrily) Lovely braids.

HERMES: (covering) Oh yeah. Lovely braids. That's it.

ZEUS: Anyway, tell her to release Odysseus.

HERMES: What if he doesn't want to be released? I know I wouldn't. You know what I'm saying?

NARRATOR: Hermes nudged Poseidon, who only shook is trident menacingly.

ATHENA: Not every man is controlled by his libido.

HERMES: Most of them are though. All right. I'll break the bad news to Calypso. If she is too upset by all this, I might stick around a while to console her. Lay on the ol' charm…

ATHENA: Just go!

HERMES: Right-o!

NARRATOR: The messenger god rocketed down toward the sea. In the midst of its wine-dark vastness, he spotted the tiny speck that was Ogygia. Hermes dropped into the island's network of glittering caves.

HERMES: Oh, Calypso, my sweet!

NARRATOR: He found Calypso seated on her ivory throne—a dinner of ambrosia and nectar laid out before her.

CALYPSO: Oh no. It's you.

HERMES: Not exactly the greeting I was hoping for.

CALYPSO: What do you expect when you're Olympus' official bearer-of-bad-news?

HERMES: Ouch. That hurts. By the way, you're looking lovely—as usual.

CALYPSO: Cut to the chase, Hermes! What news do you have for me?

HERMES: Are you doing something new with your braids? That's a lovely gown, too. It leaves little to the imagination.

CALYPSO: Keep your imagination to yourself! Now tell me—

HERMES: Oh, were you eating? That ambrosia and nectar looks delicious. Care if I pull up a stalagmite?

NARRATOR: Hermes began to help himself to the godly feast. Calypso rolled her eyes and sighed.

HERMES: (*between mouthfuls*) You know, the rest of the gods are always debating—who's better looking? Wood nymphs or water nymphs? I always say, "I'm more of a sea-nymph man myself."

CALYPSO: (*angrily*) Hermes! Deliver your message and leave me in peace!

HERMES: Touchy. Touchy. Well, you guessed it. It's not pretty. Zeus says your boy-toy has to go. You've had your fun. Now it's time to send him packing.

CALYPSO: (*quietly*) I knew it.

HERMES: I think your problem here is you're into mortals. What you need is a god. Not just any god either. Most of those fops are all flash and no substance. What you need is—

CALYPSO: (*angrily*) This is just typical of you arrogant males!

HERMES: Whoa, whoa. Don't shoot me. I'm just the messenger.

CALYPSO: The gods romance any mortal woman they want, but when we goddesses take a mortal lover, *then* we have crossed the line! Plus, I've been faithful to this man for seven years. Show me a god who has done that!

HERMES: You're right! It's an outrage! A complete double standard! (*pause*) Have I ever told you that you're beautiful when you're angry?

CALYPSO: I simply won't do it! You will tell Zeus that Odysseus is mine, and I will *not* give him up!

HERMES: Hmmm. Interesting. Instead of obeying Zeus, you're choosing suicide. Have you ever seen Zeus when he gets steamed? He starts zinging lightning bolts left and right. Gets ugly fast.

CALYPSO: *(angrily)* All I know is that I want you off my island—now!

HERMES: Hey! Hey! I know you're probably confused right now. Lots of different emotions are running through your head. But if you need a shoulder to cry on, just give me a buzz.

CALYPSO: *(screaming)* Out! Out! Out!

NARRATOR: The messenger god skittered away.

CALYPSO: *He* is impossible!

NARRATOR: When Calypso's anger had subsided, she went to Odysseus. He was sitting on the beach—facing eastward, toward home.

CALYPSO: *(quietly)* Odysseus.

ODYSSEUS: Yes?

CALYPSO: The gods have declared you free. I am releasing you.

NARRATOR: Odysseus said nothing.

CALYPSO: Did you hear me? You are allowed to return home.

NARRATOR: Odysseus turned to her, tears in his eyes. At first Calypso thought perhaps the tears might be for her. Had Odysseus finally realized how much he would miss her if he left?

ODYSSEUS: I have waited seven years to hear these words. Thank you. You have given me my life back.

CALYPSO: *(hopefully)* If you refused your freedom, the gods would allow you to stay here. You could be one of the immortals. Your handsome features would never wrinkle. Your strong arms would never weaken. Your mind would stay quick and never falter.

ODYSSEUS: It is a kind offer, but immortality is not for me. Ithaca is my home. I will live out my days, and when the Fates decree, I will pass from this earth.

CALYPSO: You know, most men would never be able to refuse such an offer.

ODYSSEUS: I would never be able to accept it.

CALYPSO: Very well. You must build a raft. I will give you the materials and all that you require for your journey. All *I* require is one more night together before you depart—to say goodbye.

NARRATOR: Odysseus toiled like a madman on his raft—constructing it from bits of driftwood and washed-up sail the nymph had collected over the years. Calypso came to the beach daily and watched Odysseus' progress with sadness. With each peg he hammered and each plank he placed, he was drawing further away from her. At last the raft was completed, and the nymph bid farewell to her love.

CALYPSO: Of all my innumerable years, these seven have been the happiest.

ODYSSEUS: Farewell.

NARRATOR: The tiny craft sailed out onto the wine-dark sea and was lost among the waves.

CALYPSO: And so my love is gone.

NARRATOR: Odysseus sailed for seven days—fighting against the waves in his makeshift vessel. But Poseidon had not yet revealed his full power. He had decided to end the hated mortal's life once and for all. The seas around Odysseus began to grow restless—churning and frothing with anger. *(storm sounds)*

POSEIDON: Rise, seas! Howl, winds! Destroy Odysseus! Pull him down into the depths! Take him to a watery grave!

NARRATOR: The waves, the mighty fists of Poseidon, began to crash against the raft of Odysseus, tearing loose its ratty sail and stripping it apart log by log.

ODYSSEUS: *(shouting)* Athena, protect me!

NARRATOR: The goddess heard her hero's cry. She descended from Olympus and began to deflect the angry blows of her uncle.

POSEIDON: You cannot calm the sea, Athena! You cannot save him from me!

ATHENA: I can, and I will!

NARRATOR: The storm continued to rage. An enormous swell flipped Odysseus from his raft into the swirling waters. Water rushed into his lungs—Poseidon choking the very life from him—and then his world went black.
    When Odysseus awoke, he was lying on his back, in an inch of water—the sun burning his vision. His head rested on soft sand.

ODYSSEUS: This is definitely not Hades.

NARRATOR: He lifted his head. A single hand-hewn plank lay by his side—the remaining piece of his ship.

ODYSSEUS: Thank you, Athena. I see Poseidon has stripped me of everything but my life.

NARRATOR: He looked down. His clothes were missing, too.

ODYSSEUS: Literally.

(sounds of giggling)

NARRATOR: Laughter drew Odysseus' gaze. Across the beach a group of young girls were playing catch with a ball in the sea-shallows. They had apparently just finished their laundry. Clothes hung on a nearby wagon to dry in the sun.

ODYSSEUS: Well, they don't look like cannibals or witches. But I've been wrong before.

NARRATOR: A bush shielded Odysseus from their sight, and he broke a branch from it.

ODYSSEUS: I'll need this for modesty. Here goes nothing!

NARRATOR: The girls looked up from their game of catch to see a grown man approaching—naked except for a branch's worth of covering.

(shriek of girls)

GIRL: Ah! *(scream)*

ODYSSEUS: No wait! This is not what it looks like!

NARRATOR: All of the girls fled behind their wagon—except for one, the tallest and the most beautiful among them.

GIRL: Run! Run, princess! He will attack you!

ODYSSEUS: No, please. I am shipwrecked. I need help.

NARRATOR: The tall girl stood her ground.

NAUSICAA: Explain yourself. You frightened my maidens. Thank the gods for that branch, or we would have died of shame.

ODYSSEUS: *(kindly)* I apologize for startling you. When I saw you standing there, I thought maybe you were a goddess—maybe Artemis herself. But now I see that you are all just mortal girls.

NAUSICAA: *(giggle)* You flatter me. What can we do for you?

ODYSSEUS: I need hospitality. Food and lodging—

NAUSICAA: And clothing.

NARRATOR: Odysseus blushed.

ODYSSEUS: Yes. Yes that, too.

NARRATOR: The young girl turned to wagon and grabbed up a drying dress.

NAUSICAA: Here. Tie this about your waist. You can't go before my father like that.

ODYSSEUS: Your father?

NAUSICAA: I am the princess Nausicaa, the daughter of Alcinous.

ODYSSEUS: Where am I?

NAUSICAA: You are in the land of Phaeacia—the home of the greatest sailors in the world.

ODYSSEUS: You are not cannibals, are you? Or witches?

NAUSICAA: *(laugh)* These are strange questions.

ODYSSEUS: The seas are more perilous than you might think.

NAUSICAA: Not for our people. Our magic ships never sink. In fact, they obey the thoughts of their captains—and sail of their own accord.

ODYSSEUS: Fantastic. May I meet with your father?

NAUSICAA: Of course. Now that you are decent, we will proceed to his palace.

NARRATOR: King Alcinous of the Phaeacians greeted Odysseus warmly and provided him with kingly robes. Odysseus feasted and drank—without ever once being asked his name or his business. Here he had encountered the hospitality that the gods decree for all men.

ODYSSEUS: You have treated me most royally, king! The gods will bless you for this.

ALCINOUS: You intrigue us, stranger. You wash up on our shores, about frighten the life out of my daughter and her handmaids, and then parade into court wearing almost nothing but a smile. We are eager to know your story.

ODYSSEUS: I will give it freely. Please let me feast more, and when I am ready to share it, I will. The belly is a shameless dog, and until it is satisfied, the mouth refuses to work.

ALCINOUS: Of course. Until then, there will be entertainment. Here in our court we have the finest bard the world has ever seen.

NARRATOR: The king clapped his hand, and an old man was led into the hearing hall. In his arms he clasped a lyre.

ODYSSEUS: The bard is blind?

ALCINOUS: His muse has mixed her blessings. She gave him the supreme gift of song, but stripped him of his sight.

ODYSSEUS: How tragic.

ALCINOUS: You will not think so once you have heard his songs.

NARRATOR: When the bard was seated, his fingers began to move nimbly across the strings, and his voice filled the air. Odysseus found himself entranced.

ODYSSEUS: He performs beautifully, but what is his song? What does he sing of?

ALCINOUS: The story that men most love to hear—the story of Troy.

NARRATOR: As the bard started to sing, a cold hand seemed to grip Odysseus' stomach. During these years of wandering at sea his only thought had been of home, of survival. Now the bard's words took him back—even

though he did not wish to go—back to Troy. The bard sang of the Trojan Horse, the fall of the great city, and the death of its many noble citizens. Tears began to stream down Odysseus' cheeks.

ALCINOUS: Stop the music! Stop! *(to Odysseus)* What is the matter, my lord?

ODYSSEUS: It is nothing. His song just moves me deeply.

ALCINOUS: Did you perhaps know someone who died in Troy? A son or a brother?

ODYSSEUS: No.

ALCINOUS: Then the story is just close to your heart?

ODYSSEUS: Yes, because I was there.

(collective gasp)

ALCINOUS: Now we *must* hear your story!

ODYSSEUS: It is a painful one—and one that does not yet have an ending. I am still making my way home from Troy.

ALCINOUS: That war ended years ago!

ODYSSEUS: You did not lie when you said this bard was the greatest at his craft. His words took me back there—to Troy. I will tell you all that happened there—how I helped bring Troy to its knees. Then I will tell you how the gods have made me suffer for it these past years.

ALCINOUS: In your words there are clues. You are Odysseus!

ODYSSEUS: I am.

NARRATOR: King Alcinous rose and clapped his hands.

ALCINOUS: We have an honored guest in our court tonight. Bring more food! More wine! Tonight we shall hear the story of Greece's greatest—the one called Odysseus.

NARRATOR: The king turned back to Odysseus.

ALCINOUS: When you are ready to speak, my lord, you may proceed.

ODYSSEUS: Thank you. I am ready.

NARRATOR: Odysseus launched out into his tale.

DISCUSSION QUESTIONS

- Would you agree to spend eternity with someone you did not love if it meant immortality? Explain.
- Does Calypso have a right to be angry with Zeus? Explain.
- Calypso's beauty is eternal. Penelope's is only temporary, but does this make her more beautiful? Explain.
- Many ancient readers saw the blind bard in this section of the *Odyssey* as Homer inserting a picture of himself into his poem—maybe even making an inside joke referring to himself as "the greatest of the bards." This led to the tradition that Homer was a blind poet. What do you think of this theory? Explain.
- Why does Odysseus now regret his actions at Troy?

IN THE CAVE OF THE CYCLOPS
TEACHER GUIDE

BACKGROUND

Hospitality was incredibly important in ancient Greek culture—to the point that it was said that Zeus himself would punish those who were inhospitable. In a time when travelers had to take refuge in the homes of strangers for the night, hospitality and safety had to be guaranteed.

Even though the cave of the Cyclops looks a bit ominous, Odysseus and his men are not afraid to seek hospitality there. They expect generosity and safety, but what they find is death and bloodshed. Many commentators have said that to a Greek audience the Cyclops would have represented Greece's barbarian neighbors who did not honor the Greek code of hospitality. Because of this breach of conduct, the Cyclops is blinded by Odysseus—teaching a lesson to all of those who are not generous givers.

SUMMARY

Previously, Odysseus and his men had barely escaped from the Lotus Eaters, a race of men who feed on the fruit and flower of a mystical plant called lotus. The plant causes those who eat of it to lose all memory of home and purpose. Only by dragging his men back to the boat was Odysseus able to save them.

Now they are moored by a strange island, which has a huge cave in the side of one of its mountains. They see sheep penned nearby and surmise that whoever lives there must be a shepherd. Odysseus picks some of his best men to go ashore and investigate.

Inside the cave they find a bounty of milk and cheese but not the master of the house. Helping themselves to these delicacies, they await the return of their host. When he arrives, they are frightened because he is an enormous, one-eyed Cyclops. The Cyclops, who is named Polyphemus, drives his sheep flock into the cave and immediately rolls a huge bolder over the entrance of the cave—sealing them in. Odysseus tells the Cyclops that his name is "Nobody" since he fears they might be in danger. Odysseus tries to reason with the brute, reminding him of the gods' rules about hospitality. The Cyclops laughs at this. He is the son of Poseidon and does not fear the gods. He gobbles up two of Odysseus' men.

Odysseus begins to formulate a plan of how to escape the cave. Polyphemus leaves every morning with his sheep. The next day, while the Cyclops is gone, Odysseus and the men whittle the monster's massive wooden club down to a sharp-pointed stake. Then they hide this within the cave. When the Cyclops returns, he gobbles up two more of Odysseus' men. Odysseus offers him some wine the travelers had brought with them to share with their host. The Cyclops drinks bowl after bowl of the wine until he passes out. Odysseus and his men retrieve their spike, hold its tip in the fire, and then jab it into the monster's eye.

Polyphemus, now blinded, frantically searches the cave for his attackers. When he fails to locate any of them, he rolls away the door-boulder and yells for assistance from his Cyclops brothers who live nearby. He shouts that Nobody has blinded him. His brothers do not come to his aid because they think he is just having a bad dream. Polyphemus decides to sit in the cave doorway, so that Odysseus and his men will have to crawl over him to escape.

Odysseus knows Polyphemus will let the sheep that are penned in the cave out to graze. He groups the sheep into groups of three and ties them together with rope. When the Cyclops releases the sheep, one man clings to the bottom of each group of sheep. As they pass beneath the Cyclops, he feels along their coats to make sure they are actually sheep. In this way Odysseus and his men escape.

Once they are back at their ships, Odysseus cannot resist taunting the Cyclops. He yells back that the Cyclops should say that Odysseus—not Nobody—has tricked him. In anger, Polyphemus rips a boulder loose from the mountain and hurls it at Odysseus' ships, barely missing them. Then he cries out to Poseidon, his father, asking the god to make sure Odysseus never reaches his home. Odysseus realizes that he has cursed the rest of his voyage.

ESSENTIAL QUESTIONS

- Is hospitality important?
- When can boasting get you into trouble?
- Why are brains more important than strength sometimes?

ANTICIPATORY QUESTIONS

- What is a Cyclops?
- How could a small man defeat a large Cyclops?
- Who are the Lotus Eaters?

CONNECTIONS

The Odyssey **(TV miniseries, 1997)** This miniseries re-tells much of the *Odyssey*. The scene featuring the Cyclops is well-done, although it omits a few key details such as the conclusion of the "Nobody" trick and Odysseus' men escaping beneath the sheep. The miniseries also excludes some major episodes from the *Odyssey* including the Sirens and the Lotus Eaters. The miniseries is rated PG-13 for some sexuality and violence.

TEACHABLE TERMS

- **Unreliable Narrator** In the *Odyssey* Odysseus narrates several of his adventures (including this episode with the Cyclops, Circe, the Sirens, and the Lotus Eaters) to the king of Phaeacia. Many have wondered: Is Odysseus, a notorious liar, telling the truth? Or is he just spinning an entertaining tale for his host?
- **Episodic Narrative** While other stories move smoothly from Point A to Point B, some are episodic. Odysseus' story has several episodes that are unrelated to one another, giving his story a choppy feel. Have your students compare the narrative of the *Odyssey* to the linear narrative of the Trojan War.
- **Pun** Polyphemus yells that "Nobody" has tricked him on pg. 131. Because the term is misunderstood by his fellow Cyclopes, this wordplay generates humor.
- **Social Custom** In ancient Greece the host-guest relationship was sacred. A host was to be generous to his guests. The Cyclops is punished in this story because he violates this custom, which has been ordained by the gods. Discuss with the students what customs are important in their culture.

RECALL QUESTIONS

1. What effect did eating the lotus fruit have on Odysseus' men?
2. What did Odysseus tell the Cyclops his name was?
3. How do Odysseus and his men wound the Cyclops?
4. Why do none of the other Cyclopes who live on the island come to help Polyphemus?
5. Who is the father of the Cyclops?

IN THE CAVE OF THE CYCLOPS

CAST

ODYSSEUS	*King of Ithaca*
EURYLOCHUS	*One of Odysseus' Men*
POLITES	*One of Odysseus' Men*
SHIPMATE ONE	*One of Odysseus' Men*
SHIPMATE TWO	*One of Odysseus' Men*
POLYPHEMUS	*Cyclops*
CYCLOPS ONE	*Brother of Polyphemus*
CYCLOPS TWO	*Brother of Polyphemus*

NARRATOR: First, it had been the Lotus Eaters. On their way home from Troy, some of Odysseus' men had gone ashore to scout out a strange island—to stock up on food and fresh water—but they never returned. They hadn't been taken by armed renegades or hostile natives. Instead the island inhabitants had offered them a fruit called lotus. The men had taken it willingly. Only whoever tasted this fruit, lost all desire to do anything—

except eat more lotus. Finally, Odysseus himself came ashore—searching for his men. He refused the lotus fruit offered to him by the natives and dragged his men one by one back to the ships. So mad were they for more lotus fruit that he had to tie each of them to their seat. When he had collected them all, the ships pushed back out to open sea.

POLITES: *(in pain)* Lotus! Lotus! I can't live without it.

ODYSSEUS: Shut up, will you? You're lucky I was there to save you fools. What were you thinking? Taking fruit from strangers.

POLITES: They were the nicest people I've ever met. They gave me lotus. *(weeping)*

ODYSSEUS: So this was our first mistake. Let's make it our last.

NARRATOR: Soon another island appeared. The ships pulled in close and moored off the shore.

POLITES: Look, Odysseus! A cave in the hillside.

NARRATOR: Sure enough a huge cave-mouth gaped in the rocky slope. Some kind of crude pen had been built around the level area before the cave-mouth. From this pen they heard the bleating of sheep. *(bleating of sheep)*

POLITES: Odysseus! Sheep! Whoever lives in that cave must have mutton and milk—and maybe even cheese. It's not exactly lotus, but it will do. We're starving!

(murmuring from all of Odysseus' men)

ODYSSEUS: We got lucky with the Lotus Eaters. Whoever lives here might be hostile.

EURYLOCHUS: Probably not, my lord. Who has ever heard of a hostile shepherd? Besides, all men must offer hospitality to strangers. It's the law of the gods.

POLITES: And he'll give us mutton! Real mutton!

ODYSSEUS: Leave it to you to make all decisions with your stomach, Polites. Well, I guess it wouldn't hurt to look around. Where is that skin of wine that we brought with us?

NARRATOR: The men produced a huge skin of wine, its top tied with a golden cord.

ODYSSEUS: All right. We'll go. We'll take the wine to barter with. There's nothing like a little wine to encourage friendly relations. Only a few of you come with me. A crowd might scare this fool shepherd out of his mind. He's got to be lonely—living alone on this rock with nothing but his sheep.

NARRATOR: Excited at the prospect of mutton, milk, and cheese, the men debated amongst themselves. Their argument resulted in a few shoves, and at last the men threw dice to decide who would go. Then Odysseus led the twelve winners up the hillside toward the mysterious cave.

ODYSSEUS: (*shouting*) Helloooo! Is anyone here? We are men from Ithaca! Friends!

NARRATOR: Only the bleating of the penned sheep was heard. Odysseus and his men passed into the gigantic mouth of the cave. When their eyes adjusted to the dimness within, they discovered that the cave was very high-roofed indeed, but did not go further than a couple of hundred feet before it ended in a blank wall. They also saw two more pens, one filled with sheep, and the entire floor was covered with a soft, flaky layer of sheep dung.

EURYLOCHUS: This man is quite a shepherd!

POLITES: (*shouting*) Cheeeeeese!

NARRATOR: Along the cave wall there were piles of cheese and the devices used in its making. The men rushed forward to partake of the cheese and the nearby jars of milk.

ODYSSEUS: Wait, men! Have you lost your manners on the sea? We must ask our host's permission first.

POLITES: (*worried*) What if he says, "No"?

ODYSSEUS: What kind of fool would say, "No"? We are his guests. Now be patient. He will be back soon enough. See? This pen has no sheep in it. He must have taken them out to graze.

POLITES: But look at these cheeses! And fresh milk!

ODYSSEUS: Fine. Eat. Our host will not care once I've explained our situation.

NARRATOR: While his men threw themselves upon these delicacies, Odysseus began to examine the cavern more closely. There was something strange about it. Everything within it seemed large—large bowls, large jars, a large hide lay over one portion of the dung-covered floor.

ODYSSEUS: Hmmmm. This shepherd must be an extremely large man.

EURYLOCHUS: Odysseus! I have an idea. Let's drive these sheep to our ships and make our getaway before the master of this house comes home.

ODYSSEUS: Have you lost your pride? We're Greeks—not a bunch of ill-mannered pirates.

POLITES: *(talking through a mouthful of cheese)* Bup we've stowen befowe.

ODYSSEUS: Besides, I am curious. I want to see what kind of man lives here in this cave. *(bleating of sheep)* And here he comes now. Get away from that cheese! As usual, let me do the talking.

NARRATOR: The sound of an approaching flock neared the cave's entrance. The men turned—their mouths still dripping with milk and stuffed with cheese—and nearly choked in their terror.

POLITES: *(in fear)* Zeus save us.

NARRATOR: A flock of sheep was pouring into the cave's entrance, but the shock was the sight of the shepherd towering above them. The creature, strong in limb and clad in a large fur, had to duck to make it into the cave. When he beheld his visitors, the one large eye in the midst of his forehead blinked in confusion.

EURYLOCHUS: Gods help us! A Cyclops! Run!

ODYSSEUS: *(sharply)* Whatever you do, don't panic. Let me handle this. Hospitality is on our side. We are his guests.

POLYPHEMUS: *(growling)* Little men, what are you doing in my cave?

ODYSSEUS: *(nonchalantly)* Oh dear me! Where did you come from, sir? You gave me

quite a start. We are sailors, and we stopped here on your island. We were just enjoying your hospitality here.

POLYPHEMUS: *(angrily) That* is not for you! It's mine!

NARRATOR: He pointed an enormous finger toward the cheese and the milk.

POLYPHEMUS: What are you? Dirty little pirates?

NARRATOR: The men were shaking in their sandals, but Odysseus remained calm.

ODYSSEUS: Pirates? Of course not. We're soldiers sailing home from Troy. Now we're here on your doorstep, begging your hospitality, hoping that you will honor the god's wishes, and give us gifts and lodging.

POLYPHEMUS: Heh. Heh. I will give you lodging.

NARRATOR: The Cyclops braced his body against a huge stone that lay beside the cave-mouth. With enormous force, he rolled it over the entrance. *(rumbling of a huge boulder)* Odysseus began to grow nervous.

ODYSSEUS: Just a friendly reminder, sir, Zeus guards all guests. Strangers are sacred.

POLYPHEMUS: You must be a fool to waltz into my cave and tell *me* to fear the gods! We Cyclopes never blink at Zeus or any other blessed god. We are mighty sons of Poseidon, and we have more strength than all of the gods put together. *(pause)* But tell me, friend, is this all of your company?

NARRATOR: Odysseus saw the clever trap laid within this question and sidestepped it with a lie.

ODYSSEUS: Yes, this is all of us.

POLYPHEMUS: I see. And where did you moor your ships? Up the coast a way or close by?

ODYSSEUS: Our ship? No, no. Your father, Poseidon smashed my ship upon the rocks at the head of this island. Now it lies at the bottom of the sea. Luckily, my men and I escaped the turbulent waters and washed up on your shore.

POLYPHEMUS: Hmmmm.

NARRATOR: Without warning, the Cyclops lunged out, grabbing one of Odysseus' men in each hand.

SHIPMATE ONE: Ahhhhhhhh!

SHIPMATE TWO: Noooooo!

NARRATOR: With terrible speed, the Cyclops smashed the men against the hard walls, knocking them dead like pups. Something red oozed out their heads as he ripped loose their limbs and gobbled them up, piece by piece. No bit of them was left behind.

Odysseus and the remaining men pressed themselves against the back wall of the cavern.

EURYLOCHUS: Oh, Zeus, save us from this monster!

POLYPHEMUS: *(loud belch)*

NARRATOR: The Cyclops grabbed up a huge jar of milk and guzzled it—washing down the human flesh. Then he reclined upon his bed of sheep dung and fell fast asleep.

POLYPHEMUS: Zzzzzzzz.

EURYLOCHUS: Now's our chance! Let's plunge our swords into his unholy heart!

POLITES: No, let's go for the liver.

NARRATOR: Eurylochus and Polites drew their swords and advanced. Odysseus threw out a hand of warning.

ODYSSEUS: Hold! Bottle up your anger and think! If we kill this monster, we will die, too. Only he is strong enough to move the boulder that blocks the entrance.

POLITES: Then we are doomed. I wish you would have left me with the Lotus Eaters.

ODYSSEUS: Have courage. A solution will present itself. Haven't I gotten us out of tougher scrapes than this one?

NARRATOR: So the men spent the night huddled against the back wall—watching the giant slumber peacefully. Odysseus turned plan after plan over in his mind. When at last morning arrived, the Cyclops yawned, stretched as he rose, and began to milk his sheep. He did all this without giving Odysseus and his men a second glance. Yet when he had finished these chores, his hands flew out again and two more men met a horrible fate. *(screams)*

POLYPHEMUS: *(laughing)* What a fine meal you've given me, strangers! I was getting sick of milk and cheese.

NARRATOR: Pushing back the boulder from the door, the Cyclops drove his sheep into the sunlight. As he slid the rock back in place behind him, he leered at the men.

POLYPHEMUS: See you at dinnertime, sweet-meats!

POLITES: What should we do, Odysseus? How will we escape?

ODYSSEUS: Athena will give me a plan. Her wisdom has never failed me before.

NARRATOR: Odysseus sat down to think. He scanned the cave for something—anything—that he could use to defeat the giant. There were the wicker baskets that the Cyclops used to make his cheese, the piles of sheep dung, the jars of milk. Only one thing held any promise: an enormous club the Cyclops had fashioned from a tree. It lay against the side of one of the sheep pens. Odysseus drew nearer to examine it.

POLITES: Will we use his club against him?

EURYLOCHUS: Don't be a fool! It's as big as a ship's mast.

ODYSSEUS: Quiet! I'm trying to think.

NARRATOR: Odysseus drew his sword and hacked at the club. Wood chips flew easily from it.

ODYSSEUS: Yes! This will work! Draw your swords and do exactly as I say.

NARRATOR: Under the instruction of Odysseus, the men hacked at the club, whittling it down into a thin pole. Odysseus himself fashioned the end, sharpening it into a deadly point.

ODYSSEUS: Now, hoist it up, lads. We'll sear the end in the fire to make it good and hard.

POLITES: Won't the Cyclops see what we've done when he comes home?

ODYSSEUS: That's why we're going to hide it. We'll bury it beneath the dung here on the floor.

NARRATOR: When this was done, Odysseus rose with a pair of dice in his hands.

ODYSSEUS: Now we cast lots—to see who will be brave enough to wield this weapon with me.

NARRATOR: The lots were cast, and Odysseus breathed a sigh of relief, for the men they fell to were the very ones he himself would have chosen.

Soon the grating of the boulder announced the return of the Cyclops. The monster drove in his whole herd this time and closed the entrance behind him. The cave was full of sheep. When he had once again performed his chores, he caught hold of two more of Odysseus' men and ripped them into edible chunks.

POLYPHEMUS: *(loud smacking)* Tastier and tastier! *(burp)* I'm beginning to wonder how you sweet-meats would taste roasted.

NARRATOR: Odysseus advanced toward the Cyclopes, smiling broadly and holding one of the huge bowls filled with a strange, dark liquid.

POLYPHEMUS: What is that?

ODYSSEUS: This, my man-eating friend, is wine. Try it. It will be the perfect thing to top off your banquet of human flesh. Even if you do not honor the gods, we do. Here is a gift to you—as our host.

POLYPHEMUS: Wine, huh?

NARRATOR: The giant snatched the bowl from Odysseus' arm and slurped its contents. He greedily smacked his lips and flung the bowl back at Odysseus.

POLYPHEMUS: More! It's good! Give me a heartier helping this time!

ODYSSEUS: Of course, your greediness.

NARRATOR: The men rushed forward with the skin of wine to fulfill his request. The Cyclops guzzled two more bowlfuls.

POLYPHEMUS: This *is* a gift! And to think I have nothing to give you in return! Heh. Heh.

NARRATOR: As he continued to drink, his eye grew dull and his words slurred.

POLYPHEMUS: (*drunk*) I must thank you for this delightful nectar of the gods. (*hiccup*) Tell me your name, friend.

ODYSSEUS: My name? You ask me my name?

NARRATOR: Odysseus paused for showmanship.

ODYSSEUS: My name is Nobody. That's my name—Nobody. So my mother called me, my father, and all my friends.

POLYPHEMUS: A strange name, but you men from far away are strange. Here is my gift to you, Nobody. I will eat Nobody *last* of all his friends.

ODYSSEUS: You are too kind.

NARRATOR: There was time for no more conversation, for the drunken Cyclops slumped over onto his side. When his head hit the floor, he vomited wine with little bits of human inside. Odysseus and his men covered their noses from the stench of rotted flesh.

ODYSSEUS: (*hissing*) He's out! No time to lose!

NARRATOR: The chosen men uncovered the sharpened pole, and Odysseus directed them to hold it in the glowing coals of the fire once again to make it sure it would sear completely. Then hoisting it high, they timidly made their way toward the sleeping giant's head.

POLITES: (*whimper*)

ODYSSEUS: Courage! Drive fast and hard, men. When you feel it hit home, run and hide. He may kill us all in his madness if we don't. (*shouting*) Now!

NARRATOR: The men drove the point forward. The Cyclops barely had enough time to open his one groggy eye before the stake rammed into it. The eyeball burst, blood came boiling from around the point, the roots of the eye crackled, and a sickening sizzling sound filled the air. (*sizzling sound*)

POLYPHEMUS: (*loud roar*) Arrrrrrrrrrg!

ODYSSEUS: It's done! Flee!

NARRATOR: The giant wrenched the stake from his eye and flung it against the wall. One hand tore at his now empty socket, while the other frantically swept the floor for his unseen enemies.

POLYPHEMUS: (*growling*) My eye! My eye! You miserable little sweet-meats have done this to me! Nobody is responsible for this! Nobody shall pay for this!

NARRATOR: As the Cyclops roared, moving from side to side within the cave, groping madly about, Odysseus' men covered their mouths to suppress their laughter.

ODYSSEUS: Not a sound, you fools! He's still dangerous!

POLYPHEMUS: Nobody, hear my words! You and your miserable man-creatures might have blinded me, but my brothers live on this island as well, and you cannot escape *their* sight! They will heed my cries. They will come to my aid and crush your bones!

NARRATOR: The Cyclops fumbled for the boulder and rolled it away from the entrance. Then, falling upon his hands and knees in the threshold, he began to bellow.

POLYPHEMUS: Help, brothers! Come to the aid of your brother Polyphemus!

NARRATOR: From the nearby hillsides voices answered.

CYCLOPS ONE: (*distantly*) What is the matter, brother? It's the middle of the night.

POLYPHEMUS: An enemy has attacked me, brothers! Avenge me!

CYCLOPS TWO: (*yawning*) Who has wronged you?

POLYPHEMUS: Nobody—Nobody has tricked me. Nobody has harmed me. Nobody has taken my eye.

CYCLOPS ONE: (*annoyed*) You're having a bad dream. Go back to sleep.

CYCLOPS TWO: Yes. If nobody has harmed you, you have nothing to worry about. (*laughing*) Stupid Polyphemus.

NARRATOR: Odysseus could not help but smile at the ingenuity of his trick.

POLYPHEMUS: Fools! Fine. I will deal with these man-creatures myself.

NARRATOR: The Cyclops sat firmly down, blocking the entrance. He extended his hands, so that they stretched from wall to wall.

POLYPHEMUS: There is only one way in and out of this cave. You will have to crawl over me to escape. And when you try it, I'll have you!

NARRATOR: Odysseus drew his men close to him.

ODYSSEUS: (*whispering*) I have a plan for our escape. He will have to let the sheep out in the morning to graze. He probably plans to feel them as they walk by—to make sure they are sheep and not men. Cut some fibers from those robes over there and help me bind these sheep together.

NARRATOR: The men, who knew better than to question the mind of Odysseus, rushed to comply. (*bleating of sheep*)

POLYPHEMUS: Quiet, my little ones. No need to be frightened. Soon these filthy man-creatures will be dead. Yes. Then Polyphemus will have quite a feast.

NARRATOR: Three sheep were placed side by side and lashed together. Odysseus and his men performed this task time and time again.

ODYSSEUS: One man will hang under the middle sheep. Then when the monster runs his hands over their fleece, he will not feel you.

POLITES: But we have no more rope. There's not enough for your sheep.

NARRATOR: Odysseus turned to the nearby pen. Within was a large ram, the aged leader of the flock.

ODYSSEUS: I will ride this one.

NARRATOR: By the time the rosy fingers of the dawn appeared in the sky, the sheep were bleating frantically. It was time for them to feed.

POLYPHEMUS: All right! All right, little ones! Come forward.

NARRATOR: The Cyclops rose from his spot, and the sheep—each tied to two others and bearing a man beneath—made their way between the giant's legs. As they passed, he ran his hand along their fluffy coats.

POLYPHEMUS: There you are. Yes. Yes. I feel my sheep. But where is the ram? Usually he leads the flock!

NARRATOR: Clinging beneath the aged ram, Odysseus began to sweat. His weight was slowing the ram's pace. At last he came under the shadow of the Cyclops, and the enormous hand descended.

POLYPHEMUS: Whoa, old friend.

NARRATOR: The hand pressed down and stopped the ram's advance.

POLYPHEMUS: Why such a slow pace? In the old days you led the flock.

ODYSSEUS: (*quietly*) Please, Athena. Spare me.

POLYPHEMUS: Are you depressed by that filthy man-creature who has taken your master's eye? If only you could speak, my ram, and tell me where that traitor is hiding, I would spill his brains for sure. Yes, that would do my heart good.

NARRATOR: His grip loosened, and the old ram continued its slow walk out into the sunlight.

Once outside the cave, Odysseus saw that all his men were free of their sheep. One man was already sprinting down the hill toward the cape where the ships were moored.

ODYSSEUS: Men, drive these sheep to our ships. We will get our guest-gift after all.

NARRATOR: The sheep were driven onto the boats, and Odysseus at last took his place at the helm of his flagship.

ODYSSEUS: Shove off! There's plenty of time to tell the tale once we're away!

NARRATOR: The cave was visible up the hillside—the ridiculous form of Polyphemus squatting just inside. Odysseus could not resist one final jab.

ODYSSEUS: (*bellowing*) Cyclops! Foolish Cyclops!

POLYPHEMUS: (*screaming*) What? Nobody? It can't be!

NARRATOR: Polyphemus ran out of the cave, craning his neck to hear the voice once again.

ODYSSEUS: (shouting) What a blind fool! You tried to eat us up, but we escaped you. Zeus and all the gods have paid you back for your crimes, you piece of filth!

POLYPHEMUS: Nobody!

ODYSSEUS: Not Nobody, you fool! If anyone asks who has blinded you—what tiny man was able to defeat the mighty Cyclops— tell them it was Odysseus: *Odysseus*, son of Laertes, who did it! (laughing)

POLYPHEMUS: Grrrrrrrr.

NARRATOR: At the sound of Odysseus' true name, the Cyclops' fury boiled over. Ripping loose a nearby hilltop, the Cyclops flung it seaward.

POLYPHEMUS: Aaaarg!

POLITES: Row! Row! Incoming!

(gigantic splash)

NARRATOR: The hilltop hit close to the ships—too close—and the spray from it knocked the men to the deck.

ODYSSEUS: Enough. Let's go!

NARRATOR: Polyphemus fell to his knees and scratched the flesh of his face with his ragged fingernails.

POLYPHEMUS: Father Poseidon! God of the sea-blue mane! Master of the earthquake, hear my cry! Odysseus has blinded me! If Polyphemus is truly your son, grant me my wish—never let Odysseus, son of Laertes, see his home again.

NARRATOR: The ground below the Cyclops began to shake—an underground cry of rage—and the seas churned.

ODYSSEUS: (to himself) What have I done?

POLITES: Odysseus, what has happened?

ODYSSEUS: Nothing. Nothing. They are empty words.

NARRATOR: He smiled reassuringly.

ODYSSEUS: No curse can stand between us and Ithaca.

NARRATOR: The ships sailed on, and soon the moaning of the Cyclops was lost in the wind.

DISCUSSION QUESTIONS

- What is Odysseus' greatest weapon? Explain.
- Does Polyphemus deserve to be blinded? Explain.
- How does Odysseus' pride get the better of him?
- Are brains more important than strength? Explain.
- This episode is the most famous part of the *Odyssey*. Does it deserve its fame? Explain.

CIRCE THE WITCH
TEACHER GUIDE

BACKGROUND

F*emme fatale*, a French term meaning "deadly woman," describes a type of mysterious and seductive woman who is an archetype from legend and myth. These women lure heroes in while plotting their destruction. Circe the witch, who just may be the original *femme fatale*, nearly succeeds in ending Odysseus' quest for home. Odysseus discovers that he may have bested the brutish Cyclops, but he will need more than wit to survive in the hall of Circe the witch. He will have to control his human desires.

Although the idea of magic-working women became much more popular in the fairy tales of Europe, there are only two witches mentioned in all of Greek mythology—Circe and her niece, Medea. The Greek concept of a witch is far removed from the character we typically imagine. Unlike fairy tale witches, who were often described as old hags, Circe is young and beautiful. A typical witch works her magic through spells (or spoken chants), but Circe's magic stems from the strange substances (or potions) she gives her victims to eat. Therefore, Greek magic was rooted in knowledge of herbs—instead of incantations. Medea also uses potions to achieve her spells. (Some have theorized that the word *medicine* might even have been derived from her name.)

SUMMARY

O*dysseus* and his men approach yet another strange island. His men are discouraged, for on the last island they were ambushed by giant cannibals who pretended to be friendly until they had them at their mercy. Many of the men were eaten, and the giants began to sink Odysseus' ships with boulders. Only one ship escaped.

When Odysseus mentions going ashore on the new island, Eurylochus leads a miniature revolt. He suggests that Odysseus go ashore alone. Odysseus complies but formulates a plan to trick his men to explore the island instead of him. Going ashore, he kills a giant stag and returns to the boat. Sharing the meat with his men, he insinuates that the island is perfectly safe and challenges his men's bravery. Seeing Odysseus' kill, his men eagerly volunteer to further explore the island the next day.

Eurylochus volunteers to lead a party ashore. They journey further inland and discover a villa built in the forest. Tame lions and wolves patrol the grounds. A group of beautiful women live there, led by Circe, and they invite the men inside. Eurylochus is suspicious and does not enter the house. Through the window he sees the women feeding the men a strange porridge. Circe taps each of them with her wand. Immediately, they are transformed into swine. Eurylochus runs back to the boat to report this to Odysseus.

Odysseus sets out to rescue his men. On his way the god Hermes appears to him, warning him that he will be transformed like his men unless he eats of a special herb called moly. He also tells Odysseus to draw his sword on Circe and make her swear not to harm him. Odysseus continues on to Circe's hall.

Circe greets Odysseus and tries to transform him as she did his men. She is shocked when her spell does not work. Odysseus draws his sword and commands her to transform his men and promise not to harm any of them. Circe agrees and then invites Odysseus to be her lover.

Odysseus and his men end up staying at the home of Circe for nearly a year. At last Odysseus remembers his quest and prepares to leave. Circe tells Odysseus that he must sail to the edge of the Underworld and ask the advice of the soul of Tiresias the blind prophet. Only he will be able to tell Odysseus how to turn aside the wrath of Poseidon. She then tells him of other trials he will have to face. Odysseus and his men then depart from the home of Circe.

ESSENTIAL QUESTIONS

- Why is it important to keep pressing on toward a goal?
- How do you become a good leader?

ANTICIPATORY QUESTIONS

- Who was Circe?
- Who are some famous wizards or witches?
- Technically speaking, what is a witch?
- What are some fairy tales (or other stories) that involve humans being transformed into animals?

CONNECTIONS

Inferno by Dante Alighieri In Dante's conception of hell, Odysseus (Ulysses in the poem) is condemned to one of the deepest circles of hell, reserved for notorious liars and those who commit fraud. Dante tells that after the events of the *Odyssey*, Odysseus grows restless and sets out for one more adventure that leads him beyond the ends of the earth. His desire for more and more adventure eventually leads him to his death.

"Ulysses" by Alfred, Lord Tennyson This famous poem features an aging Odysseus (Ulysses) who thinks on his old adventures. He finally decides to set out on yet another adventure with the mission: "to strive, to seek, to find, and not to yield."

TEACHABLE TERMS

- **Proverb**   On pg. 138 Odysseus says, "Nothing ventured, nothing gained," which is an example of a proverb or wise saying. Have the students think of some other proverbs they have heard before.
- **Reverse Psychology**   At the beginning of this episode, Odysseus uses reverse psychology on his men in order to get them to explore the island.
- **Archetype**   Circe represents the temptress, an archetype (or reoccurring character type) from myth and legend. Her plot is to compromise the hero's quest through seduction. Have your students think of another character who fits this same archetype from another myth or story.
- **Dramatic Irony**   On pg. 146 while Circe tries in vain to transform Odysseus, we know that he has taken moly and is impervious to her magic. This dramatic irony creates humor in the scene.

RECALL QUESTIONS

1. How has Odysseus' fleet been reduced down to just one ship?
2. Circe transforms Odysseus' men into what?
3. Which god appears to Odysseus and warns him about Circe?
4. What must Odysseus do to Circe after she has failed to transform him?
5. What does Circe tell Odysseus his next destination must be?

CIRCE THE WITCH

CAST

ODYSSEUS	*Lord of Ithaca*
EURYLOCHUS	*One of Odysseus' Men*
POLITES	*One of Odysseus' Men*
MAN	*One of Odysseus' Men*
CIRCE	*Beautiful Enchantress*
NYMPH	*One of Circe's Servants*
HERMES	*Messenger God*

NARRATOR: Odysseus silently surveyed his men. Some sat in the bottom of the boat—their hooded cloaks thrown over their heads to hide their tears. Others lay motionless in the bilge water—their faces buried in their arms—the only sign of life an infrequent shuddering of the shoulders.

He thought back on the past week and the horrors it had brought him and his men. They had discovered an island inhabited with hospitable giants. After the episode with the Cyclops, the Greeks were much more cautious, but these giants had invited them ashore to share in a friendly feast. The only surprise was that Odysseus and his men were actually the main course.

Odysseus would never forget the sight of his men being speared like fish and pulled apart at the joints like cooked hens. Only a handful of them had escaped with their lives. Even when they reached their ships, they were still not safe. The giants began to throw boulders, sinking their ships one by one. Only Odysseus' flagship had survived the assault.

MAN: *(terrified)* I see another island. Not again. I can't go ashore again.

NARRATOR: The man was right. An island had appeared on the horizon—a rocky line of cliffs, topped by trees. Odysseus eyed the water jars. Nearly empty.

ODYSSEUS: We need water.

NARRATOR: Odysseus turned the rudder toward the island, and as it grew closer, he saw the dread growing upon the men's faces. The ship floated in close to the craggy shore, and the rock-anchor was dropped overboard.

ODYSSEUS: *(angrily)* Who will go ashore with me to scout this island?

NARRATOR: Some of Odysseus' men lifted their heads. Others remained unresponsive.

EURYLOCHUS: Every time we go ashore on one of these islands, fewer and fewer of us come back alive! You can't ask us to keep risking our lives!

ODYSSEUS: Well, I have heard the words of a coward. What do you say, noble Polites?

POLITES: The men are frightened, my lord. They just saw all our swift ships smashed by boulders!

NARRATOR: Odysseus raised a finger.

ODYSSEUS: One ship survived! I only wish my men had survived with their courage.

EURYLOCHUS: Ha! It's *your* courage that has gotten us into so much trouble. I say if Odysseus values bravery, he shows us his own by going ashore himself.

NARRATOR: The men were shocked to hear such strong words against their king. Odysseus only smirked.

ODYSSEUS: Nothing ventured, nothing gained. Very well. I will go ashore—alone.

POLITES: My lord! What will happen to us if you should die?

ODYSSEUS: Don't worry, Polites. You will be fine without me. Like back in the cave of the Cyclops. What a brilliant plan you all had for escape! *(pause)* Oh wait. That was me.

NARRATOR: Odysseus grabbed up his massive spear and hopped nimbly over the side-rail of the ship.

ODYSSEUS: I will return soon enough with news of the island. You ladies, stay here. Let your fear master you.

(murmuring among the men)

EURYLOCHUS: Wait. I—

ODYSSEUS: Just pray that I survive. I can't imagine you all finding your way home without me!

NARRATOR: The men glanced at one another sheepishly. Odysseus turned his back on them and picked his way up the rocky hillside.

ODYSSEUS: *(to himself)* What can I do with such weak-willed men? Don't they see? If we give up now, we will never make it home! They're back there breathing a sigh of relief. They're glad that it's me who is risking my life and not them. Well, I have something they will never have—smarts.

NARRATOR: As he climbed, Odysseus began to reminisce again. Before he and his crew had happened upon the island of the cannibalistic giants, they had visited the island of King Aeolus, lord of the winds. As a gift, the supernatural king had given Odysseus all the contrary winds of the world—sewn up into a bag. Only the west wind was left free, and it blew Odysseus' ships almost home. Ithaca was in sight.

ODYSSEUS: *(angrily)* We were so close!

NARRATOR: But the men—thinking Odysseus had received some kind of treasure from Aeolus—opened the bag while he slept and unleashed all the violent winds of the world upon them.

ODYSSEUS: Now we are blown here—miles away from any known port! Those fools deserve to die out here!

NARRATOR: Odysseus had reached the top of the ridge. The land fell away quickly in front of him. The lower land was covered with thick trees. Far away, he could see a thin trail of smoke floating up out of the treetops.

ODYSSEUS: There. There is my next adventure. Will it bring me life—or death?

NARRATOR: Odysseus watched the smoke curl—examining its movements as if it could tell him something about its source. A sudden thought struck him.

ODYSSEUS: Wait! Why should I stick my neck out for those cowards? Now it's their turn to be resourceful—useful.

NARRATOR: He pulled a pair of carven dice from his pocket and smiled.

ODYSSEUS: That's it. We will leave it to chance. *(laughs)* These dice have never failed me before.

NARRATOR: There was a cry as Odysseus' men saw him returning down the rocky path.

POLITES: Odysseus returns, and he carries a kill!

NARRATOR: Across Odysseus' shoulders was slung the dead body of an enormous stag. When he reached the beach, he tossed the carcass down before his men.

ODYSSEUS: *(sarcastically)* Here is one of the vicious beasts that inhabit this island! See what you fools have to be afraid of?

POLITES: You didn't see anything else? No monsters? No giants?

ODYSSEUS: No. But while you *maids* were back here wetting yourself in fear, I did discover something.

POLITES: What?

ODYSSEUS: Someone does live upon this island. I saw the smoke of a dwelling.

NARRATOR: The men's eyes grew wide in anticipation.

ODYSSEUS: I'm sure it's the home of some rich lord—probably a hall full of wine, plump women, and treasure. I wanted to investigate further, but I didn't want to leave you alone here for so long. I thought you might die of fright.

EURYLOCHUS: *(eagerly)* Lord Odysseus, I feel foolish for my words earlier. It would be an honor for me if you would let me discover who lives here on this island.

POLITES: You? Why should you get to go? I will go!

ODYSSEUS: Hmmm. I don't know. I had planned to visit this hall myself. *(pause)* We will leave it up to chance.

NARRATOR: He held up his dice, and the lots were cast.

ODYSSEUS: *(mock anger)* Blast! It looks like the gods favor you.

EURYLOCHUS: Ha! Then it is settled. I will take half the men and scout out this strange dwelling, and then I will return with the spoils I find there. I won't fail you!

POLITES: I want to come, too!

NARRATOR: Eurylochus selected the men to accompany him, and his party began the trek in-land.

ODYSSEUS: *(to himself)* Fools. Put the thought of riches into their minds, and they would march into Hades.

NARRATOR: Satisfied that his trick had worked, Odysseus settled down for an afternoon nap.

Meanwhile, Eurylochus and his party had topped the hill and spied the smoke Odysseus had spoken of rising listlessly above the treetops.

EURYLOCHUS: The hall must be there.

NARRATOR: They descended the slope and made their way through the forest. Soon through the underbrush a columned villa appeared, its lofty roof covered in vines.

EURYLOCHUS: This hall looks deserted!

NARRATOR: A low animal growl halted their progress. (growl of an animal)

POLITES: Shhh! Did you hear that?

NARRATOR: A wolf appeared from the behind the columns, its teeth bared and its hide bristling.

EURYLOCHUS: Stay perfectly still!

NARRATOR: Polites dared not move as the beast crept closer to him. It inched its muzzle up to his hand—and extended a pink tongue.

POLITES: (dumb laugh) This beast is tame!

NARRATOR: Suddenly, a huge beast sprang forth from the darkness of the porch and toppled Polites to the ground. (roar of a lion)

EURYLOCHUS: (frightened) A lion! Kill it, men! It's mauling Polites!

POLITES: Wait! Wait! (laughing) That tickles!

NARRATOR: The large cat was purring and licking Polites' face. (purring noise)

EURYLOCHUS: What is the meaning of this? Tame predators? This doesn't add up.

NARRATOR: The sound of many women's voices singing in unison filled the air. (angelic singing) The lion and the wolf scampered away.

POLITES: It's coming from inside the hall!

NARRATOR: The villa doors slowly swung open, and a procession of young girls—perfect in every way—filed out onto the columned porch. The eyes of the men began to bug out.

POLITES: Helloooo there!

NARRATOR: The procession was followed by a stately lady with beautiful braids looped about her head. She wore a draped gown that left much of her beautiful body exposed.

CIRCE: Greetings, gentlemen. I hope my pets did not startle you. My name is Circe, and this is my hall. Would you care to come inside for some—refreshment?

NARRATOR: Half of the men bolted forward without thinking.

EURYLOCHUS: (to the men) Halt! What are you doing? We didn't come here to sup with a bunch of strange women! We should report back to Odysseus.

POLITES: We can always report back later. Right now, we have better things to do!

CIRCE: Well said. Come inside, and we will serve you sumptuous dishes with our lovely arms.

NARRATOR: The otherworldly girls raised their graceful arms in unison. (cooing from the girls)

EURYLOCHUS: No! No! This is too strange!

CIRCE: Strange? *(laugh) You* are the one who is acting strange. We have offered you hospitality, and you refuse us. How unkind.

NARRATOR: All the girls pouted beautifully. *(disappointed sounds from the girls)*

EURYLOCHUS: It is nothing personal, your ladyship, but we have our orders.

CIRCE: Orders. Orders. People who follow orders have no fun! Your master will not mind if you are a few hours late. I promise you will find us most *amusing*.

POLITES: Eurylochus, stop being a kill-joy. Just look at those women!

EURYLOCHUS: It could be dangerous!

CIRCE: Dangerous? *(musical laugh)*

NARRATOR: The girls laughed musically. *(laughter from the girls)*

CIRCE: What can poor, defenseless women do against strong men such as yourselves? Your only fear should be that you will love the pleasures of my hall so greatly that you will never want to leave.

POLITES: *(eagerly)* I'm sold!

EURYLOCHUS: *(angrily)* Fine! Go ahead, but I'm warning you—

NARRATOR: The men had bounded up the stairs and disappeared into the hall of Circe before he could finish his sentence. The mistress of the house blew Eurylochus a kiss.

CIRCE: If you change your mind, you know where to find us. Come, pets.

NARRATOR: The wolf and the lion came obediently to her side, and all of them— women and beasts—disappeared into the hall. The doors slowly closed behind them.

EURYLOCHUS: I don't like this at all!

NARRATOR: A side window of the villa stood open, and Eurylochus moved to it to peer inside. He saw the girls serving steaming bowls of a strange, red substance to the men and playfully toying with their hair while they partook of it.

POLITES: Mmmmm. It's good!

EURYLOCHUS: That fat fool would eat anything!

NARRATOR: On various ornate couches the men were reclining—fanned and caressed by the pure white hands of the maidens. The men's beards were smeared red with the strange substance, and their intoxicated laughter rose and fell. *(laughter from the men)* Circe presided over them from her throne in the midst of the hall—smiling strangely.

CIRCE: Ladies, have all these men had their supper? Are they ready for dessert?

NARRATOR: The maidens nodded and giggled. *(giggling from the girls)*

POLITES: *(drunkenly)* We are! We are!

CIRCE: Oh, good.

NARRATOR: Circe pulled a carved stick from the folds of her gown and began to stroll about the room.

CIRCE: We are so happy that you big, strong men decided to stop by our hall! We've been needing a man around the house! And, now, look. We have so many. Let me count. One…two…three…

NARRATOR: As Circe passed behind each man, she touched his head gently with her wand.

CIRCE: Nineteen…twenty…

NARRATOR: She neared fat Polites.

CIRCE: Dear me, we'll have to count you for two!

POLITES: (roaring with laughter)

NARRATOR: As Circe seated herself back upon her throne with an elegant sweep, a worried look came over her face.

CIRCE: But wait a minute, my nymphs. I have made a mistake. These are not men at all!

POLITES: (roaring with laughter) Not men!

CIRCE: Oh no. If they are not men, what are they?

NYMPH: They are pigs, my mistress!

(all nymphs shout, "Pigs!")

NARRATOR: The men laughed drunkenly, thinking this was all a joke. (laughter from the men)

CIRCE: (strangely) Pigs? But pigs root and grunt. They eat garbage and live in their own filth. They are beasts!

POLITES: Oink! Oink! Ha-ha!

CIRCE: (commanding voice) Now, nymphs! Disengage yourselves from these beasts! It is time for us to see their true nature. If you say they are pigs, then pigs they shall be!

(loud laughing from all the men)

NARRATOR: As the foolish men roared with laughter, their voices increased in pitch. (higher laughing from all the men) Higher and higher it went until it was no longer laughing—but a shrieking, a collective squeal. (squealing)

CIRCE: (shrieking) Pigs! Pigs! Pigs!

NARRATOR: Spasms of pain wracked the men, and they fell writhing to the ground.

POLITES: (in pain) What—is—happening?

NARRATOR: Their features began to change. Their noses and ears painfully lengthened—stretched by Circe's magic. Their fingers clenched down into their palms and solidified into hooves. Their bodies doubled over and painfully compacted down into those of tiny, four-legged beasts. (loud squealing) When the shrieking had subsided, Circe stood in the midst of a group of rudely grunting pigs.

CIRCE: Hmmm. They *were* pigs all along, weren't they? See, my nymphs! Didn't I tell you that pig-forms would suit them most nicely? You barely notice the change. (pig call) Souu-eeee! Before long, we will have quite the zoo around here.

NARRATOR: Eurylochus, who had witnessed all this with horror, bolted from the villa window and ran all the way back to the ship, back to Odysseus.

When Eurylochus scrambled down the

hillside and fell upon the beach, breathless before his master, Odysseus sprang up in shock.

ODYSSEUS: *(urgently)* Eurylochus! What has happened?

EURYLOCHUS: M-m-master! A witch has taken them—pigs—all of them—pigs.

ODYSSEUS: Calm down. Tell me what you saw.

NARRATOR: Eurylochus told his master of the horrors he had beheld. Odysseus listened to the entire ordeal in grim silence.

ODYSSEUS: I should have been there.

EURYLOCHUS: No, Odysseus. You would have been taken, too. She cast some kind of spell over them and drew them in.

ODYSSEUS: You say that she had them eat of the substance *before* she touched them with the wand?

EURYLOCHUS: Yes!

ODYSSEUS: Hmmm. *(pause)* I will go.

MAN: No! You can't!

(shouts of "No!" from the men)

NARRATOR: Odysseus held his hand up for silence.

ODYSSEUS: Eurylochus, you must come with me!

EURYLOCHUS: I refuse!

ODYSSEUS: What? You would leave your comrades in such a state?

EURYLOCHUS: Better them than me.

ODYSSEUS: Fine. I will go, and I go alone. If I return, I will return with the men. If I am not back by tomorrow, sail on.

MAN: We would never leave you!

ODYSSEUS: Then you are fools! Dead is dead! Sail on, I say!

NARRATOR: Without another word, Odysseus departed. As he climbed the hillside once again, he ran what Eurylochus had told him over in his mind.

ODYSSEUS: *(to himself)* I've heard that sorceresses use potions to work their magic. The red porridge she gave the men must have been drugged. I have never matched wits with a witch before. Oh, Athena, give me the cunning to save my men! They may be stupid, but they are mine to look after!

NARRATOR: He thought of the lion and the wolf that his men had seen at Circe's villa.

ODYSSEUS: Those beasts were tame because they were once men. So we are not the first travelers to fall under Circe's trap.

NARRATOR: He came to the hilltop and beheld the smoke of Circe's hall amidst the forest.

ODYSSEUS: How can I save them?

NARRATOR: He heard a fluttering—the sound of a bird perhaps—but then a clear voice above him spoke.

HERMES: You know, talking to yourself is one of the first signs of insanity.

NARRATOR: Odysseus started and glanced upward. Floating above him was a youth holding a golden staff in his hand. The fluttering noise came from the wings that flapped on the clasps of his sandals. Odysseus quickly bowed down before the god.

ODYSSEUS: Hail, Hermes!

HERMES: Oh please. It's not like Zeus himself is appearing to you. I'm just a humble messenger. But grovel—if you must.

ODYSSEUS: What are you doing here, most clever of the gods?

HERMES: Good address! I had heard you were smart, Odysseus, and now I see it for myself. Flattery will get you *everywhere* with me! I am here at my sister Athena's behest.

ODYSSEUS: What do you mean?

HERMES: *Behest.* Um. It means "request" or something like that.

ODYSSEUS: No, I mean, why hasn't Athena come herself?

HERMES: What am *I*? Chopped mutton? Well, she wanted to come, of course. You *are* her favorite mortal. But I said, "No, Odysseus is family. I'll go."

ODYSSEUS: Family? So it's true! My father always told me that he was the grandson of Hermes!

HERMES: Of course, it's true. Where did you think you got your brains from? Brains don't grow on trees. *(pause)* Or is that money? Oh well.

ODYSSEUS: Have you come to tell me how to fight this witch?

HERMES: Actually, I have. I won't have a great-grandson of mine ending up as a pig. It's bad for the family image. I guess you could say I was saving your bacon.

ODYSSEUS: You could say that…

HERMES: All right. Enough jokes. There is an herb that grows at the base of the trees in this forest called moly. Eat some before you reach Circe's hall. Circe is quite a looker and *very* persuasive. You won't be able to refuse her hospitality—and probably won't want to! But the moly herb will counteract her magic.

ODYSSEUS: So I'm protected, but what about my men? How do I change them back?

HERMES: Why do you care about them?

ODYSSEUS: I'm a king. I must take care of my subjects. You're a god. Surely, you care for the mortals beneath you?

HERMES: Oh yeah—sure. *(pause)* Anyway, once Circe sees that her magic is worthless, you should draw your sword and threaten her.

ODYSSEUS: Sounds kind of barbaric.

HERMES: You're not exactly on a Sunday picnic here! If Circe likes one thing more than transforming men into animals, it's herself! Tell her you will only spare her life if she agrees to return your men to their rightful form. Then she will invite you to be her lover.

ODYSSEUS: How do you know so much about this?

HERMES: Yeesh. Don't ask. If you choose to become her lover, make her swear that she will in no way harm you—or you might end up leaving there less of a man—if you get my drift…

ODYSSEUS: Yikes.

HERMES: Exaaactly. She's a tough customer, but if you follow my suggestions, she'll be eating out of the palm of your hand.

ODYSSEUS: Thank you, great-grandfather.

HERMES: Great-grandfather? Don't call me that. You'll make me feel old.

NARRATOR: The god swooped down and plucked up the moly plant from the ground. A white flower bloomed upon it and below it dangled a black root.

HERMES: Now eat your veggies, young man. Hopefully, the next time I see you, you won't be a couple of pork chops. Farewell.

NARRATOR: The god slapped the plant into Odysseus' hand and disappeared. The Greek continued down through the forest—chewing the root as he walked. Soon the stone villa of Circe came into view, her wolves and lions lying tamely across the front steps. Odysseus stopped and took a deep breath to steady his nerves. The root's bitter taste still lingered in his mouth.

ODYSSEUS: *(loudly)* Hello! It is I, Odysseus, king of Ithaca.

NARRATOR: The gilded doors of the villa at once swung open, and Circe appeared.

CIRCE: *(sweetly)* Ah, welcome! Welcome, Odysseus.

NARRATOR: Once he beheld Circe, Odysseus was seized by a sudden attraction, one he had not expected. Something about the witch called to him—her milky skin, her glorious braids.

CIRCE: I was expecting you. I have a feast prepared. Come and dine at my table.

NARRATOR: She extended her hand grandly, and Odysseus felt himself moving forward, up the stairs, and into the dwelling of the witch. Within in the hall the nymphs that Eurylochus had spoken of reclined on the many couches and high-backed chairs that filled the room. In the midst of the atrium was an enormous loom—a weaving taking shape in its midst.

CIRCE: Pardon the mess. I am in the middle of my weaving.

(grunting of pigs)

NARRATOR: The grunting of pigs drew Odysseus' attention to the far corner of the hall to where a herd of swine was penned. Some of them looked strangely familiar.

CIRCE: Oh, ignore those smelly beasts. Our main course will be roasted pig, but, first, why don't you enjoy some *hors d'oeuvre?*

NARRATOR: One of the nymphs came forward, bearing a steaming bowl of red porridge. The smell was one that Odysseus could not resist, so he lifted it to his lips and drank.

ODYSSEUS: Hmmm. Tasty.

CIRCE: Oooh! I love a man with an appetite!

NARRATOR: She set the empty bowl aside and placed her lovely arms around Odysseus' neck.

CIRCE: Now, sit down. Relax.

ODYSSEUS: I have come here looking for my men. Have you perhaps seen them?

CIRCE: Men? Hmmm. No, I don't think I have. But if they are as half as attractive as you, I'm sorry I missed them!

NARRATOR: Circe stealthily reached within the folds of her gown and drew forth her wand. She touched it to Odysseus' head.

CIRCE: (*yelling*) Now, Odysseus, lord of men! Run off to your sty and wallow in the mud with your piggy friends! Ha-ha!

NARRATOR: Odysseus stared at her blankly.

ODYSSEUS: Excuse me?

NARRATOR: The witch looked strangely at Odysseus and then to her wand.

CIRCE: I—uh—nothing. Nothing. Just a joke.

NARRATOR: Circe forced a smile and tucked the wand behind her back.

ODYSSEUS: Could I have some more of that porridge that you fed me? It was delicious.

CIRCE: Uh. Of course. Of course.

NARRATOR: The witch crossed behind Odysseus again and struck him once again upon the head with the wand—only harder this time.

CIRCE: Now! Run! Run like a swine, I say! Squeal, piggy, squeal! (*maniacal laughter*)

NARRATOR: Odysseus turned toward her, rubbing his head in mock confusion.

ODYSSEUS: (*mock confusion*) Is this how strangers are treated here on your island?

CIRCE: It should have worked. I—I don't understand.

ODYSSEUS: (*forcefully*) Here. Let me *help* you understand.

NARRATOR: Odysseus stood and drew his sword. (*shing*)

CIRCE: What are you doing? Stay away from me! Nymphs! Attack!

NARRATOR: Odysseus caught the witch's wrist and drew her to him, placing his sword blade against her tender throat.

CIRCE: Please! I'm too beautiful to die!

ODYSSEUS: Now, witch. This little game is over!

NARRATOR: Circe began to sob.

CIRCE: (*crying*) You must be a mighty man indeed if you can resist my magic! Please do not take my life!

ODYSSEUS: I will only spare you if you return my men to their rightful form.

NARRATOR: Circe clung desperately to Odysseus.

CIRCE: (*softly*) It's just that I'm so terribly lonely here. I saw you, and I knew I just had to have you for my own! Haven't you ever felt that way about someone?

ODYSSEUS: Nice try. Transform my men.

NARRATOR: The witch snarled.

CIRCE: *(suddenly angry)* Fine! I'll transform your men! *(sadly)* Most men find my vulnerability irresistible. I guess my beauty has no effect on you!

ODYSSEUS: I didn't say that.

NARRATOR: The witch rose and swayed close to him.

CIRCE: *(sweetly)* I see. So would you be opposed to...staying with me—and being my husband?

NARRATOR: She stroked his face with the back of her hand.

ODYSSEUS: If I agree to stay, you must swear not to harm me or my men ever again.

NARRATOR: A thin smile spread across the witch's lips.

CIRCE: Oh, very well. I promise not to harm you or your men in any way. You *are* crafty, Odysseus. I planned to lure you into a daze of love—and then undo you.

NARRATOR: She drew a carefully concealed dagger from the folds of her gown and smiled.

CIRCE: But I'm done with tricks. You've beaten me. You know, you are the first man to have gotten the better of me in five hundred years.

NARRATOR: The witch seated herself and angrily crossed her arms. She looked at her wand in disgust and tossed it away.

ODYSSEUS: You have been doing this for five hundred years?

CIRCE: Of course. What else is there to do on this gods-forsaken island? My nymphs and I lure men in, and I turn them into beasts. At first it was only cute things like kittens and puppies. Then we tried bigger beasts like elephants and hippos, but the noise was too much—not to mention the clean-up.

ODYSSEUS: So why pigs?

CIRCE: Why not?

ODYSSEUS: *(playfully)* So you thought I would make a good pig?

CIRCE: More like a boar—but yes. Normally, my failure would enrage me, but, luckily for you, I find your intelligence incredibly adorable. *(pause)* Now that you have agreed to stay and be my husband, how would you like to spend the rest of our evening?

ODYSSEUS: Ahem. Aren't you forgetting something?

CIRCE: *(innocently)* I don't think so, my dear.

ODYSSEUS: My men. You said you would transform my men.

CIRCE: Oh, that can wait surely.

ODYSSEUS: Now.

CIRCE: *(sigh)* Very well. I don't understand why you are so fond of that bunch of swine.

NARRATOR: She motioned to her nymphs, who retrieved jars full of a strange oil, and poured it into the feeding trough of the pigs.

CIRCE: No matter what their form, they're still pigs. You should have seen them, ogling my nymphs like a bunch of sailors.

ODYSSEUS: They *are* a bunch of sailors.

CIRCE: Eh. That's no excuse.

(squealing of the pigs)

NARRATOR: There was a commotion as Odysseus' men suddenly materialized amid the hog pen—down all fours, rooting around among the slop. With astonishment they examined their reformed bodies. *(cheering of the men)*

POLITES: Odysseus! You saved us!

ODYSSEUS: You have never looked filthier, but you are a sight for sore eyes!

NARRATOR: Polites suddenly noticed Circe standing at Odysseus' side.

POLITES: *(in shock)* Master! That's the witch who transformed us!

ODYSSEUS: She is no longer our enemy. In fact, we will be staying here for a time.

NARRATOR: Polites nodded toward the nymphs.

POLITES: Are they still our enemies?

ODYSSEUS: They are friends.

NARRATOR: Polites rubbed his grimy hands together.

POLITES: All right!

CIRCE: Nymphs, these men are covered in filth. Take them to the springs and see that they are cleaned!

NARRATOR: The nymphs led the smiling men away.

CIRCE: Here you shall be safe. You can stay as long as you wish.

ODYSSEUS: We will stay only for a week.

CIRCE: A week? *(laugh)* We'll see. We'll see.

NARRATOR: A week in the hall of Circe turned into a month and then a year. The men enjoyed the company of the beautiful nymphs and had taken wives among them.

Circe spent each day weaving at her loom, singing with her enchanting voice, and each night in the arms of Odysseus. Only slowly did the thought of Ithaca—of home—creep back into Odysseus' mind.

ODYSSEUS: Eurylochus, how many days have we been here in Circe's hall?

EURYLOCHUS: Days? More like months! The seasons have gone around full circle. We have tarried here almost a year.

ODYSSEUS: A year? I guess the time just got away from me.

EURYLOCHUS: You haven't forgotten our home, have you? Our Ithaca?

ODYSSEUS: Of course not!

NARRATOR: Eurylochus nodded to the other men.

EURYLOCHUS: They have. They would be content to stay here. It was easy for them to forget their wives and children at home, but I know you are not like them. You won't forget so easily.

ODYSSEUS: You are right, Eurylochus. We must depart—at once.

NARRATOR: That night, when he and Circe were alone, Odysseus broke the troubling news to her.

CIRCE: You're leaving?

ODYSSEUS: Remember, you promised to spare my life and to help me on my voyage when the time came.

NARRATOR: The witch's eyes began to glisten.

CIRCE: I know! I know! Oh, those stupid oaths. Why did I make them? Now I must keep my word. At least, I still have one hope.

ODYSSEUS: What is that?

CIRCE: I hope after I tell you all the dangers that lay ahead for you, you will reconsider and stay here with me.

ODYSSEUS: I have faced many dangers already. There is nothing that can stand between me and my Ithaca—my home.

CIRCE: Any place can be a home. What could possibly be there that you don't have here?

ODYSSEUS: A son. A wife.

CIRCE: (thoughtfully) Huh. Never in all my life did I think I would envy a mortal woman.

ODYSSEUS: Tell me. What lies ahead? You told me once that you possessed great knowledge.

CIRCE: Well, I can tell you one thing—you picked a mighty god to offend when you blinded the one-eyed son of Poseidon. He has not forgotten his anger.

ODYSSEUS: Is there a way that I can appease him?

CIRCE: Of course, but it is not for the faint of heart. You must sail to the very edge of Hades—to where the line between life and death becomes blurred. There you must embark upon that dark shore and speak with the soul of Tiresias.

ODYSSEUS: The blind prophet?

CIRCE: Yes. That poor soul can't even get rest in Hades. Even in death he still has people asking his advice. Only he can tell you how to turn aside Poseidon's wrath. Otherwise, you will spend your life a hunted man.

ODYSSEUS: I guess that's not so bad. Other men have gone into Hades and lived to tell about it.

CIRCE: I have not told you all.

NARRATOR: Then the beautiful witch spoke of further trials that Odysseus would have to face—monsters and creatures beyond imagination—that stood between him and his home. As she spoke, Odysseus felt his heart grow cold.

ODYSSEUS: Your words leave me with no hope.

CIRCE: You will always have hope, Odysseus. You are too sure of yourself not to. There is something inside of you that draws you home. Even if all the world stood against you, you would still find a way.

NARRATOR: Odysseus left the witch's presence and went to speak to his men. His news would not be well received.

ODYSSEUS: It is time for us to leave. We must sail next to a dark land—the land of death.

NARRATOR: Many of the men's faces went white with fear at the mention of Hades.

EURYLOCHUS: What? Why are we not sailing for home?

ODYSSEUS: This is the path that I must take. If you do not want to come with me, I can understand. You may stay here with Circe and her nymphs.

NARRATOR: As the men looked to one another in confusion, Polites rose to speak in front of his comrades.

POLITES: Odysseus came back and saved us. We would all still be pigs if it weren't for him! I for one, would follow him anywhere.

EURYLOCHUS: I agree! There is no captain for me but Odysseus!

(shouts of approval from the men)

ODYSSEUS: Then to Hades it is! And after those dark shores, Ithaca!

POLITES: Ithaca!

(all men shout "Ithaca!")

NARRATOR: Rain dripped down from the roof of Circe's villa the morning Odysseus and his men departed from that hall. Circe stroked the matted fur of her wolf as she and her nymphs watched their departure. Just for a second—through the drizzle—she thought she saw Odysseus look back before he and his men disappeared among the trees.

CIRCE: Well. It was fun while it lasted. Now back to business as usual. *(pause)* How do you girls feel about badgers?

NARRATOR: Circe and her servants filed back within the darkened hall, and the doors closed silently behind them.

DISCUSSION QUESTIONS

- At the beginning of this episode, do you think Odysseus is afraid of what he might find on this island? Does he have a right to be afraid? Explain.
- Does Odysseus value the life of his men? Explain.
- Throughout his journey, Odysseus has seemed eager to reach his home. Why does he decide to stay with Circe for such a long time?
- What lesson do Odysseus' men learn during this episode? Explain.
- Is Circe the witch the greatest threat that Odysseus and his men have faced? Explain.
- How does Circe present Odysseus with a different type of test than the Cyclops did?
- How is Circe different from the typical conception of a witch?
- Is Odysseus a good husband? Explain.

RETURN TO ITHACA
TEACHER GUIDE

BACKGROUND

For centuries Penelope has been praised as the ultimate example of a virtuous wife. She remained faithful to a husband, whom most considered dead, for twenty long years. A woman under extreme pressure from a group of strong-armed suitors, Penelope rises to the challenge of faithfulness and keeps her cool. She also shows herself to be her husband's match in intelligence and cunning. A trick nearly as famous as Odysseus' Trojan Horse is Penelope's tapestry, which she weaves during the day and unravels at night.

Some believe that Penelope actually sees through Odysseus' disguise when he appears in court disguised a beggar. After all, could a woman this crafty really be fooled by Odysseus' disguises? Why else would she immediately propose an archery contest that she knows only her husband can win? Maybe she is playing along with her wily husband.

Penelope is not given a voice in Homer's poem, and we are left to imagine her inner thoughts for ourselves. Modern writers have often tried to reinterpret the story from Penelope's point-of-view. What was going through her mind during these many years of separation? Did she ever doubt Odysseus' loyalty to her? If not, should she have?

SUMMARY

Adventure after adventure has been told by Odysseus to his hosts, King Alcinous and the Phaeacians. The king is so impressed that he offers Odysseus the opportunity to rule his kingdom by giving him the hand of his beautiful daughter, Nausicaa, in marriage. Odysseus politely refuses this offer, and the Phaeacians promise to transport the traveler back to Ithaca in one of their magical ships.

Once back in Ithaca Odysseus is greeted by Athena, who tells him that he has at last reached his home. She warns him about the suitors who hold his household hostage and directs him to the hut of Eumaeus, the swineherd. Athena disguises Odysseus as a dirty beggar.

Telemachus is just returning from his own voyage and seeks out the hut of Eumaeus. He is shocked when the old beggar man he sees in the hut transforms into his long-lost father. The two have a tearful reunion, and then they hatch a plan to retake Ithaca from the suitors.

Telemachus and Odysseus, disguised as a beggar, go to the royal hall. Eurycleia, Odysseus' old nurse, takes pity on the beggar, feeds him, and washes his dirty body. As she does, she recognizes Odysseus by a birthmark on his ankle. She agrees to keep his identity a secret and assist in the suitors' deaths.

The suitors lure Telemachus into a fistfight, hoping to kill him in the process. Odysseus sees that they are planning to beat the boy to death, so he intervenes. The suitors mock the old beggar and break a chair across his back. This puts an end to the fight. Penelope comes to thank the beggar for his intervention. This is the first time Penelope and Odysseus have spoken in twenty years.

Penelope, apparently unaware that Odysseus is the beggar, decides to choose between the suitors by having a contest. Whichever one of them that can string Odysseus' massive bow and shoot an arrow through twelve axe rings will be her husband. Each of the suitors tries this contest, but at last the beggar steps up to attempt it. As he completes the task, Odysseus' disguise fades away, and Telemachus steps forward and helps his father slay all of the suitors.

After putting the traitorous servants of the household to death, Odysseus is reunited with Penelope. But before she accepts him as her husband, Penelope tests Odysseus, telling him that she has moved their wedding bed from its original chamber. This shocks him as one of its legs was a live tree growing up through the palace floor. Because of his shock, Penelope realizes that he is truly Odysseus and welcomes him home.

ESSENTIAL QUESTIONS

- What is true love?
- How many obstacles can love overcome?
- Where is *home*? Why is it important?

ANTICIPATORY QUESTIONS

- How do you think the *Odyssey* will end?
- How long has Penelope been waiting for Odysseus?
- How can you tell that Penelope is very intelligent?
- How can Odysseus defeat the suitors that have taken over his hall?

CONNECTIONS

The Penelopiad by Margaret Atwood This humorous novel re-tells events of the *Odyssey* from Penelope's point-of-view, exploring several feminist issues within the epic poem. There are several portions that may not be appropriate for younger audiences, but certain excerpts would lead to interesting discussion with your students concerning point-of-view.

TEACHABLE TERMS

- **Denouement (Resolution)**   Resolution is an important part of every story. Does the

resolution of the *Odyssey* effectively wrap up the story?
- **Story Arc** Have the students view the Trojan War and the *Odyssey* as one continuous story arc and examine how far the characters have come since the beginning. Have them map out the story on a sheet of paper to see how the plot has unfolded.
- **Poetic Justice** Considering it is a literary device in which virtue is rewarded and vice is punished, is poetic justice present at the ending of the *Odyssey*? Do the suitors deserve their fate? Does Odysseus deserve a happy ending?
- **Theme** Judging the *Odyssey* as a whole, what is its theme? Answers might vary—the importance of family, the importance of home, the importance of intelligence, etc.

RECALL QUESTIONS

1. How does Odysseus reach Ithaca?
2. How is Odysseus disguised by Athena?
3. How does Eurycleia, Odysseus' old nurse, recognize him through his disguise?
4. What test does Penelope propose for the suitors?
5. How does Penelope test Odysseus after they are reunited?

RETURN TO ITHACA

CAST

ODYSSEUS	*King of Ithaca*
ALCINOUS	*King of Phaeacia*
NAUSICAA	*Young Princess*
TELEMACHUS	*Son of Odysseus*
PENELOPE	*Wife of Odysseus*
EURYCLEIA	*Old Nurse*
ANTINOUS	*Suitor to Penelope*
EURYMACHUS	*Suitor to Penelope*
EUMAEUS	*Swineherd*
ATHENA	*Goddess of War*
SUITOR	*Suitor to Penelope*

NARRATOR: Odysseus had been the guest of the Phaeacian king, Alcinous, for many days. Each night he would regale his court with a new episode from his adventures. The princess Nausicaa, who had discovered him washed up on their shores, became his most devoted admirer and sat at his feet each night as he told his tales.

ALCINOUS: I cannot remember a more joyous time here in the palace than the time you have spent with us, Odysseus. You have had the most adventurous life of any man I've ever met. You saved your men from the Lotus Eaters, passed Scylla and Charybdis, heard the song of the Sirens, and lived to tell of it.

NAUSICAA: Don't forget defeating the Cyclops, Father!

NARRATOR: The young girl smiled up at Odysseus.

ALCINOUS: Of course. How could I forget? Now what story shall you tell us tonight?

ODYSSEUS: I'm afraid there is nothing else to tell. I told you all that befell me before I landed upon your shores. All that remains is for me to sail home to Ithaca.

NARRATOR: This comment caused the princess to jump in shock.

NAUSICAA: Father! Tell him your plan.

ALCINOUS: As you know, Odysseus, Phaeacia is a great kingdom—surrounded by an impenetrable mountain range on all sides but one. Our sailors are the best in the world, and our ships are piloted by magic. We have all the wealth a people could ask for.

ODYSSEUS: Yes. This is an enchanting place. I've loved it since I first laid eyes on it.

ALCINOUS: I'm glad to hear you say that. We hoped that you might stay among us.

ODYSSEUS: Me?

ALCINOUS: We have never met anyone like you, Odysseus. Stay and be a prince among us. You may even take my young daughter as your bride.

NARRATOR: The princess beamed at Odysseus in anticipation. The Greek only smiled sadly.

ODYSSEUS: You are too kind.

ALCINOUS: Then you shall stay?

ODYSSEUS: No. I'm afraid not. I did not stay with Calypso or Circe, and I cannot stay here. Your kingdom is truly beautiful, but Ithaca is my home.

NARRATOR: Nausicaa began to weep.

ODYSSEUS: Please understand, princess. I have a wife at home, whom I love very much, and a son I have not seen since he was just a baby.

ALCINOUS: There is no need to explain, my friend. We hoped our offer might entice you. We are sad to see you go, but we wish you all the happiness in the world.

ODYSSEUS: Your hospitality has been excellent. All I ask are some materials from which build a ship.

ALCINOUS: Nonsense! You will go in one of our ships.

ODYSSEUS: I could not. I have told you that Poseidon is my mortal enemy. He would curse you forever if you helped me.

ALCINOUS: Oh, Poseidon has always hated us. Our ships never wreck—no matter how strongly he rages. It infuriates him.

ODYSSEUS: And he does nothing to stop you?

ALCINOUS: There is a prophecy that one day, he will turn one of our ships into stone and cause an avalanche that will completely seal our kingdom from the outside world forever.

ODYSSEUS: I cannot ask you to risk so much for me.

ALCINOUS: After what you have risked during these ten years at sea, our risk seems small in comparison. You will need no pilot. The ship knows the way. We will stow mighty treasures aboard your vessel so that you will never forget your friends the Phaeacians.

NARRATOR: The Phaeacians gathered at the port to bid farewell to the famous traveler. Nausicaa still hung her head in sadness. The Phaeacian ship was like no ship Odysseus had ever seen before, and once he put both feet aboard, it began to skim out across the waves of its own accord. Odysseus raised his hand in farewell, and the land of Phaeacia was soon lost from view.

ODYSSEUS: Well, if there is no need to steer, I might as well lie down.

NARRATOR: Odysseus lay down in the bottom of the boat and was soon lost in sleep.

It seemed no time before he was jolted from sleep. The magical ship had run ashore. Odysseus rose in confusion—the world around him was shrouded in mist. All that was visible was a rocky shore.

ODYSSEUS: This can't be right! Magic, my foot! This boat has taken me off course.

NARRATOR: He swung himself over the edge of the boat onto the dry land. Ahead of him in the mist, there stood a tall figure—heavily armed.

ODYSSEUS: Who's there?

NARRATOR: The mist dissipated around the figure—revealing its face.

ODYSSEUS: Lady Athena! Is it really you?

ATHENA: Yes, Odysseus. I have been protecting you these many years. It has been my mission to see you safely home.

ODYSSEUS: No offense, my lady. But there is still more to go. How will I reach my home from here?

ATHENA: You *are* home, Odysseus.

ODYSSEUS: This can't be Ithaca! I was days away and—

ATHENA: The magical ships move swiftly.

NARRATOR: A bubbling sound filled the air, and Odysseus turned back to the ship. The water around it was boiling, and in an instant the ship transformed—from a craft of wood to a craft of stone. It disappeared beneath the waves.

ATHENA: See? Poseidon has cursed the ship that carried you home to this shore. Now he will seal up Phaeacia, so that no man will find their kingdom ever again. Their race is lost to us forever.

ODYSSEUS: Then they have lost a home, and I have regained mine.

ATHENA: Behold! Ithaca!

NARRATOR: The mist rose like a curtain, and Odysseus' rocky island home spread out before him. The Greek fell to his knees.

ODYSSEUS: I can't believe it! I'm finally here—after all these years. Tell me, goddess, where is my wife? Where is my son? I must go to them.

ATHENA: I am afraid not. In your absence there have been dark times here. Telemachus has fled from these shores. Your Penelope is a prisoner in her own house.

ODYSSEUS: No! Tell me all that you know.

NARRATOR: The goddess spoke at length to Odysseus, telling him of the suitors who had invaded his household.

ODYSSEUS: I will kill them all!

ATHENA: The Odysseus I know is not foolish enough to face all one-hundred-and-eight suitors singlehandedly. Go to the hut of Eumaeus the Swineherd. He is one of the few who is still loyal to you. I will disguise you until it is time for you to reveal your true identity.

NARRATOR: Odysseus felt his body begin to change. Scraggly white hairs grew out from his chin, the hair already upon his head receded into his scalp, and as he held up to view his hands and arms, they withered before his very eyes.

ODYSSEUS: (*old man voice*) A cunning disguise.

ATHENA: Now, go, Odysseus! Meet with your son, and together you will cleanse your household.

ODYSSEUS: My son?

NARRATOR: But the goddess was already gone. Odysseus—in the stooped and gnarled form of a beggar—hobbled to the hut of Eumaeus the swineherd.

Meanwhile, Telemachus was just returning from Sparta. He had followed Athena's advice and avoided Ithaca's port. Instead he had moored on the western side of the island and sought out the swineherd. When he found Eumaeus' dwelling, the prince saw that he had company. Some dirty old man sat in the corner of his hut, absentmindedly running his hands through the pig droppings.

EUMAEUS: My lord, you have returned! Your mother was so worried that you would be killed. Those villains set an ambush for you! They were going to kill you as you sailed home.

TELEMACHUS: Then I guess I cheated death by sailing here first. Who is—?

NARRATOR: Telemachus nodded toward the old man.

EUMAEUS: Some crazy old beggar. But far be it from me to disobey the gods and not offer him some hospitality.

TELEMACHUS: Eumaeus, I need you to go to my mother in secret and tell her I have returned. I will stay here until I have made a plan to get rid of these suitors once and for all.

EUMAEUS: A secret mission, eh? Well, you can trust me! You know, I always thought I would have made an excellent spy.

NARRATOR: The swineherd scampered off toward the palace.

ODYSSEUS: (old man voice) Eumaeus may not be smart, but he is loyal.

TELEMACHUS: Excuse me?

ODYSSEUS: So, you are Odysseus' boy, huh?

TELEMACHUS: (annoyed) Yes. Do you know Odysseus?

ODYSSEUS: Very well. In fact, I would say that he and I were almost twins.

TELEMACHUS: Twins? You must be twice his age. (under his breath) Crazy old loon.

NARRATOR: Suddenly the old man seemed to shift, his wrinkles dissipating, his spine straightening, his eyes growing brighter— eyes that Telemachus saw resembled his own.

ODYSSEUS: (emotionally) My son!

TELEMACHUS: Father? What—is it really you?

NARRATOR: Telemachus had always wondered what would happen when he and his father finally met. Would they clasp hands? Embrace? Would it be the awkward meeting of two strangers? But it was just the opposite. Odysseus held his son in his arms—just as he did twenty years before— and cried tears of happiness upon his head.

ODYSSEUS: (happily) My son! My son!

TELEMACHUS: Father!

NARRATOR: Odysseus and Telemachus spent hours talking. Odysseus told of his whole journey: the Cyclops, Scylla, Charybdis, the mystical song of the Sirens that only he had heard. Telemachus could only sit there—like an enchanted five-year-old—and listen to the amazing story of his voyage.

ODYSSEUS: But tell me of how it goes here, my son. *(laughing) My son!* How great it is to speak those words!

NARRATOR: Telemachus told him of the suitors, of Penelope's tricks. When Telemachus spoke of Penelope's tapestry, Odysseus' proud smile spoke volumes. His affairs with Circe and Calypso may have satisfied his body but never his heart.

ODYSSEUS: Ha-ha! You have a clever mother, boy. There is not a finer woman under the sun than Penelope! Now listen, we must form a plan!

NARRATOR: For Telemachus it was amazing to watch his father's mind in action. Ten years of wandering seemed to have only strengthened Odysseus' wits.

ODYSSEUS: I will resume my disguise as a beggar and make my way to the palace. You must go to your mother and tell her of your quest, but give her no hope for my return.

TELEMACHUS: But—

ODYSSEUS: Penelope must not know that I live! The shock would be too great for her to conceal!

TELEMACHUS: What must I do?

ODYSSEUS: You and Eumaeus must remove the weapons from the palace storeroom. Then we will wait for our chance to strike. We must catch the suitors off their guard.

TELEMACHUS: A trick!

ODYSSEUS: Naturally.

NARRATOR: Telemachus bid his father a fond farewell and returned to Ithaca. His return caused quite a stir among the suitors. Since he had avoided their ambush, they were more determined than ever to destroy him.

ANTINOUS: He must be sneakier than we thought. What we need to do is draw him out into a fight.

EURYMACHUS: How about a boxing match?

ANTINOUS: Perfect. You've killed men in a match before, haven't you?

EURYMACHUS: Leave it to me.

NARRATOR: Upon their reunion, Penelope clung desperately to her son.

PENELOPE: Don't ever do that to me again! I can't lose you!

TELEMACHUS: Forgive me, mother. I visited many places, but no one had any news of Father.

PENELOPE: Perhaps it is better that way.

TELEMACHUS: What do you mean?

PENELOPE: I have decided to choose.

TELEMACHUS: You can't!

PENELOPE: I must. Tomorrow I make my announcement.

NARRATOR: Telemachus went at once to the courtyard—to find his disguised father. He spotted the beggar sitting against the meeting room wall. The disguise was so good he almost did not recognize his father. A shaggy shock of hair and a tangled beard covered his face. He'd smeared himself in the dung of swine and hobbled like a hunchback.

TELEMACHUS: *(whispering)* Mother said she is going to choose among the suitors—tomorrow.

ODYSSEUS: Then this is perfect. We will use the decision as a diversion.

EURYCLEIA: Telemachus! Telemachus!

TELEMACHUS: It is Eurycleia!

ODYSSEUS: Lead her away.

NARRATOR: The old nurse neared the prince and the beggar.

EURYCLEIA: You're back, my boy! You're back! It does my old heart good to see you.

NARRATOR: She noticed the grimy beggar against the wall.

EURYCLEIA: Who is this?

TELEMACHUS: Nobody. An old beggar. I was just telling him to be on his way.

EURYCLEIA: Be on his way? No. No. Not in the house of Odysseus. Come, sir. You must have a bath.

TELEMACHUS: Please. Leave him. I will attend to him.

EURYCLEIA: Look at his feet. Look how they're blistered! A nice hot bath will do him some good. Now come and let me—

NARRATOR: The nurse froze in mid-speech. She was staring at a spot on Odysseus' ankle.

EURYCLEIA: My, my. That is strange. There is only one person in the whole world who bears such a strange scar upon his ankle. It was given to him by a boar, high on the mountain.

NARRATOR: She stared into the old beggar's eyes and suddenly saw past Athena's disguise.

EURYCLEIA: My Odysseus!

TELEMACHUS: No! You must be mistaken.

EURYCLEIA: I think I can recognize the men I raised up from children.

ODYSSEUS: Shhh! Yes, old nurse. It is I, Odysseus. But we are keeping my presence here a secret.

EURYCLEIA: A wise idea. The house is full of spies. Even my lady's handmaidens have become spies for those foul suitors!

NARRATOR: Telemachus and Odysseus filled the old woman in on their plan.

EURYCLEIA: I will sneak into the common room where the suitors sleep tonight and relieve them of their weapons.

NARRATOR: As Eurycleia left them, they heard men approaching.

EURYMACHUS: There he is!

ANTINOUS: Prince Telemachus! Welcome home.

NARRATOR: Telemachus turned with a snarl of hatred upon his face.

TELEMACHUS: What do you want?

ANTINOUS: We were just discussing your predicament. Here you are, a young boy on the verge of manhood without a father—no one to show you exactly how to become a man.

TELEMACHUS: My father will return.

ANTINOUS: Will he? I would sooner expect pigs to fly or that old nurse of yours to give birth. *(laughter from the men)*

TELEMACHUS: Fine. What must I do to "become a man"?

ANTINOUS: What every boy does—fight.

TELEMACHUS: I have no desire to fight you.

NARRATOR: Telemachus turned his back on the suitors. Eurymachus grabbed the boy roughly from behind and shoved him violently into the wall. Odysseus the beggar began to rise instinctively.

ANTINOUS: Uh-oh. Look out. The prince's filthy beggar friend is going to come to his rescue.

EURYMACHUS: What are you going to do, beggar? Wipe pig dung on me?

NARRATOR: The brute slapped Odysseus in the face. Telemachus—his nose bleeding from his fall—faced the suitors angrily.

TELEMACHUS: You want a fight? I'll give you a fight!

ANTINOUS: Good. I was beginning to think you didn't have any manliness about you at all. Prepare yourself. We'll invite in the others to watch.

NARRATOR: All the suitors were called into the open-air courtyard, and Eurymachus prepared for the fight. He stripped to the waist and wrapped his fists in shreds of cloth. In between his fingers he clenched shards of pottery.

EURYMACHUS: Perfect. I'll rip that pretty boy to shreds.

NARRATOR: The gathered men formed a ring, and Odysseus tried to push himself to the forefront.

SUITOR: Get away, you mangy beggar!

NARRATOR: The suitors pushed him from the ring. Telemachus and Eurymachus began to circle one another. Telemachus made a jab, but the older, more experienced fighter grabbed his wrist and twisted his arm painfully to the side.

TELEMACHUS: Ah!

NARRATOR: Eurymachus punched him hard in the side, and when he drew his fist away from the boy's side, it dripped blood. Odysseus watched all this in horror.

ODYSSEUS: *(in horror)* They're going to kill him!

NARRATOR: Telemachus sprang up, holding his side, and rushed at his opponent. Eurymachus let loose with a roundhouse punch that cut into the prince's cheek. Telemachus stumbled and spat blood.

EURYMACHUS: This will be over sooner than I thought!

ANTINOUS: Do it! Do it now!

NARRATOR: Eurymachus rearranged the bits of pottery between his fingers—pushing their sharp edges out even further. Then he set his eyes on the boy's tender stomach.

EURYMACHUS: Heh. Heh.

NARRATOR: He ran forward, his burly arm cocked, ready to slash.

ODYSSEUS: Noooooo!

NARRATOR: The beggar, wriggling between the legs of the men, sprang into the ring.

ODYSSEUS: Gentlemen, end this fight. It is a dishonor.

EURYMACHUS: Get out of here, you crazy old fool!

NARRATOR: Antinous seized up a chair and, raising it over his head, brought it down hard upon the beggar's hunchback.

ODYSSEUS: *(cry of pain)*

NARRATOR: The suitors began to point and laugh at the ridiculous sight of the old beggar man standing up to the two suitors.

(laughter of all the suitors)

PENELOPE: Telemachus! What is going on here?

NARRATOR: Penelope had appeared in the courtyard, Eurycleia trailing at her heels.

They stopped short when they saw the wounds that had been inflicted upon Telemachus.

PENELOPE: My son! What have they done to you?

ANTINOUS: Nothing, my lady. Just teaching the boy a lesson about manhood.

PENELOPE: And what would you know about that, you beasts? Come, Telemachus. Come away from this place.

TELEMACHUS: *(weakly)* The beggar. Take the beggar, too. He saved me.

EURYMACHUS: Your mother may have saved you today, boy, but this is not finished.

PENELOPE: Oh, yes, it is. I can't stand you brutes in my home any longer! Tomorrow I will choose between you.

ANTINOUS: What? No tricks?

PENELOPE: No. I will choose one from among you. And the rest of you can leave and never darken our door again!

NARRATOR: Penelope and Eurycleia ushered the prince and the beggar away.

ANTINOUS: Ah-ha! Now we are seeing some results! Bring in the serving wenches, and we will have a feast! Tomorrow we see who will be king here in Ithaca!

NARRATOR: Eurycleia tended to Telemachus' wounds, while Penelope came and knelt before the old beggar. How strange to see their first glimpse of each other after twenty years! Odysseus didn't miss a beat and acted his part. A weaker man would have never had such patience, but Odysseus did.

PENELOPE: I want to thank you, stranger, for stepping in when you did.

ODYSSEUS: *(hoarsely)* I only did what I would have done for my own son.

PENELOPE: You are welcome here at Ithaca.

NARRATOR: She glanced down at his ankle, but he slid it quickly beneath his cloak.

PENELOPE: I—*(pause)* please let me know if I can do anything else for you.

NARRATOR: Penelope left their presence quickly. When she was gone, Telemachus spoke.

TELEMACHUS: You're amazing! You haven't seen her for twenty years? How can you act so cool?

ODYSSEUS: Years of experience have taught me that, my boy. It is better this way. This way only one of us will have to act a part.

NARRATOR: The conspirators reviewed their plans for the following day. Telemachus and Eumaeus would be on hand—weapons at the ready. The only unexpected twist in their plan came from Penelope. All the household had gathered in the hearing hall to witness her choice.

PENELOPE: Men of the surrounding isles! Lords who desire my hand! I have reached a decision. Before he left, Odysseus commanded me—in his absence—to select a mate when Telemachus had reached manhood. Since it seems that my husband will never return, I have decided to choose among you. Since I refuse to wed a man who

is not the measure of my husband, I will only marry one who can string the bow of Odysseus and shoot an arrow through twelve axe rings.

TELEMACHUS: *(whispering)* What is she saying? She will ruin our plan.

ODYSSEUS: No. You have a clever mother. Just watch.

ANTINOUS: Lady, no one could shoot an arrow through twelve axe rings!

PENELOPE: Odysseus could. So if none of you are his match in skill, I say, go home—and leave me in peace!

NARRATOR: The enormous bow was brought forth—a rough and hardened weapon, nearly inflexible. In all of Telemachus' days he had never seen it strung. Of course, as with everything to do with Odysseus, there was a trick to it. The twelve axes were driven into the floor, their handle-rings lined up perfectly. The contest was ready.

EURYMACHUS: Back, you dogs! I'll try it first!

ANTINOUS: I'm next. After you fail, of course.

NARRATOR: The one-hundred-and-eight suitors fell over one another to have their chance. They grunted and tugged until the veins bulged out in their foreheads. Try as they might, none of them could pull the string tightly enough to secure it.

Even Telemachus stepped forward to have a turn. He struggled against the hardened weapon, but it was no use. After all had tried and tired, the cracked voice of the beggar was heard.

ODYSSEUS: (*old man voice*) I'll have a try.

(*loud jeers and laughing*)

SUITOR: You? Ha!

NARRATOR: The suitors howled at him. And Telemachus had to chuckle as well. Here was Odysseus' final trick. As the beggar stepped forward to try the bow, Telemachus nodded to Eumaeus who moved silently and bolted the door to the hall.

EURYMACHUS: (*howling with laughter*) Look at this fool!

(*laughter from the suitors*)

NARRATOR: The beggar took the bow into his gnarled hands. He placed one end beneath his foot and began to slowly bend the bow as he pulled the string-loop upward. The suitors stopped laughing.

ODYSSEUS: (*regular voice*) You see, gentlemen. Things are not always as they appear. You thought that *I* was an old beggar, but nothing could be further from the truth.

NARRATOR: The beggar—who now looked nothing like a beggar—turned, bow and arrow in his hands. He took the axe rings into his sights and let the shaft fly. It clipped neatly through all twelve rings. (*twelve shings*) (*gasping from everyone*)

ODYSSEUS: Hmmm. I guess appearances can be deceiving. A fine lesson for any man to learn. A lesson, gentlemen, that you will not live long enough to use. (*cries of panic*)

EURYMACHUS: (*screaming*) It's Odysseus! Zeus preserve us!

NARRATOR: The next arrow of Odysseus found its mark in Antinous' throat. (*twang*)

ANTINOUS: (*hacking and gurgling*)

NARRATOR: Telemachus unsheathed his sword and stepped between the fleeing suitors and the bolted door. Eurymachus was the first suitor to approach him, and the prince hacked him down without mercy.

TELEMACHUS: Eumaeus, to arms!

NARRATOR: The swineherd drew his spear and began to skewer the fleeing suitors. The arrows of Odysseus cut through the air. When the fighting was done, the blood of one-hundred-and-eight men ran upon the floor.

ODYSSEUS: Good job, son! We have struck a blow for the gods this day!

TELEMACHUS: We are not done yet. We must deal with the traitors in our household.

NARRATOR: Eurycleia came forward and identified the twelve handmaids who had sold themselves to the suitors, as well as other traitorous servants. Odysseus and Telemachus strung them up one by one.

ODYSSEUS: Now where is your mother? We have waited twenty years for this reunion.

TELEMACHUS: Eurycleia took her to her chambers to spare her from the sight of this bloodshed.

ODYSSEUS: Very well. I go to my wife.

NARRATOR: Odysseus placed a firm hand upon Telemachus' shoulder and said these words like he'd journeyed his ten years just to say them:

ODYSSEUS: I'm proud of you, my boy.

TELEMACHUS: Thank you, Father. I think that Mother will be wanting to see you now.

NARRATOR: Odysseus ran through the palace—toward the room that he and Penelope had once shared. A long hallway stretched out before him, and there she was, standing breathless at the other end. They ran into each other's arms and shed tears of joy.

ODYSSEUS: I thought I would never see you again.

PENELOPE: I never gave up hope. I knew you would come back to me.

ODYSSEUS: It only took me ten years, but here I am. What has happened in my absence? I want to hear every detail!

PENELOPE: Where to start? There has been so much that you've missed.

ODYSSEUS: I know. But now I need to make up for lost time.

NARRATOR: He swept Penelope up into his arms.

ODYSSEUS: Now let me see if I remember the way to our bedroom.

PENELOPE: You might be surprised. I had our bed moved into a different room.

ODYSSEUS: What? How can that be? I hand-carved it from the tree that grows up through the palace floor! It can't be moved!

PENELOPE: Just testing. I guess you really are my husband. You never know.

ODYSSEUS: How could you doubt me? You saw me shoot an arrow through twelve axe rings. *(pause)* Wait a minute. When I was disguised as a beggar, I saw you look at my scar. Did you recognize me? Was that why you proposed a contest that you knew only I could win?

PENELOPE: *(innocently)* Of course, not. I was completely fooled by your disguise.

NARRATOR: Odysseus grinned ear to ear.

ODYSSEUS: You sly devil. And I thought *I* was the best liar in the world.

PENELOPE: Odysseus.

ODYSSEUS: Yes, my dear?

PENELOPE: Welcome home.

DISCUSSION QUESTIONS

- Now that Odysseus has returned to his home, has the story of the Trojan War come full circle? Explain.
- Are Odysseus and Penelope truly in love? Explain.
- Do the suitors deserve their fate? Explain.
- Do the twelve handmaids who were executed along with the suitors deserve their fate? Explain.
- Does Odysseus deserve a happy ending? Explain.
- What obstacles did Odysseus have to overcome to once again reach his home? Which were the most difficult to overcome? Explain.
- Were all of Odysseus' obstacles external or were some internal? Explain.

UNDERSTANDING HELEN

Helen is one of mythology's most elusive characters. Many have theorized why the Greek princess decided to leave her husband, Menelaus, and become the wife of the Trojan prince Paris. Some view Helen as a victim—even going to the extreme that she was abducted against her will. Others view her as a heartless shrew, with no thought for anyone but herself. After reading "The Judgment of Paris," read this short piece on Helen. What does it have to say about her character? Does it create sympathy for her?

Sparta had always been Helen's home. The high walls of the citadel were her protection and her prison. From the day of her birth, her looks were legendary. Her royal parents, King Tyndareus and Queen Leda, knowing and fearing her reputation, took it upon themselves to shield her from the outside world. She was kept in virtual isolation. Her handmaids and serving women hated her for her perfect beauty, and the few men she encountered simply stared with grasping desire. She had become the object of all Greece's attention, but in spite of that, she felt painfully invisible.

One evening, when the princess was down in the kitchens stealing a secret snack, she heard the cooks speaking her name.

"Curse that beautiful Helen and her head-turning looks!" one was saying. "Too bad you or I weren't born a daughter of *Zeus*!"

Hiding in her corner, Helen's heart leapt.

"Rubbish! She's no god-daughter," the other cook replied. "Don't tell me you believe that lie!"

"No, it is true. I was there the day it happened. The queen was going for a stroll. I was her maidservant. All of a sudden, a swan, as big as a man, burst out of the woods. We all saw the strange look in the bird's black eyes, and the queen began to run. The rest of us stood as if in a trance, powerless to help her!"

"That's ridiculous! A swan raped the queen? Unbelievable!"

"It is true. It is true. When we found her, she said that it had been Zeus that had visited her."

"I don't believe a word of it!"

"Well, doubter, hear this: I was there the night when Princess Helen was born, and she was not born in any natural way."

"What do you mean?"

"She was hatched from an egg. I swear it to Zeus himself. We kept it in the royal bedchamber for weeks. And when it hatched, out came the princess."

"The king would raise a child that isn't his?"

"Who says he knows? Since I left that birthing chamber, I've been sworn to secrecy."

"And you're doing a good job of keeping it a secret, I see."

The two cooks laughed.

When the voices had faded away, Helen wept. Her whole life had been a lie. She was an outcast, the unwanted daughter of a god. From that day forward, she gave up any hope of ever being a part of the world around her.

Shortly after her sixteenth birthday, the news came that it was time for her to be wed. Helen was prepared, suitably numbed. She knew that every king in Greece would want her for his personal trophy. Ego could clash against ego. It would be war.

Almost every king and noble in Greece vied for her hand, showing off their riches, their land, and their power. Her one relief was that the decision was not hers to make. King Tyndareus faced the problem alone. He must choose, but his decision was bound to start a conflict. At last he resolved on a shrewd compromise. To ensure that war did not break out between the city-states, he made each of the suitors swear an oath. No matter whom he picked, the rest would protect the honor of the man he chose. If any suitor tried to take Helen by force, he would be locked into a war against the rest of Greece.

When the day came for his choice to be announced, King Tyndareus presented Helen on the walls of the city. She was adorned in the richest jewels, and her skin had been soaked in perfumes for days. She was as glorious as the goddesses of Olympus. To the spectators she had never appeared more vibrant and alive, yet in her own mind, she was already dead.

Her suitors waited below, young and old, skinny and fat. Despite their differences, she saw the same look in their eyes. It was the same look, she imagined, that her mother had seen in the swan's eyes long ago.

When her father breathlessly announced that mighty King Menelaus of Mycenae would be her betrothed, she did not falter and forced a smile from her lips. Below, she saw the fire-haired king raise his arms in triumph and rush toward the steps. She was already resolved. She would go and be the wife of a man she did not love. She would become a doll, stunning on the outside and perfectly preserved, but inside only stuffing, an empty space where *Helen* had never been given a chance to exist.

DISCUSSION QUESTIONS

- Name some ways in which Helen is more fortunate than most Greek women. In what ways is she less fortunate?
- What type of modern person is similar to Helen, someone who feels eternally trapped?
- If you were trapped like Helen and had a chance to escape, would you take it? What would the consequences be? Explain.

SACRIFICE AT AULIS

While the Trojan War leads to the deaths of many noble warriors, it also causes the deaths of many innocents. After reading "The Tides of War," read this selection and accompanying poem about the princess Iphigenia, the daughter of Agamemnon.

With Odysseus and Achilles, the two wayward warriors, back in hand, Agamemnon commanded all troops to convene at the port of Aulis. From there they would launch their "thousand ships" for Troy. As the companies marched to the sea, a seemingly unimportant event happened. A family of rabbits, trying to dart in between the feet of the marching troops, was trampled to death. When the armies arrived at Aulis, they boarded their ships, chanting for victory, and waited for the contrary winds to change direction. But for days the winds continued to blow against them, keeping them firmly in place. Their hopes began to sour. These winds could mean only one thing: The gods were unhappy.

Calchas, a prophet Agamemnon had brought to interpret the will of the gods, beseeched Olympus, asking what must be done to satisfy whomever they had angered. Artemis, the goddess of the moon and wild creatures, answered. The Greeks troops had thoughtlessly murdered a family of rabbits and shown no remorse for their actions. Therefore, she would not allow the winds to blow until Agamemnon, the leaders of the armies, agreed to sacrifice a member of his own family, his daughter Iphigenia.

Agamemnon was flabbergasted. As he stood upon the brink of the greatest military campaign in Greek history, the gods were asking him to murder his own flesh and blood. The prophet's word quickly spread through the warriors and kings. They watched their leader expectantly. Would he disband the army he had worked so hard to organize? Would he risk mutiny and possibly his own death for such a cowardly act? Or would he allow his daughter to die?

At last he decided that the gods must be appeased. Iphigenia was the apple of his wife's eye, and he knew she would never willingly let her go. Therefore, he devised a trick. He sent word to Clytemnestra, his wife and queen, to prepare Iphigenia for a long journey to the sea. The handsome Achilles has requested her hand in marriage, he said, in return for his allegiance to the cause. Reaching Mycenae, the news thrilled Clytemnestra, who eagerly prepared Iphigenia for her seaside wedding. The army had been camped at Aulis for weeks when they finally saw the wedding procession approaching. Iphigenia, flowers pinned into her hair, rode within the marriage cart, smiling broadly at the happy prospect of her future. When she came close enough to see the faces of the soldiers, they did not reflect her joy. Something was wrong, she told herself. When she finally beheld her father, he looked far older than she remembered. More importantly, he refused to meet her gaze.

As she stepped from the cart, Iphigenia felt forceful arms grab her at either side. They pulled her to the top of a rocky hill, where a makeshift altar had been prepared. The princess began to sob. Throwing her down upon the damp stones, she heard the dim voice of her father, "Behold, Artemis. Take your sacrifice, and let come the winds of war."

"IPHIGENIA" BY ALFRED, LORD TENNYSON (1809-1892)

I was cut off from hope in that sad place,
    Which yet to name my spirit loathes and fears;
My father held his hand upon his face;
        I, blinded by my tears,

Still strove to speak; my voice was thick with sighs,
    As in a dream. Dimly I could decry
The stern black-bearded kings, with wolfish eyes,
        Waiting to see me die.

The tall masts quivered as they lay afloat,
    The temples and the people and the shore;
One drew a sharp knife through my tender throat
        Slowly, and—nothing more.

DISCUSSION QUESTIONS

- What is especially tragic about Iphigenia's death?
- Does Agamemnon have a choice in sacrificing his daughter? Explain.
- What do you think of the poem, "Iphigenia" by Alfred, Lord Tennyson? Which details are the most effective?
- According to some sources, it was Odysseus who came up with the idea of a wedding to Achilles in order to trick Iphigenia. How is this trick excessively cruel? Does it sound like something Odysseus would do? Explain.
- Later Greeks were appalled by this record of human sacrifice in their past and created an alternate version of the story: The alternate version claims that a moment before the Greek kings put the knife to Iphigenia's throat, Artemis replaces the maiden with a deer and spirits her far away. What does this change about the story? Which version do you like better? Explain.
- After he survives ten years of fighting and returns from the Trojan War, Agamemnon is murdered by his wife, Clytemnestra. She has vowed revenge ever since the sacrifice of Iphigenia. Is this a fitting end for Agamemnon? Explain.

ACHILLES' LAST STAND

After reading "The Rage of Achilles," read this selection to learn about the Greek warrior's famous death (or at least one version of it).

Hector's death did not end the war as the Greeks had hoped. Without their mighty commander, the Trojans debated whether the war should be continued at all. The Trojan prince Paris swore he would never return Helen to the Greeks, and so the fighting must continue. About this time reinforcements for the Trojans arrived from afar. An army of Amazons, a race of fierce female warriors who lived on the very edge of the world, arrived under the command of their queen, Penthesilea. They had heard of the war and wished to aid the Trojans.

There were many strange tales told about this strange race of female warriors. They were said to be the daughters of Ares, and absolutely no men were allowed in their tribe. It was said that the only interaction they had with men was once a year they met to procreate and continue their line. When male babies were born to the Amazons, they would kill them on the spot. The female children were kept and trained to be warriors. According to another rumor, Amazons ceremoniously removed one of their breasts to make firing a bow easier. One thing was sure: The Amazons were fierce warriors, and they aided the Trojans well.

In the thick of battle, Achilles came face to face with the warrior-queen, Penthesilea. The two dueled, and the queen was slain when Achilles skewered her and her horse with a single spear-thrust. But when Achilles pulled loose her helmet, he was shocked by the queen's goddess-like beauty. The warrior fell instantly in love and regretted that he had killed such a glorious creature instead of making her his wife.

The loss of the Amazon queen was only a temporary setback for the Trojans as further reinforcements arrived. Prince Memnon of Ethiopia, a relative of King Priam, arrived with his own army of warriors to aid the Trojans. The Ethiopians were a dark-skinned race from lands far south of Troy. Memnon was said to be the son of Eos, the dawn goddess. With the arrival of the Ethiopians, the battle was thick once again—that is, until the ruthless Achilles met Prince Memnon in man-to-man combat and ran him through the heart. Seeing their leader fall, the Ethiopians transformed into birds and winged themselves away. The following morning the sky remained dark because Eos, the goddess of dawn, mourned her son and vowed the sun would never rise again. Finally, Zeus convinced her to put away her grief and allow the sun to rise.

Achilles did not have long to savor his victory over Prince Memnon. The god Apollo had vowed to put an end to Achilles' bloodthirsty rampages. The god did not think it was not fair that Achilles was protected by the powers of the River Styx.

As Paris watched the Greeks and Trojans battle from the safety of the city walls, Apollo appeared by the prince's side and inspired him to shoot an arrow at Achilles. Paris fired his arrow down from the heights of the Trojan walls. It was too far a distance for any mortal shot to succeed, but Apollo carried and guided the arrow directly to the one spot of weakness on Achilles' body—the warrior's heel. All of Achilles' vulnerability had been concentrated in this one spot, and Paris' arrow spelled his demise. When the shaft struck, Achilles knew that he had been dealt a mortal blow. In spite of this, he flew into a rampage and killed many men—until at last the life and strength finally drained from him and he died upon the battlefield. Never once had he been defeated in hand-to-hand combat.

Immediately a furious battle ensued over the body of Achilles. The Trojans wanted his body so they could desecrate it as Achilles had done to Hector's body. The Greeks, initially shocked by Achilles' fall, rallied around Odysseus and the great Greek warrior, Ajax. The two warriors both fought valiantly to keep Achilles' body from falling into Trojan hands. The Trojans finally retreated, and the body was safe.

Once Achilles was mourned and his body was buried, Odysseus and Ajax both made claims to Achilles' god-given armor. Their argument became so heated that Agamemnon and Menelaus had to intervene. They awarded Odysseus the armor of Achilles. Ajax was infuriated by this verdict and swore it was a slight on his honor. He swore that Odysseus had used trickery or bribery to get the armor. In retribution Ajax decided to murder Agamemnon, Menelaus, and Odysseus in their sleep. Fortunately, the goddess Athena was watching out for Odysseus and the other Greeks. As Ajax snuck toward the tents of his victims, the goddess sent a madness upon him. While he thought he was slaying his enemies, he was in actuality slaughtering livestock among the Greek herds. The horrible cries of cattle and sheep awoke the Greeks. When they found Ajax, he was surrounded by the bloody corpses of livestock, holding the severed head of a ram insulting it as if it was the head of Odysseus. Suddenly, the madness sent by Athena left Ajax's mind, and he realized what he had done. The gathered Greeks could barely contain their laughter. Ajax, even further embarrassed and shamed, drew his sword and fell upon it.

DISCUSSION QUESTIONS

- Is it ironic that Achilles is slain by Paris? Explain.
- The male writers of Greek mythology are making a statement about powerful women by their characterization of Penthesilea and the Amazons. What do you think this statement is?
- The detail of Achilles' vulnerable heel does not appear in the earliest accounts of the hero. In fact, the *Iliad* never mentions it. Homer even says that Achilles receives a wound during the Trojan War—something that could not happen if he was truly invulnerable. Some theorize that Paris' arrows must have been poisoned. This would explain why one arrow could bring down the great warrior. They believe the myth of Achilles' vulnerable heel was added later to make his death more symbolic. What do you think of Achilles' heel?
- Is Ajax's death tragic? Explain.
- Compare this version of Achilles' death with the version presented in "Wounded by Love." Which version do you like better? Explain.

WOUNDED BY LOVE

This selection tells a different version of the death of Achilles. In this version the mighty warrior is brought down by a love affair with Polyxena, one of Priam's daughters. After reading the worksheet "Achilles' Last Stand," read this selection and hear another version of Achilles' death.

Polyxena was the youngest and fairest daughter of the Trojan king Priam. When she and her young brother, Troilus, were foolish enough to leave the safety of the walls of Troy to visit a wilderness well, they were ambushed there by the warrior, Achilles. Troilus tried to defend his sister but was hacked down by the ruthless Greek. When Achilles laid eyes on the frightened and weeping Polyxena, he was instantly struck by her beauty. Achilles begged the maiden not to be frightened of him and assured her that she was in no danger. To show his goodwill, he said he would allow her to return to her people, but only if she promised to meet him in three days' time at the temple of Apollo that lay on the Trojan plain. Polyxena agreed and ran back to the safety of the city walls.

Once back in Troy, she told her older brother Paris about the death of Troilus and her meeting with Achilles. The girl had no intention of honoring her promise to the Greek. She never wanted to lay eyes on him again, but Paris saw an opportunity. He told Polyxena that Achilles must be smitten with her—otherwise he never would have left her unharmed. He instructed her to meet Achilles at the temple and feign an attraction for him. Perhaps she could learn something that could help the Trojans defeat him. Polyxena reluctantly agreed.

The night of the meeting arrived, and Polyxena made her way outside the city walls to the temple of Apollo. Achilles was there as promised—wearing the robes of a nobleman, not the armor she had seen him in earlier. It was obvious to Polyxena that the warrior was smitten with her, and she pretended to return his feelings as Paris had instructed. Achilles spoke to her for hours—about the war, about his home, about her beauty—and when the night had passed, he asked to meet Polyxena again. She agreed.

This continued for weeks. Polyxena would meet Achilles at the temple at night—sharing in chaste conversation, the light of love shining in the warrior's eyes. Yet one night, Achilles began to speak of his mother. He told Polyxena that his mother was Thetis the sea nymph and when he was just a boy she had taken him into the Underworld to dip him in the River Styx. Although he had never told anyone else, he knew there was only one spot on his entire body where he could be harmed: a tender spot upon the ankle, where the waters had failed to touch. Polyxena rolled this information over in her mind throughout the night, and when she returned to Troy, she gleefully presented it to her brother.

The next day a secret message reached King Priam. It was from Achilles. He promised to arrange a treaty between the Greeks and the Trojans if Priam would promise Polyxena to him in marriage. Priam was surprised by the proposal, unaware of the secret meetings. Paris told his father that the message must be a trick and to ignore it. Only Paris and Polyxena knew that it was in earnest. Paris himself sent word (disguised as a message from his father) to Achilles agreeing to the marriage. Polyxena would be at the temple of Apollo at midnight, and there she would become his bride.

Polyxena made her way to the temple once more. This time she wore a bridal gown. Achilles eagerly greeted her there. He told her what a happy man her father had made him, and he would do all in his power to bring peace between their peoples so that they could live in happiness. Polyxena feigned happiness herself, and the two began the ritual of marriage before the sacred altar of Apollo.

It was then that Paris sprang his trap. From the shadows of the temple, he released a shaft from his marvelous bow. The arrow found its mark in Achilles' ankle, and the warrior fell forward upon the altar. Achilles turned his eyes toward Polyxena—the truth breaking in upon him. He had been betrayed by his one and only love. Polyxena backed away from the dying warrior, no pity in her face. She remembered how ruthlessly he murdered her brother. Her unmerciful face was the last sight Achilles saw as his lifeblood pooled about him.

When the Greeks found the lifeless body of Achilles draped across the altar of Apollo, a single arrow in his heel, they could not understand how the warrior had come to such a fate. They did not know that this was, in fact, his second wound. First, he had been wounded by love.

After the fall of Troy, the Greeks take the women of the royal household prisoner, Polyxena among them. The spirit of Achilles appears to the Greeks and tells them that if they do not sacrifice Polyxena upon his grave, he will summon winds to prevent them from reaching Greece safely. The Greeks comply, and Polyxena is sacrificed upon the grave of Achilles.

DISCUSSION QUESTIONS

- Was it right for Polyxena to trick Achilles? Explain.
- Why does Paris refuse Achilles' offer of peace?
- Does Polyxena deserve her fate? Explain.
- How is Polyxena similar to Iphigenia, the daughter of Agamemnon?
- What do you think of this story? Does it "ring true" to the character of Achilles—to the rest of the story of the Trojan War? Explain.
- The story of Achilles' love for Polyxena was added by later Roman writers writing much later than Homer and others who first wrote about the Trojan War. They preferred stories to be a bit more romantic (a word that means "idealized" originating from the term *Roman*). How is this version of Achilles' death more romantic than the original?
- Other versions of this same story say that Polyxena actually returned Achilles' love and was followed to their secret meeting place by Paris, who just happened to shoot Achilles in his one vulnerable spot. Which version do you like better? Explain.
- This same version of the story paints Polyxena's sacrifice in a romantic light. Achilles' spirit asks for her sacrifice so that they can be together in the afterlife. What do you think of this "romantic" slant?

THE LOTUS EATERS AND THE SIRENS

Two of Odysseus' most memorable adventures involve a strange people called the Lotus Eaters, who spend the entire day grazing on an intoxicating fruit called lotus, and super-natural creatures called Sirens, who lure sailors to their death with their irresistible voices. Odysseus barely rescues his men from the allure of the lotus plant, for those who have tasted the fruit try to escape from the ship. Odysseus has to tie them to their rowing benches to keep them from jumping overboard. As for the Sirens, Odysseus plugs the ears of his men with beeswax to keep them from hearing the song of the Sirens. These tales need no other teller than Homer himself. After reading "Searching for Odysseus," read these two excerpts from the *Odyssey*.

THE LOTUS EATERS

"[O]ur squadron reached the land of the Lotus-eaters,
people who eat the lotus, mellow fruit and flower.
We disembarked on the coast, drew water there
and crewmen snatched a meal by the swift ships.
Once we'd had our fill of food and drink I sent
a detail ahead, two picked men and a third, a runner,
to scout out who might live there—men like us perhaps,
who live on bread? So off they went and soon enough
they mingled among the natives, Lotus-eaters, Lotus-eaters
who had no notion of killing my companions, not at all,
they simply gave them the lotus to taste instead…
Any crewman who ate the lotus, the honey-sweet fruit,
lost all desire to send a message back, much less return,
their only wish to linger there with the Lotus-eaters,
grazing on lotus, all memory of the journey home
dissolved forever." (*Odyssey* Book IX, Lines 93-110 , Trans. Robert Fagles)

THE SIRENS

"Now with a sharp sword I sliced an ample wheel of beeswax
down into pieces, kneaded them in my two strong hands

and the wax soon grew soft, worked by my strength
and Helios' burning rays, the sun at high noon,
and I stopped the ears of my comrades one by one.
They bound me hand and foot in the tight ship—
erect at the mast-block, lashed by ropes to the mast—
and rowed and churned the whitecaps stroke on stroke.
We were just offshore as far as a man's shout can carry,
scudding close, when the Sirens sensed at once a ship
was racing past and burst into their high, thrilling song:
"Come closer, famous Odysseus—[Greece's] pride and glory—
moor your ship on our coast so you can hear our song!
Never has any sailor passed our shores in his black craft
until he has heard our honeyed voices pouring from our lips,
and once he hears to his heart's content sails on, a wiser man.
We know all the pains that the [Greeks] and Trojans once endured
on the spreading plain of Troy when the gods willed it so—
all that comes to pass on the fertile earth, we know it all!"
So they sent their ravishing voices out across the air
and the heart inside me throbbed to listen longer.
I signaled the crew with frowns to set me free—
they flung themselves at the oars and rowed on harder.
Perimedes and Eurylochus springing up at once
to bind me faster with rope on chafing rope.
But once we'd left the Sirens fading in our wake,
once we could hear their song no more, their urgent call—
my steadfast crew was quick to remove the wax I'd used
to seal their ears and loosed the bonds that lashed me."
(*Odyssey*, Book XII, Lines 189-217, Trans. Robert Fagles)

DISCUSSION QUESTIONS

- What could be a modern parallel for the addictive nature of the lotus fruit?
- In the episode with the Sirens, why does Odysseus leave his own ears unplugged?
- How is the test of the Sirens similar to the test of the Lotus Eaters?
- Homer does not describe the Sirens' appearance, but later myth-makers described them as half-woman, half-bird creatures. Others said they were mermaid-like creatures. (In every case they were described as female.) How do you picture the Sirens? Is it more or less effective to leave their appearance ambiguous? Explain.

BETWEEN SCYLLA AND CHARYBDIS

Circe the Witch gives Odysseus advice on how to pass a series of dangerous tests that lie ahead for the hero. One is the Sirens. Another involves the two monsters Scylla and Charybdis. They both lived in a narrow seaway between two cliffs. Sailors had to pick which monster they would rather face because there was no way to avoid them both. (Our modern saying "between Scylla and Charybdis" means choosing between two unpleasant choices.) The third involves the golden cattle of the sun god Helios. After reading "Circe the Witch," read this piece about Odysseus' further adventures.

Before Odysseus left the witch's isle, Circe warned Odysseus of a treacherous strait he must navigate. Two monsters lived in this narrow sea-way. Three times a day, a gigantic underwater monster, Charybdis, opened its gullet, sucking the surrounding waters into the vortex of its mouth. When the terrifying whirlpool subsided, Charybdis would then spray the consumed water high into the heavens, destroying whatever had fallen into its clutches. If a ship kept close to the rocky edge of the strait in order to avoid Charybdis, it faced another monster named Scylla, a creature with six dog-faced, snake-necked heads, who picked sailors off the passing ships as an easy snack. Those who passed through the strait must choose between the twin terrors—between Scylla and Charybdis.

Odysseus set sail. They soon approached the strait that housed Scylla and Charybdis. They heard the roar of the whirlpool far away. Odysseus warned his men to row close to the shore. Although he planned to tell them of the threat of Scylla, he realized that this would only terrify them further, so he kept his knowledge to himself. The whirlpool monster appeared ahead, sucking the sea down into its belly. The crew rowed hard to shore, keeping the craft as close to the rocks as possible, avoiding the swirl of the current. As they did, Odysseus kept his eyes on the cliffs overhead. He knew Scylla was lurking there. Perhaps they would escape her notice.

At that moment Scylla struck. Six rowers disappeared from their posts in the same instant. The crew—covered with their comrades' blood—stared helplessly as the six terrifying heads of Scylla swallowed her captives down raw, barely chewing with her razor sharp teeth. "Row! Row!" Odysseus yelled. "Before the monster takes us all!" With one final burst of speech, the ship passed through the strait—beyond the reach of Scylla and Charybdis—and out of danger.

Circe had warned Odysseus, if he did in fact make it past the strait of Scylla and Charybdis, he would come to the isle of Helios, her father. Odysseus and his men should not harm the cattle they found there, for these were Helios' cattle. If Odysseus and his men harmed them in any way, the gods would take revenge.

Once Odysseus and his men were through the perilous strait, the island of Helios came into view. Odysseus knew they should simply sail on by, but his men begged him to stop. They were so hungry, so exhausted from the day's work. He reluctantly agreed with a warning: "Do not touch the golden cattle of this land."

His men obeyed, and they camped on the island for the night. In the morning they found the winds blowing against them. Many days passed in this way; the wind continued to blow against their port, and they could not sail. Supplies grew short, and Odysseus' men began to hungrily eye the shining cattle that grazed on the nearby hillside. When Odysseus went into the hills one day to call out to the gods, the men snapped: They slaughtered the cattle of Helios and cooked their golden meat. Even on the spit, the cattle continued to moo, and the cuts shone as the men gulped them down. When Odysseus returned and saw what had been done, he knew they were all doomed.

Soon enough the winds stopped, and the ship took to sea, yet they did not sail far before a raging storm overtook them. Helios had informed Zeus about the death of his cattle. As the black clouds boiled overhead, the lord of the gods himself aimed a thunderbolt at Odysseus' tiny craft. In a spray of planks and salt water, the ship was destroyed. Men flew into the brine. Only Odysseus survived—clinging to the single surviving piece of his vessel.

DISCUSSION QUESTIONS

- Is it fair for Odysseus *not* to warn his men about the dangers of Scylla and Charybdis? Explain.
- Why do you think he chooses to withhold this information?
- After the episode involving the cattle of Helios, do you think Odysseus' men deserve to die? Explain.

TROJAN WAR FIND·IT PUZZLE

CAN YOU FIND ALL THESE ITEMS HIDDEN IN THE PICTURE?

- A Copy of the *Iliad*
- A Flock of Seagulls
- Achilles
- Ajax
- Ant
- Aphrodite, Goddess of Love
- Aphrodite's Magical Cloud
- Apollo, Archer of Olympus
- Apollo's Temple
- Ares, God of War
- Artemis, Goddess of the Moon
- Athena, Goddess of Wisdom
- Battering Rams (2)
- Briseis
- Calchas the Prophet
- Catapult
- Egg
- Golden Apple
- Greek Ship
- Harpy, Half-Woman/Half-Bird
- Hephaestus, God of the Forge
- Head of Medusa
- Hearts (10)
- Hector
- Helen
- Hera, Queen of the Gods
- Hermes, Messenger God
- Horses (2)
- Ladder
- Laocoön
- Messenger Crow
- Odysseus
- Paris
- Peacock
- Pegasus Silhouette
- Pitcher
- Poseidon, God of the Seas
- *Reaching Olympus* Textbook
- Sheep (1)
- Snake
- Swan
- Swords (5)
- The Word "Homer"
- The Word "Styx"
- Thetis, Mother of Achilles
- Trojan Horse Structure
- Zeus, Lord of the Gods

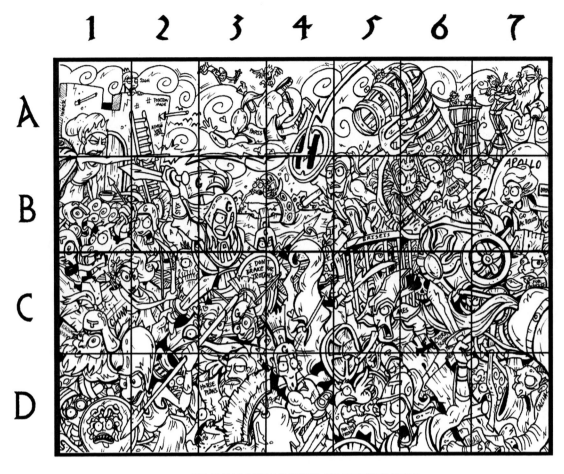

TROJAN WAR FIND·IT PUZZLE KEY

A Copy of the *Iliad*, **D6-D7**

A Flock of Seagulls, **A2**

Achilles, **B2-B3-C3**

Ajax, **B2**

Ant, **A7-B7**

Aphrodite, **C3**

Aphrodite's Magical Cloud, **B4-C4**

Apollo, **B6**

Apollo's Temple, **B7**

Ares, **C5-C6**

Artemis, **C1-C2**

Athena, **D1-D2**

Battering Rams (2), **C1, C6-D6**

Briseis, **B5-C5**

Calchas the Prophet, **D7**

Catapult, **B1-B2**

Egg, **D7**

Golden Apple, **D5**

Greek Ship, **B2-B3**

Harpy, **A3-A4**

Hephaestus, **C7**

Head of Medusa, **D1**

Hearts (10), **D3, C3, C3, C4, C4, C4, D4, C2, A3, A3, A4, A4, B4**

Hector, **B4-B5**

Helen, **A1-A2**

Hera, **A1-B1**

Hermes, **A3**

Horses (2), **C4, C7**

Ladder, **A2**

Laocoön, **B3-B4**

Messenger Crow, **D5**

Odysseus, **D3**

Paris, **A3-A4**

Peacock, **B7**

Pegasus Silhouette, **C6**

Pitcher, **D2**

Poseidon, **B5-B6**

Reaching Olympus Textbook, **C1**

Sheep (1), **D7**

Snake, **D2-D3**

Swan, **C2-C3**

Swords (5), **C5, D4, C6, C2, B2**

The Name "Homer" **A1**

The Word "Styx" **B2**

Thetis, **B7**

Trojan Horse Structure, **A5-A6**

Zeus, **A7**

THE TROJAN WAR GAME

PREMISE: In this game players assume the identity of a character from the Trojan War and "battle" one another. Players have a certain number of troops under their command. When all the troops under a character's command have been "killed," the character dies as well, and the player is out of the game. Players roll a die to determine who wins a particular battle-round. Whichever side, Greeks or Trojans, that inflicts the most "kills" on the opposing team by the end of the game wins.

NUMBER OF PLAYERS: 10-40 (over 40 can play, but you will need more Greek and Trojan character names than are listed here)

LEARNING GOALS: Since students are assigned individual characters and must respond to those character names, the roleplaying aspect will aid them in remembering which characters fought on which side of the war.

ITEMS NEEDED

3 dice
1 marker for every student
3 pairs of desks, facing each other, labeled as "battle stations"
1 piece of scratch paper

GETTING STARTED

1. Equally divide your class into two sides: Greek and Trojan. (These numbers do not have to be perfectly equal but should be as close as possible.)
2. Have the Greek players sit on the opposite side of the room from the Trojans.
3. Assign a Trojan War character to each player. (You can let them pick their own character. See the included chart for a list of characters.)
4. Make a list for yourself of every character name that is used. This will be important later.
5. Pass out the Trojan War game worksheet (copied front and back, pgs. 185-186).
6. Distribute a brightly colored marker to each player.
7. Have each player choose 20 units to command. Each type of troop costs a different number of units. Chariot warriors cost 5 units and are very powerful, while footmen only cost 1 unit but can be very easily killed. Players should indicate which troops they choose by circling them with a bright marker. Players should carefully double-check their totals, and players whose troops do not add up to a total of 20 units should be removed from the game.
8. Have players choose a patron god or goddess and a corresponding lucky number from the front side of the game sheet. This number cannot hurt them when they are being attacked. Have them write this number in the indicated space on the opposite side of the game sheet.

9. Designate at least 3 battle stations. A battle station is two desks facing one another in the middle of the room. This is where the students will "do battle." **Note:** You can create as many battle stations as you desire, but 3-4 is a good number for a typical class.
10. Place one die at each battle station.

PLAYING THE GAME

1. Using your list of character names, call out the first character name you wrote down. (Place a tally mark by each name each time you call it. This way you can make sure everyone gets the same number of turns.)
2. The character whose name you called is now the challenger.
3. The challenger makes his or her way to a battle station and chooses an opponent from the opposite side. (Example: You call the character name "Achilles." The player designated as Achilles goes forward to the battle station and says, "I challenge Hector!" The player designated as Hector must come forward to the battle station.)
4. Once both players are at the battle station, the challenger examines the opponent's sheet. The challenger chooses which type of unit on the opponent's sheet to attack. (The opponent gets no chance to attack.)
5. The challenger indicates which type of troop he or she is going to attack on the opponent's sheet. (Example: Achilles says, "I'm going to attack your chariot.")
6. The challenger and opponent re-examine the numbers needed for a kill. (This same chart is listed on each player's game sheet.)

> **Chariot Warriors**   **Challenger must roll a 5 or higher to kill**
> **Spear Warriors**   **Challenger must roll a 4 or higher to kill**
> **Javelin Throwers**   **Challenger must roll a 3 or higher to kill**
> **Footmen**   **Challenger must roll a 2 or higher to kill**

7. The opponent must reveal his or her lucky number. This number will not harm the opponent if the challenger rolls it (even if it normally would result in a kill).
8. The challenger rolls the die.
9. If the challenger rolls the needed number (and it is not the opponent's lucky number), the challenger can X out the attacked troop on the opponent's paper. (Example: Achilles is attacking Hector's chariot. He knows he must roll a 5 or higher and Hector's lucky number is 5. This means he must roll a 6. Achilles rolls and gets a 6. He reaches over and X's out one of Hector's chariots.)
10. If the challenger does not roll the needed number (or rolls the opponent's lucky number), the opponent gets to remove a troop from the challenger's paper of equal or lesser value. (Example: Achilles has to roll a 6 to kill Hector's chariot, but he rolls a 4. Hector reaches across and X's out one of Achilles' chariots.)
11. Once the challenger has attacked, both players leave the battle station and go back to their respective sides.
12. Repeat the process of calling out characters' names, keeping track of how many times each character has gone. Keep the battle stations filled. (Make sure if you call Achilles and Hector to battle at the same time, they don't battle one another. The name you call is the challenger and should choose an opponent who is not currently a challenger.)

13. When all of a player's troops have been killed, the player should bring his or her playing sheet to you. This means the player is out of the game, and the opposing side gets a point for "killing" that player. (Example: If Achilles kills Hector's last troop, Hector is removed from the game, and the Greeks get 1 point.) Also remember to remove the player's character name from the list since he or she will no longer be called to battle.

WINNING THE GAME

There are two ways of winning the game. The game can be played until every player on one side has been defeated. (Example: All the Greeks die, so the Trojans are declared the winners.) Or a certain time limit can be declared. (Example: The game will be played for two class periods, and the side with the most points at the end of the second class period will be declared the winner.) Depending on the time available to you, this game can be played over several class periods. **Note:** Due to set-up time, the game is probably too complicated to play in a single class period.

CLARIFICATIONS

- It is best to do several "sample" battles before actually beginning the game.
- It will take about 10 minutes before the players completely understand the rules, but once they do, they will enjoy it immensely!
- Lucky numbers do not protect a challenger, only an opponent. For example, Achilles' lucky number is 4. Achilles challenges Hector but does not roll the number he needs to kill Hector's chariot. He rolls a 4 instead, so Hector gets to kill one of Achilles' chariots. Achilles objects because his lucky number is 4, so it shouldn't hurt him. This is not correct. Lucky numbers do not protect challengers. Hector is allowed to take the chariot.
- When challengers fail to roll the needed number (and should lose a troop equal to the one they were trying to kill) but have no troops of equal value, they must lose a troop from the closest value. (For example, Achilles is supposed to lose a footman for attacking Hector's footman and failing to roll the needed number. Achilles only has chariots at this point of the game. Since chariots are the closest to a footman Achilles has, he must lose a chariot.)

FUN ADDITIONS

- At the beginning of a class period ask several questions about the Trojan War. Those students who answer correctly can be given extra units to add onto their game sheet.
- Take on the role of a Greek god and choose to enter the battle at any point with your own playing sheet.
- Take on the role of Zeus and threaten to "zap" any players that get too rowdy or don't follow the rules.
- Give a fun prize to the side that wins the war.
- Divide the room into two sides (Greek and Trojan) several days before you actually play the Trojan War game. Have the two sides face their desks toward one another. Have each group make a banner for their team and hang it on the wall.

- Assign characters a few days before you actually play the game. Have the players research their characters, finding out what role they played in the Trojan War.
- Incorporate the Trojan War game into several days' worth of lessons. For example, read a little about the Trojan War and then spend the last half of class playing the game. Once the students are familiar with the game, they will be able to set up quickly.
- Make a spying rule. When characters "die," it frees their spirit from the rules of the mortal world. They can cross over to the opposite side and scout out opponents' sheets, looking for characters who are near death and reporting this back to their teammates.

GREEK CHARACTERS	TROJAN CHARACTERS
Achilles	Aeneas
Agamemnon	Andromache
Ajax	Aphrodite
Athena	Apollo
Briseis	Ares
Calchas	Artemis
Chryseis	Astyanax
Diomedes	Cassandra
Hera	Hector
Menelaus	Hecuba
Nestor	Helen
Odysseus	Helenus
Palamedes	Iulus
Patroclus	Laocoön
Philoctetes	Memnon
Polites	Pandarus
Poseidon	Paris
Pyrrhus	Penthesilea
Sinon	Polyxena
Thetis	Priam

THE TROJAN WAR GAME

TROOPS: Every player (that's you) is allowed 20 units of troops under his or her command. Different types of troops count as more or fewer units. For example, chariot warriors count as 5 units, while footmen count for only 1. Of course, a chariot warrior is much harder to kill than a footman. To indicate how you would like to disperse your 20 units, circle the troops you choose on the opposite side of this sheet. (Make sure the units you choose add up to 20, or you'll be removed from the game.) **Remember:** Choose wisely. When all of your troops are eliminated, your character "dies," you are out of the game, and the opposing team gets a point.

TYPE OF TROOP	COST	ADVANTAGE
Chariot Warriors	5 units	Challenger must roll a 5 or higher to kill
Spear Warriors	4 units	Challenger must roll a 4 or higher to kill
Javelin Throwers	3 units	Challenger must roll a 3 or higher to kill
Footmen	2 units	Challenger must roll a 2 or higher to kill

PATRON GOD OR GODDESS: Every player should choose a patron god or goddess, who will give you a lucky number. When you are attacked, this number will not be able to harm you. Choose a patron god or goddess, and write the associated number in the indicated space on the reverse side of this sheet.

GREEKS	LUCKY NUMBER
Athena	6
Poseidon	5
Hera	4
Thetis	3

TROJANS	LUCKY NUMBER
Apollo	6
Artemis	5
Ares	4
Aphrodite	3

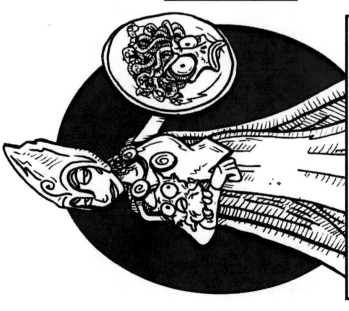

PREPARE FOR BATTLE!

Using the reverse side of this sheet:

1. Write down your character's name.
2. Choose your troops. (Make sure your troops add up to 20 units.)
3. Select a patron god or goddess and write down the lucky number.

NAME: _____

LUCKY NUMBER: _____   GREEK/TROJAN NAME: _____

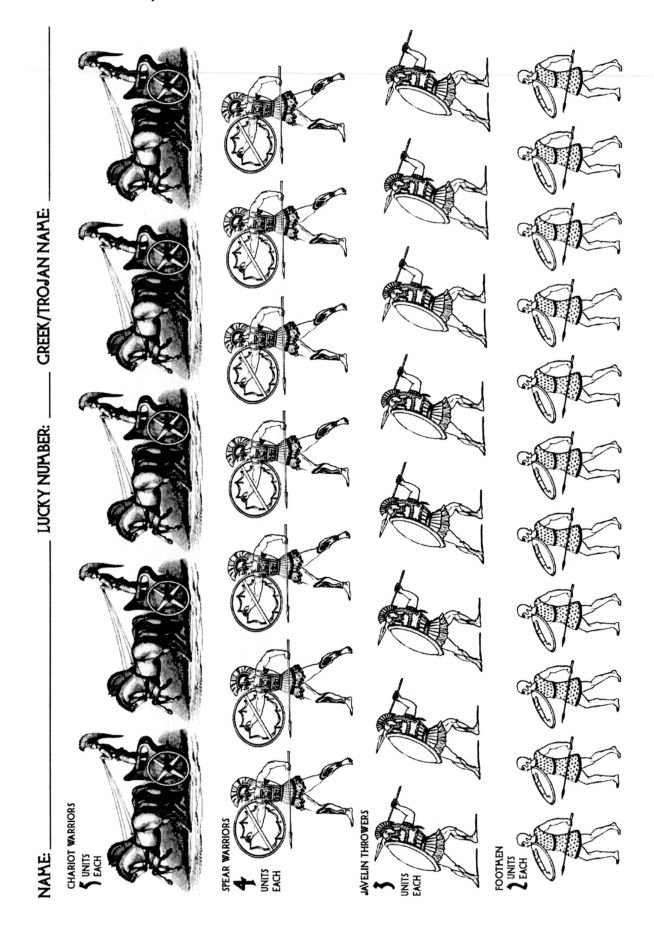

CHARIOT WARRIORS
5 UNITS EACH

SPEAR WARRIORS
4 UNITS EACH

JAVELIN THROWERS
3 UNITS EACH

FOOTMEN
2 UNITS EACH

WHO'S WHO IN THE TROJAN WAR

Below is a list of some of the key players in the Trojan War and their affiliations.

GREEKS

Achilles The most powerful Greek warrior

Agamemnon Leader of the Greek armies

Ajax Mighty warrior, cousin of Achilles

Athena Goddess of battle and wisdom

Briseis Captured Trojan girl, concubine

Calchas Greek prophet

Chryseis Captured Trojan girl, concubine

Diomedes Warrior of great renown

Hera Queen of the gods

Menelaus King, brother of Agamemnon, husband of Helen

Myrmidons Achilles' troop of fighting men

Nestor Oldest and wisest Greek at Troy

Odysseus Warrior known for his tricky mind

Patroclus Warrior, beloved friend of Achilles

Philoctetes Warrior, fights with a famed bow

Poseidon God of the seas and oceans

Pyrrhus Warrior, son of Achilles

Thetis Sea nymph, mother of Achilles

TROJANS

Aeneas Second-best warrior for the Trojans, son of Aphrodite

Andromache Wife of Hector

Aphrodite Goddess of love and beauty

Apollo God of light, truth, and poetry

Ares God of war

Artemis Goddess of the moon and the hunt

Astyanax Hector's young son

Cassandra Princess of Troy, cursed prophetess

Hector Oldest prince of Troy, greatest warrior for the Trojans

Hecuba Queen of Troy

Helen Wife of Menelaus, elopes with Paris

Helenus Son of Priam, prophet to the gods

Laocoön Son of Priam, prophet to the gods

Memnon Ethiopian king, ally of Troy

Paris Young prince of Troy

Penthesilea Amazon warrior queen

Polyxena Young princess of Troy

Priam Aged king of Troy, father of fifty sons

GLOSSARY OF IMPORTANT CHARACTERS

Achilles Greatest Greek warrior in the Trojan War, son of Thetis the sea nymph, trained by Chiron the centaur, took one of Paris' arrows in the heel and died during the Trojan War.

Aegisthus Lover of Clytemnestra, accomplice in the murder of Agamemnon, killed by Orestes

Aeneas Trojan son of Aphrodite, after the sack of Troy set out on his own quest to start a new city-state based on the legacy of Troy

Aeolus Lord of the winds

Agamemnon Ruler of Mycenae, brother of Menelaus, leader of the united Greek armies, slain by his wife, Clytemnestra

Ajax Greek chieftain who committed suicide during the Trojan War

Andromache Wife of Hector, taken into captivity after the Trojan War by Pyrrhus, the son of Achilles

Aphrodite (Roman: Venus) Goddess of love and beauty, born from the foam of the sea, sister of Zeus, wife of Hephaestus, lover of Ares, mother of Eros and Aeneas

Apollo (Roman: Apollo) God of light and truth, twin brother to Artemis, son of Zeus, gifted in poetry and the playing of the lyre. Apollo's oracle in Delphi was renowned throughout ancient Greece for her prophetic wisdom.

Ares (Roman: Mars) God of war, son of Zeus

Artemis (Roman: Diana) Goddess of wild things, goddess of the moon, twin sister to Apollo, daughter of Zeus, virgin goddess

Astyanax Infant son of Hector and Andromache, during the sack of Troy he was flung from the walls of the city to his death

Atalanta Heroine of ancient Greece, known for her nearly superhuman speed, helped to kill the giant boar of Calydon, joined Jason on his quest for the Golden Fleece

Athena (Roman: Minerva) Goddess of wisdom, goddess of handicrafts, protector of the city, daughter of Zeus, inventor of the bridle, patroness of Athens, leader of the virgin goddesses. One day on Mount Olympus, Zeus complained of a terrible headache. Hephaestus was summoned and was instructed to strike his Olympian father upon the head with his mighty axe. He complied, and once Zeus' skull was split, Athena sprang forth, fully formed.

Atlas The titan who is forced to forever bear the weight of the sky received his eternal punishment for joining with his titan brothers and sisters in the war against Zeus and the gods of Olympus. Titans were giant beings, the first children of the Father Heaven and Mother Earth. After their defeat, almost all were subjugated and imprisoned by the mistrustful Zeus. Over the years it became common for a book of maps to show a depiction of Atlas holding up the world on its cover. Through time this type of book came to be called an "atlas."

Bellerophon Hero of ancient Greece, tamer of Pegasus, slayer of the Chimaera

Briseis Beautiful Trojan captive awarded to Achilles as a spoil of war

Calypso Sea nymph, lover of Odysseus

Cassandra Sister of Hector and Paris, prophetess, taken as a concubine by Agamemnon after the fall of Troy. Cassandra was once courted by Apollo, who gave her the gift of prophecy as an incentive to return his love. When she rejected him, he cursed her so that no one would ever believe the prophecies that came forth from her lips.

Centaur Half-man, half-horse creature known for its wild and violent tendencies

Cerberus Three-head hell-hound that prevents entrance into the Underworld

Charon Aged boatman who ferries souls across the river Styx in the Underworld

Charybdis Gigantic whirlpool, notorious for sucking ships down to their destruction

Chimaera Fearsome creature, part-lion, part-goat, part-snake, defeated by Bellerophon

Chiron Wise centaur who was renowned as a trainer of heroes, raised Jason up from a child, trainer of Achilles

Chryseis Trojan girl taken captive by the Greek army, daughter of Apollo's priest.

Circe Famous witch who transforms the men of Odysseus into pigs

Clytemnestra Wife of Agamemnon, mother of Electra and Orestes, lover of Aegisthus, sister of Helen, together with her lover plotted and carried out the murder of her husband

Cyclops (plural: Cyclopes) Large beings that have only one eye, said to be the sons of Poseidon

Daedalus Famous Athenian inventor, designer of the Labyrinth

Demeter (Roman: Ceres) Goddess of the harvest and nature, mother of Persephone

Diomedes Famed warrior of the Greeks, during the Trojan War earned the distinction of physically harming two gods

Dryad Tree nymph

Electra Daughter of Agamemnon and Clytemnestra

Eros (Roman: Cupid) Son of Aphrodite, shoots arrows that cause extreme infatuation

Fates Three ancient beings that control the lives of all living things, one spins out the thread of life, one measures out its length, one cuts the thread at the time of death

Furies Three foul spirits who torture those who commit offensive crimes

Gorgon (see "Medusa")

Gray Women Three old hags who all share a single eyeball

Hades (Roman: Pluto) Ruler of the Underworld and the dead

Harpy Evil creature, head of a woman, body of a bird, repugnant stench

Hebe Goddess of youth, cupbearer of the gods

Hector Greatest prince of Troy, defended his brother Paris against the Greeks

Hecuba Queen of Troy, wife of Priam, taken into slavery after the fall of Troy, stoned to death by the men of Odysseus

Helen Most beautiful woman in the world, daughter of Zeus, wife of Menelaus, given back to Menelaus after the fall of Troy. Zeus came to Helen's mother, Leda, in the form of a swan and raped her. From that union Leda produced two eggs. When one egg hatched, inside were two girls. In the other were two boys. The first contained the breath-taking Helen and her less-beautiful sister, Clytemnestra. The second contained Helen's twin brothers, Castor and Polydeuces, the Gemini Twins.

Hephaestus (Roman: Vulcan) God of fire and the forge, only ugly god, husband of Aphrodite, son of Zeus. When Hera saw that she had born such an ugly son, it is said that she flung the infant Hephaestus to the earth, and in that moment he became lame. Zeus took pity on him and, marveling at his abilities in shaping weapons and armor, allowed him to return to Olympus. The word "volcano" comes from his Latin name, Vulcan. Hephaestus was said to have a fiery forge under the mountain.

Hera (Roman: Juno) Queen of Olympus, protector of marriage, jealous wife of Zeus, busied herself making life miserable for Zeus' many mistresses and illegitimate children

Heracles (Roman: Hercules) The mightiest of Greek heroes, endowed with superhuman strength, mortal enemy of Hera, Queen of Heaven. The exploits of Heracles are too many to name. After being struck with a madness sent by Hera, Heracles unintentionally murdered his wife and young sons. In repentance for his sin, he sought the Oracle of Delphi who commissioned him to complete twelve great labors to earn his pardon. It was during these labors that many of Heracles' major feats occurred. Upon his death, Zeus took his favorite son to Olympus, making him a god.

Hermes (Roman: Mercury) Messenger god of Olympus, god of commerce, guides souls down to the Underworld after death, master thief, inventor of the lyre, wears winged sandals upon his feet and a winged cap upon his head, carries a magical wand bearing the image of spread wings and intertwined serpents. On the first day of his life, Hermes robbed his brother Apollo of his cattle.

Icarus Son of Daedalus, died while attempting human flight

Iphigenia Daughter of Agamemnon and Clytemnestra, offered as a human sacrifice to appease the anger of Artemis.

Iris Goddess of the rainbow, secondary messenger of the gods. The colorful part of the eye is named for her.

Jason Leader of the Argonauts, trained by Chiron, husband of Medea

Medea Witch, wife of Jason, murdered her young sons

Medusa Snake-haired gorgon, possessed the power to turn men into stone if they met her gaze

Menelaus Brother of Agamemnon, ruler of Sparta, husband of Helen, could not kill his wife as he planned to do after he reclaimed her

Midas Foolish king who wished for everything he touched to turn to gold

Minos King of Crete, who refused to sacrifice the bull Poseidon gifted him. Because of this, Poseidon made Minos' wife Pasiphaë lust for the bull. The queen gave birth to the Minotaur, a half-man, half-bull creature.

Muses Nine immortal beings who inspire every form of art

Myrmidons Fighting men of Achilles, their race is said to have been created from ants

Naiad Water nymph

Nestor Oldest Greek chieftain who fought in the Trojan War, known for his great wisdom

Nymph Nature spirit, known for a promiscuous disposition (see "Dryad" and "Naiad")

Odysseus (Roman: Ulysses) King of Ithaca, vowed to protect the honor of Helen with the other kings of Greece, formed the idea of the Trojan Horse, wandered ten years at sea to reach his home after the fall of Troy

Oedipus King of Thebes, murdered his father and married his mother

Olympus Home of the gods, said to be a floating mountain in the sky, the palace of Zeus sits at its peak

Oracle One who speaks the wisdom of the gods, traditionally the priestess of a god or goddess' temple

Orestes Son of Agamemnon and Clytemnestra, avenges the murder of his father

Orpheus Famed musician, accompanied Jason on his quest for the Golden Fleece

Pan Satyr, god of shepherds

Paris Exiled prince of Troy, lover of Helen, son of Priam, judged the beauty contest of the goddesses, killed by Prince Philoctetes in the Trojan War

Patroclus Beloved friend of Achilles, his death caused Achilles to re-enter the Trojan War

Pegasus Famed winged horse, ridden by Bellerophon

Penelope Queen of Ithaca, wife of Odysseus

Persephone (Roman: Proserpine) Goddess of spring, abducted by Hades, queen of the Underworld

Perseus Hero, illegitimate son of Zeus, slayer of Medusa, went on to found the city-state Mycenae, married to the princess Andromeda

Philoctetes Prince who bore the bow and arrows of Heracles, abandoned by the Greeks on the island of Lemnos for ten years

Polyphemus Famous Cyclops, tricked by Odysseus (Ulysses) and blinded by his men

Poseidon (Roman: Neptune) God of the sea, brother of Zeus, giver of the horse to man, carries a trident (a three-pronged spear)

Priam Elderly king of Troy, defended his son Paris against the Greeks, killed by the son of Achilles during the sack of Troy

Prometheus Titan who stole fire from the gods and gave it to man

Proteus Shape-shifting creature, known as "the old man of the sea"

Pyrrhus Red-haired son of Achilles, sired by Achilles during his stay at the court of Lycomedes, brought to Troy by Odysseus

Satyr Half-goat, half-man creature

Scylla Many-headed monster rooted to a rock in the middle of the ocean, notorious for sinking ships

Sphinx Creature with the head of a woman, the body of a lion, the wings of an eagle, and the tail of a snake, great teller of riddles, defeated by Oedipus

Telemachus Prince of Ithaca, son of Odysseus

Theseus Famous Greek hero, slayer of the Minotaur

Thetis Sea nymph, mother of Achilles, wife of Peleus

Tiresias Blind prophet of Thebes, lived for seven generations of men

Troy City of legend, located on the shores of Asia Minor, known for its richness of gold and its people's love of horses, walls of Troy were built with the help of both Apollo and Poseidon

Zephyr The west wind

Zeus (Roman: Jupiter, Jove) Ruler of the gods, wielder of the mighty thunderbolt, father of many heroes, represented by his bird, the eagle. Zeus, along with his brothers and sisters, fought against their titan father, Cronus, for control of the world. Cronus feared that his children would one day usurp him, and to prevent them from ever getting that chance, he swallowed them one by one as they were born. Rhea, Zeus' mother, could see this happen no more, and when it came time for her youngest son to be born, she substituted a rock in his place. Cronus gobbled up the rock, never suspecting it was not a real child. The child Zeus was spirited away and raised by the nymphs of Mount Ida. When he came of age, he returned in disguise, poisoned his father, and when Cronus vomited up Zeus' brothers and sisters, they joined him a battle against the titans that shook the very foundations of the world.

PRONUNCIATION GUIDE

Achates	(UH-KAY-TEEZ)	Cerberus	(SER-BUH-RUS)
Acheron	(ACK-UH-RUN)	Charon	(KAH-RUN)
Achilles	(UH-KILL-EEZ)	Charybdis	(KUH-RIB-DIS)
Acrisius	(UH-KRIH-SEE-US)	Chimaera	(KY-MEE-RUH)
Actaeon	(ACT-EE-ON)	Chiron	(KY-RUN)
Æetes	(EE-UH-TEEZ)	Chryseis	(KRY-SEE-ISS)
Aegeus	(EE-GEE-US)	Circe	(SER-SEE)
Aegina	(EE-JY-NUH)	Clio	(KLEE-OH)
Aeneas	(EE-NEE-US)	Clytemnestra	(KLY-TIM-NESS-TRUH)
Aeneid	(EE-NEE-ID)	Colchis	(KOL-KISS)
Aeolus	(EE-OH-LUS)	Creon	(KREE-ON)
Agamemnon	(AG-UH-MEM-NON)	Cumae	(KOO-MEE)
Alcema	(AL-SEE-MUH)	Cupid	(KEW-PID)
Alcinous	(AL-SIN-OO-US)	Cyclops	(SY-KLOPZ)
Alecto	(UH-LEHK-TOE)	Cyclopes	(SY-KLOPE-EEZ)
Amata	(UH-MAY-TUH)	Daedalus	(DAY-DUH-LUS)
Anchises	(AN-KY-ZEEZ)	Danaë	(DUH-NAY-EE)
Andromache	(AN-DRAH-MUH-KEE)	Deidamia	(DEE-UH-DAH-MEE-UH)
Andromeda	(AN-DRAH-MEE-DUH)	Delphi	(DEL-FY)
Antigone	(AN-TIG-UH-NEE)	Dido	(DY-DO)
Antinous	(AN-TEN-YOO-US)	Diomedes	(DY-O-MEE-DEEZ)
Aphrodite	(AF-RO-DY-TEE)	Dryad	(DRY-AD)
Apollo	(UH-PAW-LO)	Electra	(EE-LEK-TRUH)
Arachne	(UH-RAK-NEE)	Epeios	(EE-PAY-OS)
Ares	(AIR-EEZ)	Eris	(EE-RUS)
Argos	(AR-GOS)	Eros	(EE-ROS)
Argus	(AR-GUS)	Eumaeus	(YOO-MAY-US)
Ariadne	(AIR-EE-AHD-NEE)	Eurycleia	(YOOR-IH-KLEE-UH)
Artemis	(AR-TUH-MIS)	Eurydice	(YOO-RIH-DIH-SEE)
Astyanax	(UH-STY-UH-NAX)	Eurylochus	(YOO-RIL-UH-KUS)
Atalanta	(AT-UH-LAN-TUH)	Eurymachus	(YOO-RIM-UH-KUS)
Athena	(UH-THEE-NUH)	Gorgon	(GOR-GUN)
Atreus	(UH-TRAY-OOS)	Hades	(HAY-DEEZ)
Aulis	(O-LIS)	Harpies	(HAR-PEEZ)
Bacchus	(BAHK-US)	Hector	(HEK-TER)
Bellerophon	(BEH-LEHR-UH-FUN)	Hecuba	(HEK-YOO-BUH)
Briseis	(BRIH-SEE-US)	Helenus	(HEL-UH-NUS)
Cadmus	(KAHD-MUS)	Helios	(HEE-LEE-OS)
Calchas	(KAL-KUS)	Hephaestus	(HEE-FESS-TUS)
Calliope	(KUH-LY-O-PEE)	Hera	(HEE-RUH) (HEH-RUH)
Calydon	(KAL-IH-DUN)	Heracles	(HEER-UH-KLEEZ)
Calypso	(KUH-LIP-SO)	Hercules	(HER-KYOO-LEEZ)
Carthage	(KAR-THIJ)	Hermes	(HER-MEEZ)
Cassandra	(KUH-SAN-DRUH)	Hermione	(HER-MY-O-NEE)
Castor	(KAS-TER)	Icarius	(IH-KAR-EE-US)
Centaur	(SIN-TAUR)	Icarus	(IH-KAR-US)

Iliad	(IH-LEE-AD)	Palamedes	(PAL-UH-MEE-DEEZ)
Ilium	(IH-LEE-UM)	Pallas	(PAL-US)
Iphigenia	(IF-UH-JUH-NY-UH)	Pandarus	(PAN-DARE-US)
Iris	(EYE-RIS)	Parnassus	(PAR-NAH-SUS)
Ithaca	(ITH-UH-KUH)	Pasiphaë	(PASS-IH-FAY-EE)
Iulus	(YOO-LUSS)	Patroclus	(PAH-TRO-KLUS)
Janus	(JAY-NUS)	Peleus	(PEE-LEE-US)
Jocasta	(YO-KAS-TUH)	Pelias	(PEL-EE-US)
Juno	(JOO-NO)	Penelope	(PEH-NEL-O-PEE)
Jupiter	(JOO-PIH-TUR)	Penthesilea	(PEN-THUS-SIH-LEE-UH)
Lacedaemon	(LAH-SEE-DEE-MUN)	Perseus	(PER-SEE-US)
Laertes	(LAY-ER-TEEZ)	Phaeacia	(FAY-EE-SHUH)
Laius	(LAY-US)	Philoctetes	(FIL-OK-TEE-TEEZ)
Laocoön	(LAY-O-KO-UN)	Phineus	(FIN-EE-US)
Latinus	(LUH-TY-NUS)	Phoebus	(FEE-BUS)
Latium	(LAY-SHI-UM)	Phrygia	(FRIH-GEE-UH)
Leda	(LEE-DUH)	Pisistratus	(PIH-SIH-STRAH-TUS)
Lemnos	(LEM-NUS)	Plautus	(PLAW-TUS)
Lethe	(LEE-THEE)	Pluto	(PLEW-TO)
Leto	(LEE-TOE)	Polites	(PO-LY-TEEZ)
Lycomedes	(LY-KO-MEE-DEEZ)	Polyphemus	(PO-LEE-FEE-MUS)
Lyre	(LY-ER)	Polyxena	(POL-EK-ZEE-NUH)
Maenad	(MEE-NAD)	Poseidon	(PO-SY-DUN)
Maron	(MAH-RUN)	Priam	(PRY-UM)
Medea	(MEE-DEE-UH)	Proserpine	(PRO-SER-PEEN-UH)
Medusa	(MEH-DOO-SUH)	Proteus	(PRO-TEE-US)
Memnon	(MEM-NUN)	Pylos	(PY-LOS)
Menelaus	(MEN-UH-LAY-US)	Pyrrhus	(PEER-US)
Mentes	(MEN-TEEZ)	Remus	(REE-MUS)
Mercury	(MER-KOO-REE)	Rhea	(REE-UH)
Minerva	(MIH-NER-VUH)	Romulus	(ROM-YOO-LUS)
Minos	(MY-NUS)	Satyr	(SAY-TER)
Minotaur	(MY-NO-TAR)	Scylla	(SIHL-UH)
Mycenae	(MY-SEE-NEE)	Scyros	(SKY-RUS)
Myrmidon	(MER-MIH-DON)	Silenus	(SUH-LY-NUS)
Naiad	(NY-AD)	Sinon	(SY-NON)
Narcissus	(NAR-SIS-US)	Styx	(STIKS)
Nausicaa	(NAW-SEE-KUH)	Tantalus	(TAN-TUH-LUS)
Neoptolemus	(NEE-O-TOL-EE-MUS)	Telemachus	(TUH-LEM-UH-KUS)
Neptune	(NEP-TOON)	Thalia	(THUH-LY-UH)
Niobe	(NY-O-BEE)	Thebes	(THEEBZ)
Odysseus	(O-DIS-EE-US)	Theseus	(THEE-SEE-US)
Oedipus	(ED-IH-PUS)	Thessaly	(THEHS-UH-LEE)
Oeta	(EE-TUH)	Thetis	(THEE-TIS)
Ogygia	(O-JIH-JEE-UH)	Tiresias	(TY-REE-SEE-US)
Orestes	(O-RES-TEEZ)	Troilus	(TROY-LUS)
Orpheus	(OR-FEE-US)	Tyndareus	(TIN-DARE-EE-US)
Ovid	(OH-VID)	Zeus	(ZOOS)

ABOUT THE AUTHOR

Zachary "Zak" Hamby is a teacher of English in rural Missouri, where he has taught mythology for many years. In mythology he has seen the ability of ancient stories to capture the imaginations of young people today. For this reason he has created a variety of teaching materials (including textbooks, posters, and websites) that focus specifically on the teaching of mythology to young people. He is the author of two book series, the *Reaching Olympus* series and the *Mythology for Teens* series. He is also a professional illustrator. He resides in the Ozarks with his wife and children.

For more information and products (including textbooks, posters, and electronic content)
visit his website
www.mythologyteacher.com

Contact him by email at **mr.mythology@gmail.com**

CPSIA information can be obtained at www.ICGtesting.com
Printed in the USA
LVOW132255260712

291610LV00002B/71/P